VIRTUE ETHICS A
PROFESSIONAL RO

C000231730

Professionals, it is said, have no use for simple lists of virtues and vices. The complexities and constraints of professional roles create peculiar moral demands on the people who occupy them, and traits that are vices in ordinary life are praised as virtues in the context of professional roles. Should this disturb us, or is it naive to presume that things should be otherwise? Taking medical and legal practice as key examples, Justin Oakley and Dean Cocking develop a rigorous articulation and defence of virtue ethics, contrasting it with other types of character-based ethical theories and showing that it offers a promising new approach to the ethics of professional roles. They provide insights into the central notions of professional detachment, professional integrity, and moral character in professional life, and demonstrate how a virtue-based approach can help us better understand what ethical professional–client relationships would be like.

JUSTIN OAKLEY is Director of the Monash University Centre for Human Bioethics. His publications include *Morality and Emotions* (1992) and a number of journal articles.

DEAN COCKING is Senior Research Fellow at the Centre for Applied Philosophy and Public Ethics, Charles Sturt University. He has published articles in journals including *Ethics* and the *Journal of Philosophy*.

VIRTUE ETHICS AND PROFESSIONAL ROLES

JUSTIN OAKLEY

Monash University

DEAN COCKING

Charles Sturt University

CAMBRIDGE
UNIVERSITY PRESS

CAMBRIDGE UNIVERSITY PRESS
Cambridge, New York, Melbourne, Madrid, Cape Town, Singapore, São Paulo

Cambridge University Press
The Edinburgh Building, Cambridge CB2 2RU, UK

Published in the United States of America by Cambridge University Press, New York

www.cambridge.org
Information on this title: www.cambridge.org/9780521793056

© Justin Oakley and Dean Cocking 2001

This publication is in copyright. Subject to statutory exception
and to the provisions of relevant collective licensing agreements,
no reproduction of any part may take place without
the written permission of Cambridge University Press.

First published 2001
Hardback version transferred to digital printing 2006
Digitally printed first paperback version 2006

A catalogue record for this publication is available from the British Library

Library of Congress Cataloguing in Publication data
Oakley, Justin, 1960–
Virtue ethics and professional roles / Justin Oakley, Dean Cocking.
p. cm.
Includes bibliographical references and index.
ISBN 0 521 79305 X
1. Professional ethics. I. Cocking, Dean, 1958– II. Title.
BJ1725 .C55 2001
174–dc21

ISBN-13 978-0-521-79305-6 hardback
ISBN-10 0-521-79305-X hardback

ISBN-13 978-0-521-02729-8 paperback
ISBN-10 0-521-02729-2 paperback

To my partner, Kathryn Bailey, for her patience, support, and understanding, and our loving son, Jordan Bailey Oakley, for the life that awaits him.

Justin Oakley

To my father, Gordon, whose love, humour, sensitivity, and insight I adored and continue to miss greatly. To my beautiful mother, Yvonne, loving brother, Peter, and wonderful son, Harry.

Dean Cocking

Contents

Preface

There are many people we wish to thank for their support in the course of writing this book. Work on the book began during 1992–3, with the help of a Large Research Grant from the Australian Research Council. We are grateful to the ARC for supporting this project from the outset. For his encouragement and enthusiasm about the project from the beginning, and for his helpful comments on the work in progress (especially in the early stages) we would like to thank Michael Smith. Michael's interest in the project helped to get it off the ground, and he has been an inspiration to us both, as he has been to many of his colleagues and students. For his detailed and incisive comments on every chapter, several times over, we are deeply indebted to John Campbell. John read our drafts very carefully, and his feedback was extremely valuable. He helped us refine our arguments at many points, and raised many useful questions about virtue ethics that would not otherwise have occurred to us. Warm thanks are also owed to Jennifer Radden for her valuable and stimulating comments on the entire typescript. Two anonymous readers for Cambridge University Press also provided very extensive comments on the penultimate draft, and their detailed suggestions resulted in many improvements to the typescript. We are also grateful to Jeanette Kennett, for discussing many of the issues in this book with us, and to Tim Dare, for his spirited rejoinder to a paper which was an earlier version of chapter 5.

Extensive comments on various chapters were provided by John Cottingham, Owen Flanagan, Lynn Gillam, Brad Hooker, Tom Hurka, David Sosa, Christine Swanton, and the editors of *Ethics*, and we are indebted to all of them for their help. We are also grateful for the feedback we received from Lori Gruen, R. M. Hare, Elinor Mason, Steve Matthews, Bernadette McSherry, Jeannie Paterson, Philip Pettit, Gerald Postema, Per Sandberg, Peter Saul, Julian Savulescu, Peter Singer, Michael Stocker, and Bernadette Tobin. Valuable references were suggested to us by Minou Friele, David Macintosh, Ani Satz, Merle Spriggs, and Alison Stubbs. Dean would also like to thank the Department of Philosophy at the University of Auckland, for their support in the form of a Post-Doctoral Fellowship, and in particular team captain Tim Dare. For his enthusiasm about the project and his general encouragement, we also thank Robert Young.

Earlier versions of the chapters in this book have been read to various audiences over the years, as indicated in the notes to each chapter. Along with those audiences, we would also like to thank Rae Langton and Michael Smith for organising the 'Consequentialism, Kantianism, and Virtue Ethics' conference at Monash University in June 1995, which was an excellent international forum at which to read an earlier version of chapter 1. We are also grateful to Tony Coady and Megan Laverty, for helping organise the symposium on 'Virtue Ethics and Professional Roles', at the Australian Association for Professional and Applied Ethics Fourth Annual Conference held at the University of Melbourne in September 1997, where we read an earlier version of Chapter 5. Justin would also like to thank Daisuke Arie of Yokohama City University, Yasunori Fukagai of Tokyo Metropolitan University, and Satoshi Kodama of Kyoto University for organising ethics symposia in Tokyo and Kyoto, where a version of Chapter 1 was read in January 2000.

On a more practical level, we wish to express our appreciation to Hilary Gaskin, Philosophy Editor at Cambridge University Press, for her patience, professionalism, and promptness. We also thank copy-editor Pauline Marsh for her meticulousness and her suggestions for stylistic improvements. Monash University generously provided Justin with two periods of study leave, which enabled significant progress to be made on this project. Justin also wishes to thank David and Beverley Macintosh, for their kindness in making available the library of their wonderful house as a peaceful area in which to write, and the Faculty of Arts staff at Monash Caulfield Campus, who provided a quiet temporary office away from the distractions of the Clayton campus. Dean is especially grateful to Seumas Miller for providing him with the research time to finish work on this book and for his tremendous support and encouragement more generally. For general administrative assistance, Justin would like to thank Heather Mahamooth, from the Monash University Centre for Human Bioethics.

We are personally indebted to a number of people for their support over the years this book was written. Justin wishes to express his heartfelt appreciation to his partner, Kathryn Bailey, for her unfailing loyalty and support, and to his son Jordan, for the lightness and joy he has brought during these years. Most of all Dean would like to thank his mother, Yvonne, whose continuing devotion and support have been enormous and contributed so much to his life.

Acknowledgements

Sections of the following chapters draw on our previously published material, as indicated. Permission to adapt and use parts of that material has been kindly granted by the publishers, as noted.

Chapter 1: 'Varieties of Virtue Ethics', *Ratio* 9, no. 2, September 1996, pp. 128–52. Copyright (c) 1996 by Blackwell Publishers Ltd. 'A Virtue Ethics Approach', in Helga Kuhse and Peter Singer (eds.), *A Companion to Bioethics*, Oxford, Blackwell, 1998, pp. 86–97. Copyright (c) 1998 by Blackwell Publishers Ltd.

Chapter 2: 'Indirect Consequentialism, Friendship, and the Problem of Alienation', *Ethics* 106, no. 1, October 1995, pp. 86–111. Published by The University of Chicago Press. Copyright (c) 1995 by The University of Chicago. All rights reserved.

Chapter 5: 'Doing Justice to the Lawyer's Role', in Andrew Alexandra, Tony Coady, and Bruce Langtry (eds.), *Proceedings of the Fourth Annual Conference of the Australian Association for Professional and Applied Ethics*, Melbourne, University of Melbourne Centre for Philosophy and Public Issues, 1998, pp. 77–86. Copyright (c) 1998 by A. Alexandra, T. Coady, and B. Langtry.

Chapter 6: 'The Ethics of Professional Detachment', *Journal of Law and Medicine* 7, no. 2, November 1999, pp. 150–5. This article has been incorporated into chapter 6 with the express permission of (c) LBC Information Services, a part of Thomson Legal and Regulatory Group Asia Pacific Limited.

Introduction

Professionals, it is said, have no use for simple lists of virtues and vices. The complexities and constraints of professional roles create peculiar moral demands on the individuals who occupy them. Traits that are vices in ordinary life are praised as virtues in the context of professional roles. Should this disturb us, or is it naive to presume that things should be otherwise?

It is natural to turn for guidance on such matters to recent work in virtue ethics. Unfortunately, however, much of this writing suffers from a lack of detail about how the approach is to be applied to practical issues. This book is an attempt to address that problem. In what follows we develop a clear and rigorous account of virtue ethics, which explains how it differs from contemporary versions of rival ethical theories. We show why virtue ethics is to be preferred to those views, and explain how it offers a natural and promising approach to the ethics of professional roles. In doing so, we bring out how a properly developed virtue ethics can offer a promising way to resolve a central issue in professional ethics, in its ability to account for how professional roles can legitimately have their own action-guiding force, without compromising the broader values to which those roles are answerable.

Our general aim is to show how a theoretically advanced virtue ethics offers a plausible and distinctive alternative to utilitarian and Kantian approaches to understanding and evaluating professional roles – in particular, the role morality of medical and legal practice. We argue for the merits of virtue ethics over these other approaches on both theoretical and practical grounds. In the theoretical chapters of the book, we develop the notion of a 'regulative ideal' as a way of explicating the relation between an ethical theory's criterion of rightness and its account of how agents are to be guided by this criterion. We draw on this notion in outlining a rigorous virtue-based account of moral justification, and in comparing and defending this account against its Kantian and consequentialist rivals. Following this, we go on to provide an outline of a virtue-based approach to professional roles, which we then apply to medical and legal practice.

The rise of systematic approaches to professional ethics in the 1970s saw traditional practices in various professions subjected to critical scrutiny by broad-based ethical theories, such as utilitarianism and Kantianism. For instance, doctors were told that it is unethical to withhold a diagnosis from a patient out of concern for the patient's welfare, for telling patients the truth here respects their rights or maximises utility overall. Similarly, lawyers acting for the defendant in a rape trial have been advised to avoid making gratuitous courtroom references to the plaintiff's sexual history in order to impugn her character, as such conduct violates her rights and is in any case counterproductive to the administration of justice overall, because it deters many rape victims from reporting the assault in the first place. Many have welcomed this sort of external critical evaluation of previously accepted professional norms, which they rightly feel was well overdue. Indeed, some have gone on to suggest that professional norms are themselves redundant and that reliance upon them is pernicious. Robert Veatch, for instance, argues that 'the use of a professionally generated ethic makes no sense in theory or in practice', and he suggests that we instead appeal directly to more general moral standards.[1]

However, other writers have recently criticised the suggestion that professional ethical norms should be abandoned in favour of an approach which judges professional behaviour directly in terms of broad-based moral standards. They feel that something important is lost in the move to the general here. For example, Larry Churchill and Charles Fried have argued that utilitarianism and Kantianism fail to register certain role-generated commitments and characteristic sensitivities of good doctors, and Fried has put forward a similar argument about the distinctive requirements of the lawyer's role. Lawrence Blum has likewise made claims about the inadequacies of universalist ethical theories in capturing what it is to be a good teacher.

These critics seem to us correct in saying that an approach which judges the legitimacy of all professional behaviour directly in terms of broad-based moral standards will not do justice to the responsibilities and sensitivities proper to various professional roles, and that a satisfactory ethic for a given profession must be able to recognise the particular

---

[1] Robert M. Veatch, *A Theory of Medical Ethics*, New York, Basic Books, 1981, p. 106.

roles, responsibilities, and sensitivities appropriate to that profession. In the later chapters of the book, we discuss a range of problems that consequentialist and Kantian ethical theories might have in accommodating the distinctive requirements and sensitivities appropriate to various professional roles. But whatever implications such difficulties have for Kantian and utilitarian approaches to professional roles, we argue that virtue ethics has the resources to deal with the various problems we raise here.

Indeed, the topic of professional roles presents a particularly good example of how virtue ethics may be applied in practice, as the focus of virtue ethics on functions and ends fits well with professional practice, which can be readily regarded as having a teleological structure. The proper goals of a particular profession also tend to be clearer, more specific, and more widely recognised than do the characteristic functions and ends of human beings generally.

Chapter 1 provides a systematic account of the essential and distinctive positive features of a virtue-based approach to normative ethics. We explain how a virtue ethics form of character-based ethics differs from recent character-based forms of Kantian and consequentialist theories, and we defend virtue ethics against several important criticisms which are commonly made in philosophical discussions of the approach.

In chapter 2 we argue for the superiority of a virtue ethics approach to contemporary consequentialist and Kantian theories, on the grounds that virtue ethics can appropriately recognise the nature and value of friendship, whereas consequentialism and Kantianism are unable to do so. The inadequacies we identify in consequentialist and Kantian treatments of friendship are instructive for our purposes in this book. For, as many recognise, the plausibility of any ethical theory rests importantly on its capacity to recognise great human goods, of which friendship is clearly one, and consequentialists and Kantians have done much work recently in attempting to accommodate the value of friendship. But further, the problems which impartialist ethical theories like consequentialism and Kantianism have in accommodating friendship will be helpful, by way of contrast and similarity, in understanding the problems these theories have in giving due acknowledgement to the value and normative force of various professional roles. Both friendship and professional roles may license departures from what universalist or impartialist ethical theory would ordinarily require of us, and the values inherent in both friendship and various professional roles seem significantly independent of the values contained in universalist and impartialist ethical theories. However, as we show in chapter 4, section 1, the nature of and justifications for this independence and these departures from broad-based ethical theory that might be claimed for friendship and professional roles are importantly different.

Chapter 3 outlines how virtue ethics can provide a plausible framework for evaluating professional roles. We argue that good professional roles must be part of a good profession, and that a good profession is one which involves a commitment to a key human good, a good which humans need to live flourishing lives. Several virtues specific to medical practice are then outlined and defended at the end of this chapter.

Our arguments against consequentialism in chapters 2 and 4 complement each other. Two distinct sorts of critique can be made of consequentialist justifications of friendship. One might attack the empirical claim made by many consequentialists that engaging in relationships such as friendship is by and large the way in which individuals can produce the most agent-neutral good. Alternatively, one might question whether the sorts of relationship a consequentialist agent is permitted to have with others would really qualify as friendships, quite apart from whether the agent's engaging in those relationships does produce the most agent-neutral good. For example, one might examine whether the governing conditions that consequentialist agents must impose on their relationships preclude any such relationship from being a friendship. In chapter 2, we offer an argument against consequentialism along the lines of this second critique, and we leave aside consequentialists' empirical claim about friendships maximising the good. Some consequentialists have justified certain professional roles by making the empirical claim that those professionals produce the most agent-neutral good by engaging in such roles. When we go on to discuss professional roles, we attack this empirical claim made by certain consequentialists in relation to a general practitioner's commonly accepted partiality towards their own patients. Thus, in chapter 4 we argue that there are good reasons for thinking that such devotion to one's own patients will not in fact maximise the good, and we bring out the complacency on the part of consequentialists who provide little evidence for the plausibility of such a claim. We also demonstrate some limitations of influential personal relationship models of the partiality which might be thought appropriate to various professional–client relationships.

Chapter 5 addresses the limits which the general conception of the virtuous agent might be justifiably thought to impose on the exercise of role-based virtues in professional life. Here we focus on lawyers' roles, and we argue that virtue ethics can consistently recognise the distinctive value of a lawyer's role and its associated virtues, while also holding that a lawyer ought not to fulfil those role requirements where doing so would involve a gross violation of justice.

In chapter 6 we examine what sorts of psychological integration between their personal and professional life would characterise a virtuous person, and we discuss what virtue ethics might say about various sorts of psychological distancing from one's professional role and its apparent requirements. Here, by drawing attention to the Kantian conception of the limits of the moral self, we also provide a critique of how Kantian ethics might understand the morality of professional roles.

There has been much writing in virtue ethics, and a good deal said about its promise, yet comparatively few works have really delivered on that promise. Much work in virtue ethics, for all its value, often lacks crucial details about the nature of the approach and about how it differs from the more sophisticated forms of rival theories which have been developed recently. As a result, there has been a certain lack of engagement, both in ethical theory and applied ethics, between the advocates of virtue ethics and those who take more traditional views. Our hope in writing this book is that it initiates greater dialogue between the advocates of virtue ethics and utilitarian and Kantian approaches, and that it reveals the richness and strength of a more developed and rigorous account of virtue ethics.

CHAPTER I

The nature of virtue ethics[1]

The current renewal of philosophical interest in the virtues is one of the most noteworthy developments in contemporary ethical theory. The first signs of this revival appeared in 1958, when Elizabeth Anscombe called for the restoration of Aristotelian notions of goodness, character, and virtue as central concerns of moral philosophy.[2] While initial reactions to Anscombe's call were modest, interest in the virtues gathered momentum during the 1980s, largely because of the work of philosophers such as Philippa Foot, Bernard Williams, and Alasdair MacIntyre. The philosophical literature on the virtues is now vast, and there is a great variety of different views which advertise themselves as forms of virtue ethics.[3] Many of those who hold such views argue that virtue ethics can lay serious claim to rival Kantianism and utilitarianism as comprehensive normative ethical theories. But what exactly is virtue ethics? What are the central claims which the variants of virtue ethics

---

[1] Earlier versions of this chapter were read at the 'Consequentialism, Kantianism, and Virtue Ethics' conference at Monash University, at an Ethox seminar at Oxford University, at Kyoto University, and at a seminar in Tokyo organised by the utilitarian studies research group in Japan. We would like to thank those audiences for useful discussion on those occasions. We are especially grateful to John Campbell, John Cottingham, Brad Hooker, Per Sandberg, and Christine Swanton, for their very helpful comments on previous versions, and to Kazunobu Narita for his detailed critique of a late draft of this chapter.

[2] G. E. M. Anscombe, 'Modern Moral Philosophy', *Philosophy* 33, 1958.

[3] A comprehensive bibliography of material on virtue ethics can be found in Robert B. Kruschwitz and Robert C. Roberts, *The Virtues: Contemporary Essays on Moral Character*, Belmont, Wadsworth, 1987. For good recent collections of papers on virtue ethics, see Roger Crisp (ed.), *How Should One Live? Essays on the Virtues*, Oxford, Clarendon Press, 1996; Roger Crisp and Michael Slote (eds.), *Virtue Ethics*, Oxford, Oxford University Press, 1997; Peter A. French, Theodore E. Uehling, and Howard K. Wettstein (eds.), *Midwest Studies in Philosophy, Volume 13: Ethical Theory: Character and Virtue*, Notre Dame, Notre Dame University Press, 1988; and Daniel Statman, *Virtue Ethics: A Critical Reader*, Edinburgh, Edinburgh University Press, 1997. See also the survey articles on virtue ethics by Gregory E. Pence, 'Recent Work on the Virtues', *American Philosophical Quarterly* 21, 1984; and Gregory Trianosky, 'What is Virtue Ethics all About?', *American Philosophical Quarterly* 27, 1990. Pence summarises and compares certain key texts in the recent history of virtue ethics, while Trianosky offers a more systematic guide to the different forms of virtue ethics, in terms of a range of common targets which unite various writers in the field.

share, and how is virtue theory distinct from other, more familiar ethical theories?

There is a somewhat bewildering diversity of claims made by philosophers in the name of virtue ethics. Many of those claims are put in negative form, and are expressed in terms of an opposition to an 'ethics of principles', or to an 'impartialist ethics', or to 'abstract ethical theory', or simply to an 'ethics of action'. Unfortunately, this negative emphasis has resulted in virtue ethics becoming better known to many by what it is *against*, rather than by what it is *for*. Of course, given that the revival of virtue ethics has been sparked by dissatisfaction with standard Kantian and utilitarian ethical theories, it is not surprising that those negative claims have gained prominence. However, to focus only on those claims in an outline of virtue ethics and its variants would be inadequate, for this would not sufficiently distinguish it from other approaches – such as an ethics of care, and various forms of feminist ethics – which are also often advanced in terms of a rejection of similar features of orthodox ethical theories. While virtue ethics does share certain common targets with these and other ethical theories, it can be more clearly distinguished from them by its positive features.

When virtue ethicists *do* enunciate their positive claims, however, there is often a lack of clarity and specificity which does not help in fixing the theory's distinctive content. Thus, when virtue ethicists suggest how the theory can overcome many of the perceived vices of Kantianism and utilitarianism, there is often a failure to articulate virtue theory in ways which make clear how or why its features cannot simply be appropriated by more sophisticated or ecumenical forms of these more familiar ethical theories. For example, many regard virtue ethics' emphasis on an agent's character in justifying right actions as a feature which distinguishes virtue ethics from other ethical theories. However, while the virtue ethics movement has helped bring considerations of character to the fore in contemporary ethics, it is not alone in emphasising the important connections between right action and an agent's character. For recent influential versions of Kantianism and consequentialism have also moved towards endorsing the idea that the morally good person would have a certain sort of character.[4] So, while many writers on virtue ethics assume that arguments for the importance of character necessarily lend support to a

[4] See, for example, Barbara Herman, 'The Practice of Moral Judgment', and other essays in her *The Practice of Moral Judgment*, Cambridge, MA, Harvard University Press, 1993; and Peter Railton, 'Alienation, Consequentialism, and the Demands of Morality', in Samuel Scheffler (ed.), *Consequentialism and its Critics*, Oxford, Oxford University Press, 1988.

virtues-based approach to ethics, the moves by contemporary Kantians and consequentialists to recognise the importance of character in evaluating actions indicate that this broad assumption is unjustified. What virtue ethicists need to show, in addition to the importance of character, is what makes a *virtue ethics* form of character-based ethics distinctive, and why such an approach is to be preferred to character-based forms of Kantianism and consequentialism. Thus, in order to show how virtue ethics resists assimilation to a form of Kantianism or utilitarianism, one needs to bring out which features of virtue ethics could not consistently be endorsed by someone who holds one of those theories.

In this chapter we set out the basic features of virtue ethics, by presenting a systematic account of its main positive claims, and by showing how these claims help to distinguish it from other approaches. We also develop certain aspects of this basic virtue ethics approach, introducing the concept of a 'regulative ideal', and demonstrating how this concept helps to clarify and strengthen virtue ethics. At the end of the chapter, we consider several criticisms of virtue ethics which are commonly made by philosophers, and we discuss how virtue ethics might be defended against these criticisms.

I THE ESSENTIAL FEATURES OF VIRTUE ETHICS

There are at least *six* claims which seem to be essential features of *any* virtue ethics view. The first and perhaps best-known claim, which is central to any form of virtue ethics, is the following:

(a) An action is right if and only if it is what an agent with a virtuous character would do in the circumstances.

This is a claim about the primacy of *character* in the justification of right action. A right action is one that is in accordance with what a virtuous person would do in the circumstances, and what *makes* the action right is that it is what a person with a virtuous character would do here.[5] Thus, as Philippa Foot argues, it is right to save another's life, where life is still a good to that person, because this is what someone with the virtue of benevolence would do. A person with the virtue of benevolence would act in this way because benevolence is a virtue which is directed at the good of others, and to have the virtue of benevolence, according to Foot,

---

[5] For an explicit statement of this claim, see, e.g., Rosalind Hursthouse, 'Virtue Theory and Abortion', *Philosophy and Public Affairs* 20, 1991, p. 225. See Aristotle, *Nicomachean Ethics* II.6.1107a1–2.

is to be disposed to help others in situations where we are likely to be
called upon to do so.[6] Similarly, as Rosalind Hursthouse argues, it is right
in certain circumstances to reveal an important truth to another, even
though this may be hurtful to them, because a person with the virtue of
honesty would tell the truth here. For example, if my brother asks me
whether his wife is being unfaithful, and I happen to know that she is, I
ought to answer him truthfully because this is what a person with the
virtue of honesty would do here.[7] Likewise, in regard to justice, Foot
argues that I ought to repay you the money I have borrowed, even if you
plan to waste it, because repaying the money is what a person with the
virtue of justice would do.[8]

Now, as we noted above, the primacy given to character in (a) might
also seem to be endorsed by recent influential forms of Kantianism, consequentialism, and utilitarianism, which invoke one of these theories to
give content to the notion of a 'virtuous person'. For example, Barbara
Herman has argued that the Kantian Categorical Imperative, which
provides the standard of rightness for actions, is best understood as a
normative disposition in the character of a good agent to rule out certain
courses of conduct as impermissible.[9] Similarly, Peter Railton has
argued that the consequentialist requirement to maximise agent-neutral
value can be understood as a normative disposition in the character of
the good agent, and R. M. Hare suggests that the utilitarian requirement
to maximise utility can be thought of in the same way.[10] How can (a) help
distinguish virtue ethics from these other theories?

Virtue ethics gives primacy to character in the sense that it holds that
reference to character is *essential* in a correct account of right and wrong
action. However, the examples from Foot and Hursthouse do not bring
out fully how virtue ethics envisages (a) operating as a standard for determining the rightness of actions. For (a) might be proposed as providing
a purely 'external' criterion of right action, which a person may meet no
matter what kinds of motives, dispositions, or character they act from in
performing the action the criterion directs them to do. On this interpretation, acting rightly would not require modelling oneself on a virtuous

---

[6] See Philippa Foot, 'Euthanasia', p. 54; and 'Virtues and Vices', p. 4, both in her *Virtues and Vices*,
   Berkeley, University of California Press, 1978. Foot sometimes calls this virtue 'benevolence',
   while at other time she refers to it as 'charity'.
[7] See Hursthouse, 'Virtue Theory and Abortion', pp. 229, 231.
[8] See Foot, 'Euthanasia', pp. 44–5, and 'Virtues and Vices'. See also William Frankena, *Ethics*, 2nd
   edn, Englewood Cliffs, Prentice-Hall, 1973, pp. 63–71.
[9] See Herman 'The Practice of Moral Judgment'.
[10] Railton, 'Alienation'; and R. M. Hare, *Moral Thinking*, Oxford, Oxford University Press, 1981.

person or a particular aspect of their character, but would involve just having a good idea of what kinds of acts such a person would perform in various circumstances. In that case, (a) would be analogous to the role in certain ethical theories of an Ideal Observer, whose deliverances may guide one even though one lacks the qualities of such an observer oneself (and indeed, even if there were no 'natural' persons who embodied all the characteristics of an Ideal Observer).[11] Alternatively, the criterion of right action in (a) might be proposed as carrying certain 'internal' requirements, such that a person can act rightly only if they themselves have and act out of the kinds of motives, dispositions, or character-traits that a virtuous agent would have and act out of in the circumstances.

Now, it is clear from (a) that virtue ethics makes character essential to right action at least in the sense that its criterion of rightness contains an essential reference to the character of a hypothetical figure – namely, a virtuous agent. And this feature is already enough to distinguish virtue ethics from forms of act-utilitarianism and act-consequentialism which evaluate an act according to the consequences that it *actually* results in, as Railton's act-consequentialism does. For unlike virtue ethics, these actualist approaches allow us to say what acts are right, with no reference to the character of a hypothetical agent (or, for that matter, to the character of the real agent whose action is being evaluated) at all. For these actualist versions of act-utilitarianism and act-consequentialism hold simply that an act is right if and only if it results in the best consequences.[12]

However, many contemporary utilitarians and consequentialists repudiate actualism in favour of some form of expectabilist approach, where actions are evaluated according to their *likely* consequences, rather than their actual consequences. One widely held expectabilist form of act-consequentialism evaluates an act according to the consequences it is *objectively* likely to result in, and this approach can be interpreted as having a criterion of rightness containing an essential reference to the character of a hypothetical figure.[13] For this form of

---

[11] See Roderick Firth, 'Ethical Absolutism and the Ideal Observer', *Philosophy and Phenomenological Research* 12, 1952. We thank John Campbell for pointing out this similarity between virtue ethics and an Ideal Observer theory.

[12] Railton uses the term 'objective consequentialism' to refer to what many call 'actualism'.

[13] For one account and defence of this approach, see Graham Oddie and Peter Menzies, 'An Objectivist's Guide to Subjectivist Value', *Ethics* 102, no. 3, April 1992. This form of expectabilism is to be distinguished from that form which evaluates an act according to the consequences it is *subjectively* likely to result in. This subjectivist approach holds that the consequences relevant to the act evaluation are those which the agent *believes* are probable consequences of the act (rather than those which are *objectively* probable consequences of the act). For one account and

expectabilism can be presented as evaluating the rightness of an act by looking at which of its possible consequences a reasonable person in the agent's position would judge to be likely (whether or not the act does actually result in those consequences). And so, the essential reference in virtue ethics' criterion of rightness to the character of a hypothetical figure might be seen as insufficient to distinguish the approach from this expectabilist version of consequentialism.

But in addition to its essential reference to the character of a hypothetical figure, unlike the expectabilist approach described above virtue ethics' criterion of rightness also contains an essential reference to the character of *this particular agent* who is performing the act. That is, 'doing what a virtuous person would do' in (a) is to be understood as requiring not merely the performance of certain acts, but also acting out of certain dispositions and (in many cases) motives. So, acting rightly requires our acting out of the appropriate dispositions and, for many virtues, suitable motives also. Or better, we cannot meet the criterion of right action in (a) in a particular case unless we ourselves have and act out of the virtuous disposition appropriate to the circumstances.[14] For example, to act as a person with the virtue of benevolence would do, I must not only provide help to another, but I must do so out of a benevolent disposition and a genuine concern for their welfare. And it should be noted that, as this also illustrates, while virtue ethics holds that acting out of the appropriate dispositions is *necessary* for right action, it does not claim that acting out of such dispositions is *sufficient* for right action. Not only is a virtuous agent well disposed (and with many virtues, well motivated) when they act, but they also perform appropriate actions from those dispositions (and those motives, where the relevant virtue requires this). (As we

Footnote 13 *(cont.)*

    defence of this subjectivist approach, see Frank Jackson, 'Decision-Theoretic Consequentialism and the Nearest and Dearest Objection', *Ethics* 101, no. 3, April 1991. (As Oddie and Menzies explain on pp. 515–16, the objectivist version of expectabilism is still distinct from actualism, since acts sometimes actually result in consequences which – at the time of the act – are objectively highly *im*probable.)

    Note that we are talking here about genuinely expectabilist theories, rather than about theories which tell us to use the reasonably expected best consequences as a useful heuristic for identifying right actions, on the grounds that this provides us with the most reliable 'rule of thumb' to determining which of our actions will result in the *actual* best consequences (but it is upon the latter which rightness is ultimately based).

[14] In making this claim, we agree with Aristotle, who held that: 'It is not merely the state in accordance with the right rule, but the state that implies the *presence* of the right rule, that is virtue' (*Nicomachean Ethics* VI.13.1144b26–9; see also II.4.1105a26–33). See John Cooper, *Reason and Human Good in Aristotle*, Indianapolis, Hackett, 1986, p. 78; and Christine Korsgaard, 'Aristotle on Function and Virtue', *History of Philosophy Quarterly* 3, no. 3, 1986, pp. 266–8.

discuss later, virtue ethics recognises that there is a variety of reasons why good dispositions and motives may on occasions lead someone to act wrongly.)

The essential reference in virtue ethics' criterion of rightness to the character of the agent performing the act distinguishes the approach from actualist versions of act-consequentialism and from the expectabilist version of act-consequentialism described above, since these consequentialist theories allow us to say what acts are right without referring to the character of the agent at all.[15] For act-consequentialists hold simply that an act is right if and only if it results in (or can reasonably be expected to result in) the best consequences. They typically add that the best humanly possible character is the one with the best (actual or expected) consequences. But the best humanly possible character *may* be one that will *not* allow the agent in every possible situation to do the act with the best (actual or expected) consequences. Thus, act-consequentialists admit that a person with a virtuous character might not always perform the act with the best (actual or expected) consequences – i.e. may not always do what is right according to act-consequentialism.[16]

Nevertheless, there are forms of utilitarianism, consequentialism, and Kantianism which *do* give the character of the agent performing the act an essential role in the justification of right action, for they hold that right actions must be guided by a certain sort of character, and that such actions are justified because they flow from agents' having the requisite kind of character. For example, Richard Brandt proposes a form of rule-utilitarianism which

orders the acceptable level of aversion to various act-types in accordance with the damage . . . that would likely be done if everyone felt free to indulge in the kind of behaviour in question . . . The worse the effect if everyone felt free, the higher the acceptable level of aversion.[17]

On this view, we cannot say what rightness is without referring to the aversions in the character of the agent. Indeed, some have taken the idea of a character-based utilitarian or Kantian ethics to suggest that these

---

[15] Note that this feature is not sufficient to distinguish the virtue ethics criterion of rightness from that form of expectabilism which relies on what consequences of an act *the agent* believes to be likely, since this approach also contains an essential reference to the character of the agent performing the action. Nevertheless, virtue ethics is distinguishable from this subjectivist form of expectabilism in terms of how virtue ethics grounds the normative conception to govern the character of the good agent, which we discuss below.

[16] We are indebted to Brad Hooker here.

[17] Richard B. Brandt, 'Morality and its Critics', *American Philosophical Quarterly* 26, 1989, p. 95. See also Brad Hooker, 'Rule-Consequentialism', *Mind* 99, 1990.

theories can actually be recast as derivative forms of virtue ethics. For example, Philippa Foot has suggested that we could consider utilitarianism a form of virtue ethics, insofar as it tells us that we ought to act and be motivated as a person with a good utilitarian character would. The character of such a person, as Foot sees it, would be governed by just *one* disposition – the virtue of universal benevolence – and the rightness of their actions would be judged according to whether they conformed with what such a disposition would have them do.[18] Likewise, Barbara Herman suggests that Kant (especially in his later work) tells us to act as a good Kantian agent would, and that such an agent would have and act out of certain emotional and partial dispositions, which are regulated by a commitment to not acting impermissibly.[19]

These forms of utilitarianism and Kantianism indicate that it will clearly not do to talk about virtue ethics as distinctive simply by the primacy it gives to *character* in the determination of right action.[20] One

[18] Philippa Foot, 'Utilitarianism and the Virtues', in Scheffler (ed)., *Consequentialism and its Critics*, pp. 224–42.

[19] See Barbara Herman, 'Agency, Attachment, and Difference', and other essays in her *The Practice of Moral Judgment*. See also Kurt Baier, 'Radical Virtue Ethics', in P. French et al. (eds.), *Midwest Studies in Philosophy, Volume 13: Ethical Theory: Character and Virtue*; Robert B. Louden, 'Kant's Virtue Ethics', *Philosophy* 61, 1986, esp. pp. 478–9, 484–9; Robert Louden, 'Can we be too Moral?', *Ethics* 98, 1988; Onora O'Neill, 'Consistency in Action', in N. Potter and M. Timmons (eds.), *Morality and Universality*, Dordrecht, Reidel, 1985; and Nancy Sherman, 'The Place of Emotions in Kantian Morality', in Owen Flanagan and Amélie O. Rorty (eds.), *Identity, Character, and Morality: Essays in Moral Psychology*, Cambridge, MA, MIT Press, 1990. A criticism analogous to that which Foot makes of a utilitarian virtue ethics may also be made of a Kantian virtue ethics, which took conscientiousness (as the disposition to act according to duty) as the only virtue. See N. J. H. Dent, *The Moral Psychology of the Virtues*, Cambridge, Cambridge University Press, 1984, pp. 27–31; and James D. Wallace, *Virtues and Vices*, Ithaca, Cornell University Press, 1978, p. 130.

[20] The primacy of character is taken as distinctive of virtue ethics by Frankena, *Ethics*, pp. 63ff.; Pence, 'Recent Work on the Virtues'; Gregory E. Pence, 'Virtue Theory', in Peter Singer (ed.), *A Companion to Ethics*, Oxford, Blackwell, 1991; and Gary Watson, 'On the Primacy of Character', in Flanagan and Rorty (eds.), *Identity, Character, and Morality*.

There is an important body of research in social psychology which provides substantial evidence that the variations in behaviour displayed by different individuals in a given context are often better explained by relatively minor situational variations than by the assumptions we commonly make about differences in character-traits. (For a good summary of this research, see Lee Ross and Richard Nisbett, *The Person and the Situation: Perspectives of Social Psychology*, New York, McGraw-Hill, 1991, esp. chapters 2 and 5.) Some take this as a reason for scepticism about the value or legitimacy of talk of character-traits at all, while others see the research as indicating that whatever character-traits we have are significantly less powerful determinants of our behaviour than is commonly thought. This research has been argued by some to pose particular problems for virtue ethics, given its reliance on the notion of character. However, given the moves by contemporary Kantians, utilitarians, and consequentialists to develop their own forms of character-based ethics, the normative upshot of these research findings may be broader than is usually realised. In any case, the apparent fact that the standing dispositions we take ourselves and others to have are often swayed by relatively trivial situational factors does not mean that we should not *try* to have more robust dispositions, as virtue ethics suggests; and so these research

needs to point to additional features in order to show what is distinctive about virtue ethics as a form of character-based ethics.

One important way of distinguishing virtue ethics from Kantian and utilitarian forms of character-based ethics is by bringing out the differences in how each theory grounds the relevant normative conception which would govern the character of a good agent. These differences should become more apparent as we go on, but let us say something about them here. Kantians claim that the goodness of an agent's character is determined by how well they have internalised the capacity to test the universalisability of their maxims, while utilitarians claim that a person with a good character is one who is disposed to maximise utility. Virtue ethicists, however, reject both Kantian universalisability and the maximisation of utility as the appropriate ground of good character, and instead draw on other factors in substantiating the appropriate normative conceptions of a good agent.

There are broadly speaking two main kinds of approach taken by virtue ethicists in grounding the character of the good agent. The more prominent of these approaches draws on the Aristotelian view that the content of virtuous character is determined by what we need, or what we are, qua *human* beings. Many virtue ethicists develop one particular version of this approach, taking the eudaimonistic view that the virtues are character-traits which we need to live humanly flourishing lives. On this view, character-traits such as benevolence, honesty, and justice are virtues because they feature importantly among an interlocking web of intrinsic goods – which includes courage, integrity, friendship, and knowledge – without which we cannot have *eudaimonia*, or a flourishing life for a human being. Moreover, these traits and activities, when coordinated by the governing virtue of *phronesis* (or practical wisdom), are regarded as together partly *constitutive* of *eudaimonia* – that is, the virtues are intrinsically good components of a good human life.[21] Aristotle

findings may not undermine virtue ethics' claim to provide appropriate normative ideals of character (although achieving those ideals might perhaps be significantly more difficult than people usually think). For discussion of the implications of this research for virtue ethics and moral psychology, see John Campbell, 'Can Philosophical Accounts of Altruism Accommodate Experimental Data on Helping Behaviour?', *Australasian Journal of Philosophy* 77, no. 1, March 1999; John M. Doris, 'Persons, Situations, and Virtue Ethics', *Nous* 32, no. 4, 1998; John M. Doris, *Lack of Character: Personality and Moral Behaviour*, New York, Cambridge University Press, 2001; Owen Flanagan, *Varieties of Moral Personality*, Cambridge, MA, Harvard University Press, 1991; and Gilbert Harman, 'Moral Philosophy Meets Social Psychology: Virtue Ethics and the Fundamental Attribution Error', *Proceedings of the Aristotelian Society* 99, 1998–1999.

[21] See Aristotle, *Nicomachean Ethics*. See also Cooper, *Reason and Human Good in Aristotle*, pp. 79–88; and J. L. Ackrill, 'Aristotle on *Eudaimonia*', in Amélie O. Rorty (ed.), *Essays on Aristotle's Ethics*, Berkeley, University of California Press, 1980.

thought that humans flourish by living virtuous lives because it is only in doing so that our rational capacity to guide our lives is expressed in an excellent way. Human good is a function of our rational capacity because what counts as good in a species is determined by its character- istic activity, and the exercising of our rational capacity is the character- istic activity of human beings.[22] It is this Aristotelian approach to the grounding of the character of the good agent that we take in this book. On this view, the good is not a passive external consequence of acting virtuously, and so it would be incorrect to say (as utilitarians might) that acting virtuously typically results in our living a good human life; rather, the good is active, and acting virtuously is a constituent part of what a good human life consists in.

Some virtue ethicists develop this general approach by grounding the virtues not so much in the idea of a good human being, but rather in what is good *for* human beings. The best-known exponent of this view is Philippa Foot, who in her early work argued that a feature of the virtues is that they are beneficial to their possessor. Foot thought that this helped explain why courage and temperance count as virtues. However, she later found this rationale unpromising with such common-sense virtues as justice and benevolence; so she broadened her account to derive virtues from what is beneficial to humans either individually or as a com- munity.[23] This brought her closer in some respects to Alasdair MacIntyre, who argues that such qualities as truthfulness, courage, and justice are virtues because they enable us to achieve the goods internal to the characteristically human practices which strengthen traditions and the communities which sustain them.[24]

An alternative version of a broadly Aristotelian approach is put forward by perfectionists, who reject both the eudaimonistic idea that virtuous living is necessary for happiness and the idea that such a life must be overall beneficial to the person living it. Perfectionism derives the virtues from those characteristics which most fully develop our essen- tial properties as human beings. For example, love of knowledge, friend- ship, and accomplishment count as virtues because these states most fully realise our essential capacities for theoretical and practical ration- ality. And further, loving these goods would count as virtuous even where a person would lead a happier life, and would benefit more, by not loving

---

[22] This is Aristotle's well-known *ergon* argument, found in *Nicomachean Ethics* I. 7.
[23] See Foot, 'Virtues and Vices', and 'Moral Beliefs', both in her *Virtues and Vices*.
[24] See Alasdair MacIntyre, *After Virtue*, 2nd edn, Notre Dame, University of Notre Dame Press, 1984, esp. chapter 14.

them – say, because his accomplishment can be gained only at the cost of enormous personal hardship.[25] Nevertheless, despite the differences between this and the eudaimonistic development of the Aristotelian approach, the two views agree that to live a life without the virtues would in some sense be to go against our basic nature.

A different kind of approach to grounding virtuous character also rejects the eudaimonistic idea that the virtues are given by what humans need in order to flourish, and instead derives the virtues from our common-sense views about what character-traits we typically find admirable. According to this non-Aristotelian approach, developed principally by Michael Slote, there is a plurality of traits which we commonly find admirable in human beings in certain circumstances, and one way we can determine what these are is by examining our responses to the lives led by various admirable exemplars. Further, when we look at such exemplars, we see that some are quite different from those which would be held up by Kantians and utilitarians. For example, while people like Mother Teresa are undoubtedly thought admirable on account of the benefits they have bestowed on humanity, Slote claims that we may well regard people like Albert Einstein or Samuel Johnson as just as admirable as Mother Teresa, even though Einstein and Johnson were not exactly *benefactors* of mankind.[26] On this view, then, benevolence, honesty, and justice are virtues because, even if they are not necessary for human flourishing, they are nevertheless character-traits which we ordinarily find deeply admirable in human beings.

The differences between these forms of virtue ethics, on the one hand, and character-based forms of Kantianism and utilitarianism, on the other hand, would become apparent in practice in their different ways of handling cases where certain values conflict. Thus, consider a case where the requirements of duty or utility conflict with what a good or admirable friend would do. For example, suppose I console a close friend of mine who is grieving over the irretrievable breakdown of his marriage, and that in consoling him, I stay with him longer than would be required by my duty to him as a friend. A virtue ethicist might regard

---

[25] See Thomas Hurka, 'Virtue as Loving the Good', in Ellen F. Paul, Fred D. Miller and Jeffrey Paul (eds.), *The Good Life and the Human Good*, Cambridge, Cambridge University Press, 1992, esp. pp. 153–5; Thomas Hurka, *Perfectionism*, New York, Oxford University Press, 1993; and L. W. Sumner, 'Two Theories of the Good', in Paul et al. (eds.), *The Good Life and the Human Good*, esp. pp. 4–5. See also John McDowell, 'The Role of *Eudaimonia* in Aristotle's Ethics', in Rorty, *Essays on Aristotle's Ethics*, esp. pp. 370–1; and Korsgaard, 'Aristotle on Function and Virtue', pp. 277–8.

[26] See Michael Slote, *From Morality to Virtue*, New York, Oxford University Press, 1992; and Michael Slote, *Goods and Virtues*, Oxford, Clarendon Press, 1983.

my staying longer to console him as right, even if my doing so meant cancelling an appointment with a business associate I had promised to meet for lunch, and also meant that I thereby failed to maximise overall utility. As we explain in our chapter 2 discussion of similar cases, what makes it right to console the friend here is that this is the sort of thing which someone with an appropriate conception of friendship will be disposed to do, rather than that this brings about the best overall consequences, or that this is our duty as a friend. (In chapter 2 we go on to explain that this is not, of course, to suggest that just *any* other significant conflicting values will be justifiably trumped by such reasons of friendship.)

In this book, we base our arguments on the Aristotelian approach to grounding the character of the virtuous agent, and we take the eudaimonistic view that the virtues are character-traits which we need to live humanly flourishing lives. We take this broad approach because it seems to us to provide a more promising rationale for why certain dispositions are to count as virtues than do the rival accounts which we described briefly above. For example, while the dispositions proper to friendship might often be admirable, in our view what makes such dispositions virtues is their inextricable links with our basic nature as creatures who are social and who pursue understanding. Without friendship, our self-development and self-understanding would be stunted in ways alien to our condition as human beings. This view might be interpreted as deriving virtues from what humans as a species *tend* to do, and so might seem to count traits like aggression as virtues, insofar as humans tend to be aggressive. However, the central idea of this Aristotelian approach is the connection that various character-traits have to living a flourishing human life. And so while acts of aggression, or indeed, of nepotism, might be things that humans as a species tend to do, they are not – unlike friendship – tendencies that contribute to the flourishing of human beings. (Of course, as we argue in later chapters, some character-traits which are not virtues in general might nevertheless qualify as virtues in particular contexts – we would allow that character-traits such as aggression might form an important part of the virtues appropriate to, say, certain sporting or business activities.) So, on this approach, there is an interdependent network of intrinsically valuable activities which together are *constitutive* of a well-lived human life. And it is a *conceptual* requirement of the realisation of some of these goods (for example, love and friendship) that agents act out of certain *motives*, while other goods (for example, justice) have no such requirement with regard to motives.

Further, while some goods (for example, justice) are agent-neutral, virtue ethics holds (unlike standard versions of utilitarianism and Kantianism) that the value intrinsic to certain other goods is *agent-relative*. Thus, according to this conception of virtue ethics, what is intrinsically valuable ranges from agent-relative motive-dependent goods such as love and friendship to agent-neutral and motive-independent goods such as justice. Further, as we explain in section 2, virtuous dispositions embody conceptions of excellence or what we call 'regulative ideals', which guide us in our actions, and provide a standard against which our actions can be assessed.

A second claim made by all varieties of virtue ethics is:

(b) Goodness is prior to rightness.

That is, the notion of goodness is primary, while the notion of rightness can be defined only in relation to goodness: no account can be given of what makes an action right until we have established what is valuable or good. In particular, virtue ethics claims that we need an account of *human* good (or of what are commonly regarded as admirable human traits) before we can determine what it is right for us to do in any given situation. In terms of a familiar taxonomy of normative theories, claim (b) makes virtue ethics a *teleological* rather than a *deontological* ethical theory, and so would seem to place virtue ethics in the same family as utilitarianism and standard forms of consequentialism.[27] However, as we explain shortly, there are important differences between virtue ethics' account of the good and those given by most versions of utilitarianism and consequentialism, and in the light of this, it is misleading to group virtue ethics as a theory of the same type as utilitarianism and consequentialism. Indeed, we shall see that virtue ethics has important similarities with non-consequentialist and deontological ethical theories.

Claim (b) is actually implicit in (a) above, but making the claim explicit brings out an important difference between virtue ethics and any form of character-based ethics derived from traditional forms of Kantianism

---

[27] This way of classifying normative theories is increasingly coming under attack as inadequately sensitive to the issues which divide contemporary consequentialists and non-consequentialists. See Herman, *The Practice of Moral Judgment*, esp. chapter 10, 'Leaving Deontology Behind'; and Watson, 'On the Primacy of Character', p. 450. John Rawls, in *A Theory of Justice* (Oxford, Oxford University Press, 1972), p. 24, assumes that all teleological theories must be consequentialist, and indeed, John Broome, in *Weighing Goods* (Oxford, Blackwell, 1991), chapter 1, argues that *all* ethical theories can be regarded as forms of consequentialism. On the other hand, Watson sees the possibility of teleological theories which are not consequentialist. For a good discussion of these issues, see James Dreier, 'Structures of Normative Theories', *The Monist* 76, 1993.

and deontology. For according to these latter theories, rightness is not derived from notions of goodness or accounts of human good, well-being, or virtue. Indeed, the Kantian notions of a morally worthy action or agent are derived from prior deontic notions of rightness and right action – a good Kantian agent, as contemporary Kantians explain, is one who is disposed to act in accordance with certain moral rules or requirements (which themselves are derived from, for example, the nature of practical rationality). By contrast, virtue ethics derives its account of rightness and right action from prior aretaic notions of good-ness and good character, which (in Aristotelian virtue ethics) are them-selves grounded in an independent account of human flourishing that values our emotional as well as our rational capacities, and recognises that our goodness can be affected for the better or worse by empirical contingencies.

A third claim made by virtue ethics is:

(c) The virtues are irreducibly plural intrinsic goods.

The substantive account of the good which forms the foundation for virtue ethics' justification of right action specifies a range of valuable traits and activities as essential for a humanly flourishing life, or as central to our views of admirable human beings. These different virtues embody irreducibly *plural* values – i.e. each of them is valuable in a way which is not reducible to a single overarching value.[28] The virtues them-selves are here taken to be valuable *intrinsically* rather than *instrumentally* – i.e. they are valuable for their own sake, rather than as a means to pro-moting or realising some other value. For example, Aristotle argued that friendship is 'choiceworthy in itself', apart from any advantages it may bestow upon us.[29] The plurality of the virtues distinguishes virtue ethics

---

[28] On the evaluative pluralism of virtue ethics, see Aristotle's criticisms of Plato, in *Nicomachean Ethics* I. 6; Wallace, *Virtues and Vices*, e.g. pp. 27–32; Hursthouse, 'Virtue Theory and Abortion'; and Lawrence Becker, *Reciprocity*, London, Routledge & Kegan Paul, 1986, e.g. chapter 4. Note that the Aristotelian notion of *eudaimonia* is not itself to be construed in an evaluative monist way. See the discussions of 'inclusivist' versus 'dominant' conceptions of *eudaimonia* in W. F. R. Hardie, 'The Final Good in Aristotle's Ethics', *Philosophy* 40, 1965; Ackrill, 'Aristotle on *Eudaimonia*'; and Cooper, *Reason and Human Good*, pp. 96–9.

[29] See John M. Cooper, 'Aristotle on Friendship', in Rorty, *Essays on Aristotle's Ethics*, e.g. p. 338 n. 18. It should be noted that to claim that a virtue is intrinsically good is not yet to claim that it is unconditionally good. For example, that (the dispositions of) friendship is intrinsically good does not entail that friendship is *always* a good, wherever it is instantiated. When combined with intrinsic bads, friendship may no longer be a good, and may even be a bad. For instance, a rela-tionship between two murderous gangsters that is governed by the dispositions and counterfac-tual conditions characteristic of friendship (rather than a disposition, say, to dispose of the other should he become a nuisance) might not be a good in that context. This raises large issues, which we cannot discuss here.

from older, monistic forms of utilitarianism, which reduce all goods to a single value such as pleasure.[30] Claim (c) would also distinguish virtue ethics from a simple 'utilitarianism of the virtues', which would regard the virtues as good, but only *instrumentally* – i.e. insofar as they produce pleasure.[31]

However, the evaluative pluralism of the virtues in (c) does not distinguish virtue ethics from contemporary preference-utilitarianism, which seems able consistently to recognise a plurality of things which are, at least in one sense, intrinsically valuable. For preference-utilitarianism attributes value to the plural things desired, and can allow that certain things – such as knowledge, autonomy, and accomplishment – have intrinsic value, at least in the sense that we desire to have these things for themselves, rather than for any consequences which having them may bring.[32] On this kind of view, the concept of 'utility' is not a substantive value, but is given a formal analysis in terms of the fulfilment of informed preferences. Thus, as James Griffin puts it,

> Since utility is not a substantive value at all, we have to give up the idea that our various particular ends are valuable only because they cause, produce, bring about, are sources of, utility. On the contrary, they [our various particular ends] are the values, utility is not.[33]

Such a view might therefore allow that the virtues are plural, intrinsic values, in the sense that agents attach value to having them for their own sake.

Nevertheless, there is a further claim made by virtue ethics, which helps to distinguish it from any preference-utilitarian approach to the virtues, namely:

(d) The virtues are objectively good.

Virtue ethics regards the virtues as objectively good in the sense that they are good independently of any connections which they may have with

---

[30] See, for example, Bentham's hedonistic utilitarianism. But as Michael Stocker points out, in *Plural and Conflicting Values* (Oxford, Clarendon Press, 1990), pp. 184–93, hedonistic utilitarians need not have been evaluative monists; for pleasure, when properly understood, can itself can be plausibly thought of as plural.

[31] See, e.g., Henry Sidgwick, *The Methods of Ethics*, 7th edn, Indianapolis, Hackett, 1981, pp. 391–7, 423–57.

[32] See James Griffin, *Well-Being: Its Meaning, Measurement, and Moral Importance*, Oxford, Clarendon Press, 1986, e.g. p. 31: 'It seems to me undeniable that we do value irreducibly different kinds of things . . . The desire account is compatible with a strong form of pluralism about values . . . On the desire account one can allow that when I fully understand what is involved, I may end up valuing many things and valuing them for themselves.' See also R. M. Hare, 'Comments', in D. Seanor and N. Fotion (eds.), *Hare and Critics*, Oxford, Clarendon Press, 1988, pp. 239, 251.

[33] *Well-Being*, p. 32 n. 24. See also p. 89.

desire.[34] What the objective goodness of the virtues means in positive terms depends on the particular rationale given for them. As we saw earlier, one approach bases the goodness of the virtues on the connections they have with essential human characteristics, such as theoretical and practical rationality; another approach derives the goodness of the virtues from admirable character-traits. But neither approach makes the value of any candidate virtue depend on whether the agent desires it (either actually or hypothetically). For example, courageousness would still count as a virtuous trait, even in a person who had no desire to be courageous.[35] Further, the virtues can confer value on *a life*, even if the person living it does not (actually or hypothetically) desire to have them.[36] So, while preference-utilitarians might allow that certain character-traits have intrinsic value in the sense that we may desire to have them for themselves, preference-utilitarians would not allow that the value of the virtues can be independent of desire in these ways.

But while (c) and (d) distinguish virtue ethics from various forms of utilitarianism, they seem to leave open whether virtue ethics is different from those forms of consequentialism which accept the idea of irreducibly plural *intrinsic* and *objective* values. For example, some consequentialists believe that there are at least two irreducibly plural intrinsic and objective values – such as universal benevolence and fairness – while others believe that there is a whole range of such values – such as happiness, knowledge, purposeful activity, autonomy, solidarity, respect, and

---

[34] For this use of 'objective good', see Hurka, *Perfectionism*, p. 5. See also Sumner, 'Two Theories of the Good'.

[35] Could Philippa Foot allow this, given her well-known claim that we cannot have a reason to pursue something unless it is linked appropriately to some desire of ours (see 'Morality as a System of Hypothetical Imperatives', in *Virtues and Vices*)? It would seem so, for in several places Foot suggests that a virtuous person is a good example of a human being. Foot's view then would be that while a person cannot have a reason to be virtuous unless this serves some desire of theirs, the *goodness* of their being virtuous does not depend on their desires. See 'A Reply to Professor Frankena', in *Virtues and Vices* p. 178: 'propositions of the "good F" "good G" form do not, in general, have a direct connexion with reasons for choice'. See also 'Goodness and Choice', in *Virtues and Vices*, esp. pp. 145–7.

[36] This is not to say that the virtues increase one's *well-being*. There is disagreement amongst virtue ethicists about whether the virtues are good *for me*, or make me 'better off'. As we saw earlier, Philippa Foot claims that virtues generally (i.e. except justice and benevolence) make their possessor better off; however, Michael Slote rejects any such general claim: see *From Morality to Virtue*, *op. cit.*, p. 209: 'I am ruling out the possibility that a distinctive ethics of virtue would want to reduce the admirable and the idea of a virtue to notions connected with personal good or well-being'. See also pp. 8 and 130.

Some would question whether a person who achieves certain characteristic human excellences could be living a good life if they do not *desire* (either actually or hypothetically) to have those excellences. For it might be claimed that living a good life has an ineliminable *subjective* element. See Gregory W. Trianosky, 'Rightly Ordered Appetites: How to Live Morally and Live Well', *American Philosophical Quarterly* 25, 1988.

beauty.[37] What, if anything, is there to distinguish virtue ethics from these forms of consequentialism?

Two further claims are essential to any form of virtue ethics, and these help distinguish virtue ethics from most forms of consequentialism. The first is:

(e) Some intrinsic goods are agent-relative.

Among the variety of goods which virtue ethics regards as constituting a humanly flourishing life, some, such as friendship and integrity, are held to be ineliminably agent-relative, while others, such as justice, are thought more properly characterised as agent-neutral. To describe a certain good as agent-relative is to say that its being a good of *mine* gives it additional moral importance (*to me*), in contrast to agent-neutral goods, which derive no such additional moral importance from their being goods of mine.[38] For example, friendship could be regarded as either an agent-neutral or an agent-relative good. In the former case, it would be friendship per se which is intrinsically valuable, and a plura-listic consequentialist who believed that friendship is an agent-neutral value would tell us to maximise (or at least promote) friendships them-selves – say, by setting up a social club. On the agent-relative account of the value of friendship, however, the fact that a certain relationship is *my* friendship would give it more moral relevance to my acts than would be had by, say, the competing claims of your friendships. Virtue ethics sees friendship (and certain other virtues) as valuable in the latter sense – were performing a friendly act towards a friend of mine to conflict with promoting friendships between others (for example, by throwing a party

---

[37] See, e.g., T. M. Scanlon, 'Rights, Goals and Fairness', in Scheffler (ed.), *Consequentialism and its Critics*; Railton, 'Alienation', pp. 108–10; Hurka, 'Virtue as Loving the Good'; Hurka, *Perfectionism*; Thomas Hurka, 'Consequentialism and Content', *American Philosophical Quarterly* 29, 1992, pp. 71–8; the 'Ideal Utilitarianism' of G. E. Moore, in *Principia Ethica*, Cambridge, Cambridge University Press, 1903, chapter 6; and Hastings Rashdall, *The Theory of Good and Evil*, vol. 1, Oxford, Oxford University Press, 1907, chapters 7 and 8. David McNaughton and Piers Rawling, in 'Agent-Relativity and the Doing–Happening Distinction', *Philosophical Studies* 63, 1991, pp. 168–9, explain well how a consequentialist might be able to allow for plural intrinsic values. See also Derek Parfit, *Reasons and Persons*, Oxford, Clarendon Press, 1984, p. 26; and David Sosa, 'Consequences of Consequentialism', *Mind* 102, 1993.

Some might question whether the sense of intrinsic 'goodness' that certain pluralistic conse-quentialists allow such features to have really has much in common with the sense in which virtue ethics regards those features as intrinsically good, as the former are *welfaristic* while the latter are *aretaic*. (We thank one of the readers for noting this.) But if these really do turn out to be two entirely different senses of 'goodness', then this would further distinguish virtue ethics from con-sequentialist approaches.

[38] By this we do not mean to suggest that agent-relative value must be understood as *aggregative*. In describing the value of a certain trait or activity as 'agent-relative', one may be making a claim about its *qualitative* character.

for new colleagues), I would nevertheless be justified in acting for my friend.[39]

Claim (e) distinguishes virtue ethics from most forms of consequentialism, whether monistic or pluralistic, since most consequentialists regard all values as agent-neutral.[40] But there seems to be no reason in principle why a consequentialist could not allow that some values are properly characterised as agent-relative. Indeed, some consequentialists do seem to accept that certain values (such as friendship and integrity) are irreducibly agent-relative.[41] However, most of those consequentialists would stop short of endorsing the following claim made by virtue ethics.

(f) Acting rightly does not require that we maximise the good.

The core thesis of most versions of consequentialism is the idea that rightness requires us to maximise the good, whether goodness is monistic or pluralistic, subjective or objective, agent-neutral across the board or agent-relative in some instances.[42] Virtue ethics, by contrast, rejects maximisation as a theory of rightness. Thus, in a case where I can favour *my* friendships over promoting others' friendships, I am not required by virtue ethics to *maximise* my friendships. Neither am I required to have the best friendship(s) which it is possible for me to have.[43] Rather, I ought to have *excellent* friendships, relative to the norms which properly govern such relationships, and an excellent friendship may not be the very best friendship which I am capable of having.[44] Virtue ethicists hold that in

---

[39] See Stocker, *Plural and Conflicting Values*, pp. 313–14; and Dreier, 'Structures of Normative Theories'.

[40] Indeed, some theorists, such as Samuel Scheffler (in his introduction to *Consequentialism and its Critics*) and Shelly Kagan, in *The Limits of Morality* (Oxford, Clarendon Press, 1989), regard a belief in the agent-neutrality of all value as a *sine qua non* of a consequentialist theory.

[41] See, e.g., Railton, 'Alienation'; and Sosa, 'Consequences of Consequentialism'.

[42] There are *satisficing* versions of consequentialism, which hold that acting rightly does not require us to maximise the good, but to bring about consequences that are *good enough*. See, e.g., Michael Slote, 'Satisficing Consequentialism', Part I, *Proceedings of the Aristotelian Society*, Supplementary Volume 58, 1984; and Michael Slote, *Beyond Optimizing: A Study of Rational Choice*, Cambridge, MA, Harvard University Press, 1989. However, consequentialists commonly reject satisficing in favour of maximisation, as they argue that when one can have more of a certain good or less of it, it is irrational to prefer less. See the response to Slote by Philip Pettit, 'Satisficing Consequentialism', Part II, *Proceedings of the Aristotelian Society*, Supplementary Volume 58, 1984; and Hurka, *Perfectionism*, pp. 56–7. For a critique of Pettit's arguments here, see Stocker, *Plural and Conflicting Values*, pp. 325–31. For discussion of satisficing in relation to virtue ethics, see Justin Oakley, 'Varieties of Virtue Ethics', *Ratio* 9, no. 2, September 1996.

[43] On Aristotle as a non-maximiser, see Stocker, *Plural and Conflicting Values*, pp. 338–42; and Cooper, *Reason and Human Good in Aristotle*, pp. 87–8, and chapter 2.

[44] It should be noted that, in setting excellence as the standard of rightness, virtue ethics can allow that different individuals who have a certain type of disposition to varying degrees could still

acting towards my friends I ought to be guided by an appropriate normative conception of what friendship involves (such as the account of
character-friendship given by Aristotle in *Nicomachean Ethics* IX.9).

Claims (a) to (f) are made by all forms of virtue ethics, and the different varieties of the theory can be distinguished according to which of
these claims they emphasise, and their reasons for making these claims.
Some philosophers who do not (or at least, not explicitly) call themselves
virtue ethicists nevertheless endorse one or more of these claims as part
of their criticisms of Kantian, utilitarian, or consequentialist theories.[45]
However, taken as a whole, these claims help show how virtue ethics constitutes a distinct alternative to familiar forms of Kantianism, utilitarianism, and consequentialism.

2 THE NOTION OF A 'REGULATIVE IDEAL'

In this section we introduce the notion of a 'regulative ideal', which is
central to our arguments in this book. In our view, the best way to conceive of a virtue ethics criterion of right action is in terms of a 'regulative ideal'. To say that an agent has a regulative ideal is to say that they
have internalised a certain conception of correctness or excellence, in
such a way that they are able to adjust their motivation and conduct so
that it conforms – or at least does not conflict – with that standard. So,
for instance, a man who has internalised a certain conception of what it
is to be a good father can be guided by this conception in his practices
as a father, through regulating his motivations and actions towards his
children so that they are consistent with his conception of good fathering. A regulative ideal is thus an internalised normative disposition to
direct one's actions and alter one's motivation in certain ways. Principles
of normative theories, the standards of excellence embodied in the
virtues, a conception of friendship, standards of excellence in a musical
genre, or principles of grammar in a natural language could all function
as regulative ideals in various agents' psychologies.

have this disposition to an excellent degree, and so still count as virtuous in that respect. For
example, while the disposition to medical beneficence of one's local family doctor might not
reach the level of, say, Albert Schweitzer, she might nevertheless have developed her disposition
to medical beneficence to an excellent degree, and so she could properly lay claim to having this
medical virtue.

[45] See, e.g., Samuel Scheffler, *The Rejection of Consequentialism*, Oxford, Oxford University Press,
1982; Samuel Scheffler, *Human Morality*, New York, Oxford University Press, 1992; Stocker, *Plural
and Conflicting Values*; and Bernard Williams, 'Persons, Character, and Morality', in his *Moral Luck*,
Cambridge, Cambridge University Press, 1981.

Regulative ideals may be general in scope, or they may be specific to certain domains. For example, the good consequentialist's life will be guided by a general regulative ideal, as exemplified in their normative disposition to maximise agent-neutral value. However, the activities of a good person may be guided by specific regulative ideals in particular areas. For example, it may be thought part of being a good medical practitioner that one has internalised a conception of what the appropriate ends of medicine are, and one is disposed to treat one's patients in ways which are consistent with those ends. Further, since regulative ideals operate as guiding background conditions on our motivation, they can direct us to act appropriately or rightly, even when we do not consciously formulate them or aim at them. Thus suppose, for instance, that I have learnt some jazz theory and studied various jazz pianists, and have thereby developed a conception of excellence in jazz piano. I can be guided by this conception of jazz excellence when I am ensconced in playing jazz piano, without consciously formulating that conception as I play. Indeed, the absence of any need consciously to formulate such a conception while playing would probably be part of what I would take excellence at jazz piano to be. Similarly, in learning to speak Greek, I learn the principles of Greek grammar, which in the early stages I must explicitly formulate before I can string together a well-formed Greek sentence. But what I want is to shape and condition my linguistic dispositions in such a way that I no longer need to formulate the appropriate grammatical rule each and every time before I speak and respond in Greek. After I have reached that later stage, my speech will still in an important sense be informed and guided by an underlying regulative ideal which is the principles of Greek grammar. For clearly, the fact that I have now reached the stage where I do not need consciously to formulate the principles of Greek grammar before carrying on a conversation in that language is compatible with my speech being regulated by those principles – indeed, this is just what fluency in a second language *is*.[46]

---

[46] Compare this with a case in which I try to learn the underlying conception of performing a certain activity excellently, but then without going any further I jettison it entirely. For example, I may try to learn the underlying ideas of jazz theory, but then, failing to grasp them, I may go on to play excellent jazz. Here my playing jazz would not be informed or regulated by the underlying ideas of jazz theory, and so my playing jazz well may, in an important sense, not be due to *me*.

There is, of course, the further issue of how to assess actions which are truly ungoverned or uninformed by *any* underlying conception of what an excellent example of that activity involves. Of such people we sometimes say that they are 'a natural' at that kind of activity (think here of certain musicians, writers, chefs, sportspeople, etc.). Critics of virtue ethics sometimes seem to assume that *this* is what Aristotle was telling us to take as a moral exemplar. However (apart from

Further, a regulative ideal can guide us in our actions, without becoming one of our *purposes* in acting. For instance, the principles of Greek grammar guide us in having a conversation in Greek, but our purpose in having the conversation may simply be to find a good hotel, rather than to demonstrate our command of Greek grammar. Also, as we discuss later, a regulative ideal can govern our behaviour without becoming one of our *motives* in acting.

As these examples suggest, we intend our notion of regulative ideals to include both normative dispositions that govern one's actions in accordance with standards of *correctness* and normative dispositions that govern one's behaviour and motivation according to standards of *excellence*, which go beyond the merely correct or incorrect. A regulative ideal that embodies standards of correctness suggests that it involves codifiable rules and principles (although a standard of correctness could conceivably be based on values or considerations that are uncodifiable); whereas a regulative ideal that embodies a standard of excellence may indicate that the values or considerations it involves are not codifiable as a set of rules or principles.[47] In any case, the uncodifiability of the values that determine excellence in a certain regulative ideal does not preclude those values or that ideal from playing a guiding role in our motivation and behaviour. So, for instance, it would presumably be rather difficult to codify standards of correctness for good fathering, yet it would be absurd to suggest that the uncodifiability of the notion of a 'good father' entails that the sorts of values involved in good fathering cannot play any sort of guiding or governing role in the motivation and behaviour of men with their children. On our account, in order to operate as a guiding conception, a regulative ideal need not be codifiable as a set of principles or rules. The codifiability of a guiding conception varies across different human endeavours. Some guiding conceptions, such as the correct grammar of a certain language, are clearly codifiable, while others, such as those governing arts and crafts, seem less amenable to codification as sets of rules or principles.

The guiding idea of virtue ethics is the notion of *eudaimonia*, or living a flourishing life, where this is exemplified in an agent's having certain key virtues and goods, such as friendship, courage, and integrity.

---

the fact that Aristotle devoted a whole book (Bk II) of the *Nicomachean Ethics* to explaining how we can inculcate the virtues), as we have been trying to show, this is an inadequate understanding of what virtue ethics is advocating. We will leave aside the question of how such a naturally virtuous person's actions are to be judged.

[47] There are underlying issues about the nature and importance of codifiability, which we cannot settle here.

According to virtue ethics, these virtues are related to a virtuous person's life in the following ways. First, they require performing certain *activities* (since the virtuous life is, according to Aristotle, importantly one of *acting*, as well as feeling and experiencing). Second, performing these activities in a virtuous way requires acting from certain *motives*. Third, one can be properly said to have acted from these kinds of motives only if they proceed from (and are conditioned by) a certain character structure.[48] It is this third connection in particular which brings out how a virtuous person may act according to a certain regulative ideal. For, in order to act from the right sort of character structure, one must have developed one's motivation and perception to a certain level. Thus, a virtuous agent will have certain standing commitments or normative dispositions, which need not always be consciously formulated or applied, but which will govern and shape their motivations and actions. As a general explanation of the connection between character and right action, this sort of account is widely accepted. As we discuss further in chapter 2, influential recent versions of Kantianism and consequentialism both conceive of their respective criteria of rightness in terms of a regulative ideal operating on an agent's psychology.

Generally speaking, then, having a particular virtuous disposition requires internalising a certain normative standard of excellence, in such a way that one is able to adjust one's motivation and conduct so that it conforms, or at least does not conflict, with that standard. Let us illustrate this in the case of friendship. To have the virtuous dispositions appropriate to *friendship*, one must have an appropriate normative conception of what kind of relationship friendship is, and of what sorts of motives and conduct would be appropriate to such a relationship. We can observe the importance of having an underlying conception of friendship here when we consider young children and adolescents, who, in developing their sense of what it is to have and be true friends, typically revise their views about their earlier relationships' claims to be true friendships. For instance, there is evidence that young adolescents commonly place relatively minimal requirements on what sorts of relationships they count as 'friendships', since they tend to place more importance simply on the fact of having (and being seen to have) personal relationships with others than they do on the quality of those relationships, but as they grow older and more independent of peer

---

[48] This does not mean that there is only one determinate description of a virtuous character – the plural virtues may be instantiated in a virtuous person in a variety of ways.

approval, their conception of what is to count as a friendship becomes less broad and more qualified, and more oriented than previously towards the good of the other person.[49] Further, in order to exemplify the good of friendship in one's actions, one must have developed one's motivation and perception to a certain level. For in exemplifying the good of friendship, one does not act for the sake of *friendship* per se, or even for the sake of *this* friendship, but rather for the sake of this *person*, who is one's friend. And one can properly be said to be acting for the sake of this person only if one has shaped one's perception in certain ways – for example, one must have developed some kind of understanding of what this person's well-being consists of, and of which ways of acting would promote it. Unless a person's motivation were conditioned by a certain conception in this way, they would not yet have succeeded in inculcating the particular virtue or good which is appropriate to that particular activity – here friendship. It is in terms of being governed by some underlying understanding such as this that virtue ethics seeks to justify certain actions.

This is an illustration of how a virtuous person's motivational structure is governed by a *particular* regulative ideal, which is appropriate to a *particular* virtue (i.e. the virtuous dispositions appropriate to the good of friendship). But in a virtuous person, this particular regulative ideal will itself be governed by a higher-order and more *general* regulative ideal, which functions so as to co-ordinate the interplay between the particular regulative ideals which themselves govern the agent's motivation in relation to each of the plural values. This general regulative ideal is what Aristotle calls 'practical wisdom' or *phronesis*, and this involves an understanding of the general good for humans, and the capacity to deliberate well such that one realises virtuous ends in one's responses to particular situations. Aristotle provides some suggestion as to the interplay in moral deliberation between the higher-order regulative ideal of *phronesis* and

---

[49] See, e.g., the essay by Gray and Steinberg in Wyndol Furman, B. Bradford Brown, and Candice Feiring (eds.), *The Development of Romantic Relationships in Adolescence*, Cambridge, Cambridge University Press, 1999. Of course, this does not rule out the possibility that the concept of friendship may be relatively parochial, since a full account of the nature of friendship would allow some degree of cultural variation in specifying what the defining characteristics of true friends are. Therefore, the fact that a culture lacks *our* full conception of friendship does not entail that it has *no* conception of friendship which governs the actions of its members. On the contrary, the inculcation of some conception of friendship would presumably be viewed in many cultures as an important part of becoming an adult. We should also add that to require that the friend has a conception of friendship is not to require that this conception be *consciously* guiding the friend, just as this is not required of the moral conceptions embodied in the regulative ideals of the good Kantian or the consequentialist agent.

the particular regulative ideals appropriate to specific virtues in the following passage:

Practical wisdom . . . is concerned with things human and things about which it is possible to deliberate; for we say this is above all the work of a man of practical wisdom, to deliberate well . . . The man who is without qualification good at deliberating is the man who is capable of aiming in accordance with calculation at the best for man of things attainable by action. Nor is practical wisdom concerned with universals only – it must also recognise particulars; for it is practical, and practice is concerned with particulars.[50]

If our actions and our lives were not governed and co-ordinated by the general regulative ideal of *phronesis*, we would not be living a fully *human* life, but would rather be living a life akin to that of 'lower animals', who, as Aristotle says 'have no universal judgement but only imagination and memory of particulars'.[51]

   In summary, then, we might say that the deliberative and motivational structure of the virtuous person should meet a *counterfactual condition*: while he ordinarily does not do what he does for the sake of exemplifying virtue, he would nevertheless alter his dispositions and the course of his life if he thought that they did not exemplify virtue.[52] And, as we illustrated in the case of friendship, assessments of right action in virtue ethics are given in the way the general regulative ideal of *phronesis* bears on the particular regulative ideal which governs the particular virtue in question.

---

[50] *Nicomachean Ethics* VI.7.1141b9–17, trans. Ross. On the function of *phronesis* in moral deliberation in relation to particular virtues, see Martha Nussbaum, *The Fragility of Goodness*, Cambridge, Cambridge University Press, 1986, esp. chapter 10; Martha Nussbaum, 'The Discernment of Perception: An Aristotelian Conception of Private and Public Rationality', in her *Love's Knowledge*, New York, Oxford University Press, 1990; Nancy Sherman, *The Fabric of Character*, Oxford, Clarendon Press, 1989; T. H. Irwin, 'Reason and Responsibility in Aristotle', in Rorty (ed.), *Essays on Aristotle's Ethics*; Richard Sorabji, 'Aristotle on the Role of Intellect in Virtue', in Rorty (ed.), *Essays on Aristotle's Ethics*; and David Wiggins, 'Deliberation and Practical Reason', in Rorty (ed.), *Essays on Aristotle's Ethics*.

[51] *Nicomachean Ethics* VII. 3. 1147b4–6. Some (eg. particularists, Wittgensteinians, and certain feminist ethicists) who complain that utilitarianism and Kantianism lose or fail to capture certain irreducible role-generated responsibilities and special sensitivities of certain professions are motivated by a deeper scepticism about theory in ethics; however, we think that is too extreme a reaction. Our notion of 'regulative ideals' restores a level of generality in virtue ethics. Further, the regulative ideal approach shows how (contrary to Griffin, *Well-Being*, p. 63: 'It proposes an occasion-by-occasion approach, but we have never been given, and cannot easily find, an explanation of what this approach is that gets beyond the vaguely suggestive') virtue ethics is different from (and so does not succumb to the problems of) situation ethics and casuistry.

[52] For a similar formulation of the general regulative ideal of the virtuous person, see Hursthouse, 'Virtue Theory and Abortion', pp. 225–6, who puts it as follows:

P1. An action is right iff it is what a virtuous agent would do in the circumstances.
P1a. A virtuous agent is one who acts virtuously, that is, one who has and exercises the virtues.
P2. A virtue is a character trait a human being needs to flourish or live well.

We return to the notion of regulative ideals further in chapter 2, where, in arguing against consequentialist and Kantian attempts to accommodate friendship, we explain how regulative ideals impose various 'governing conditions' on relationships, and we indicate the important role which such governing conditions can play in differentiating various relationships.

3 TWO COMMON CRITICISMS OF VIRTUE ETHICS

A number of criticisms have been made of virtue-based approaches to ethics. We will describe two criticisms which we take to be particularly important, and outline how a virtue theorist might respond to them. Both of these objections centre on virtue ethics' appeal to 'what the virtuous agent would do' as the determinant of right action (as in (a) above).

The first criticism raises doubts about whether the notion of virtue is clear or detailed enough to serve as the basis of a criterion of rightness. Many writers argue that this criterion of rightness is too *vague* to be an acceptable basis of justification in ethics. How do we determine what the basic virtues are, and so, what a virtuous agent would be like? And even if we could establish the character of a virtuous agent, the practical applications of such a model are unclear. What would a virtuous agent do in the great variety of situations in which people find themselves? Further, there is a plurality of virtuous character-traits, and not all virtuous people seem to have these traits to the same degree, so virtuous people might not always respond to a particular situation in the same way. For example, is the right action in a given set of circumstances the action which would be done by an honest person, a kind person, or a just person? And even if the range of possible virtuous characters is narrower than this suggests, how do we *know* what a virtuous person would do in a particular situation? As Robert Louden puts it:

Due to the very nature of the moral virtues, there is . . . a very limited amount of advice on moral quandaries that one can reasonably expect from the virtue-oriented approach. We ought, of course, to do what the virtuous person would do, but it is not always easy to fathom what the hypothetical moral exemplar would do were he in our shoes.[53]

---

[53] Robert B. Louden, 'On Some Vices of Virtue Ethics', *American Philosophical Quarterly* 21, 1984, p. 229. Aristotle himself might be thought partly responsible for the non-action-guidingness-of-the-virtues objection, because while he does offer helpful examples of virtues and virtuous action, he also says things such as: moral virtue is determined simply as 'the way in which the man of practical wisdom would determine it' (*Nicomachean Ethics* II.6.1107a1–2).

Worse, is it possible to establish what a virtuous agent would be like without knowing what actions are right? If right action is given by what a virtuous person would do, but we are to determine who counts as a virtuous person by looking at the rightness of their actions, then virtue ethics' requirement in (a) is circular.

Now, to the extent that the criticism here expresses a general worry about appeals to 'what a certain person would do', it is worth remembering that such appeals are quite commonly and successfully used in justifications in a variety of areas. For example, novice doctors and lawyers being inducted into their professions sometimes justify their having acted in a certain way by pointing out that this is how their professional mentor would have acted here, and indeed, such justifications are crucial in situations where the usual procedures do not fully determine what is to be done there. Also, courts often rely significantly on claims about what a reasonable person would have foreseen, in determining a person's legal liability for negligent conduct. Moreover, any general worry about such appeals would also apply to many modern consequentialist theories, which hold that the rightness of an action is determined partly by appealing to what consequences would have been foreseen by a reasonable person in the agent's position.

However, those who accept reliance on such appeals in other areas might well have misgivings about the particular sort of appeal to such a standard which is made by virtue ethics. For establishing what counts as having reasonable foresight of the consequences of actions may be far easier than establishing what counts as having a virtuous character. And it may be considerably more difficult to determine which of the variety of virtuous character-traits a virtuous person would act on in a given situation than to determine what consequences of a given action a reasonable person would foresee.[54]

Now, establishing the nature of a virtuous agent's character is indeed a complex matter, but it should be remembered that virtue ethics does not derive this from some prior account of right action. Rather, which character-traits count as virtuous is determined by their involvement in human flourishing or their admirability, as explained above. It is true to say that virtue ethics does not deliver an 'algorithm' of right action (as

---

[54] See James Rachels, *The Elements of Moral Philosophy*, 2nd edn, Englewood Cliffs, Prentice-Hall, 1993, p. 178. Some writers also argue that a virtue ethics criterion of rightness is too vague to tell us what *emotions* we should feel in various conflict situations. See Kristjan Kristjansson, 'Virtue Ethics and Emotional Conflict', *American Philosophical Quarterly* 37, no. 3, July 2000.

Aristotle put it), and that a virtue ethics criterion of rightness is perhaps less precisely specifiable and less easily applicable than that given by consequentialist theories (although perhaps not compared to those given by Kantian theories). But it is perhaps an overreaction to argue that this undermines virtue ethics' claim to provide an acceptable approach to ethical justification. For virtue ethicists often give considerable detail about what virtuous agents have done and would do in certain situations, and these details can help us to identify what it is right to do in a particular situation. (We might not gain any more precision from the directives of contemporary Kantian and consequentialist theories, which advise us to do what a good Kantian or consequentialist agent would do.) And further, virtue ethics need not claim that there is only one true account of what a virtuous person would be and do, for it can allow that, sometimes, whichever of two courses of action one chooses, one would be acting rightly. In some situations, that is, whether one does what a kind person would have done, or what an honest person would have done, one would still have acted rightly.[55]

The second major criticism of virtue ethics is more fundamental than the first, as it focuses on the plausibility of a purely character-based criterion of rightness, such as that given by virtue ethics in (a) above. That is, many have argued that reference to what an agent with a virtuous character would have done (no matter how precisely specifiable and unitary virtuous character-traits are) is not sufficient to justify actions. In support of this criticism, many writers argue that people with very virtuous characters can sometimes be led by a virtuous character-trait to act wrongly. For example, a benevolent doctor may be moved to withhold a diagnosis of terminal cancer from a patient, although the doctor reveals the news to the patient's family, and asks them to join in the deception. Or, a compassionate father might decide to donate most of the family's savings to a worthwhile charity, without realising that his action is likely to result in severe impoverishment for his family in the long term. Likewise, a compassionate nurse caring for a convicted murderer in a prison hospital might be so moved by the story of a patient's deprived upbringing that the nurse may deliberately fail to raise the alarm when the patient makes a dash for freedom. As Robert Veatch puts the worry:

---

[55] See Rosalind Hursthouse, 'Normative Virtue Ethics', in Roger Crisp (ed.), *How Should One Live? Essays on the Virtues*, Oxford, Clarendon Press, 1996, p. 34.

I am concerned about well-intentioned, bungling do-gooders. They seem to exist with unusual frequency in health care, law, and other professions with a strong history of stressing the virtue of benevolence with an elitist slant.[56]

If we agree that thoroughly virtuous people can sometimes be led by their virtuous character-traits to act wrongly, then this seems to cast strong doubt on the plausibility of virtue ethics' criterion of rightness in (a) above. Many critics have been led by such examples of moral ineptitude to claim that virtue ethics is incomplete, and must therefore be underwritten by a deontological or a utilitarian criterion of rightness.[57]

Now, some virtue theorists would question whether the agent does act wrongly in these sorts of cases.[58] However, suppose it is granted that the agent concerned does indeed act wrongly in some such cases. There is no reason to think that virtue ethics is committed to condoning such moral ineptitude. For most virtues are not simply a matter of having good motives or good dispositions, but have a practical component which involves seeing to it that one's action succeeds in bringing about what the virtue dictates. Therefore, we might question the extent to which the agent really does have the virtuous character-trait which we are assuming they do here. Is it really an act of benevolence to withhold a diagnosis of terminal cancer from a patient, leaving that patient to die in ignorance of their true condition? Alternatively, in cases where the action does not seem to call into question the degree to which the agent has the virtuous character-trait under scrutiny, it might be that the agent was lacking in some other virtue which was appropriate here. Thus, the father seems to have an inadequate sense of loyalty towards his own family, and the nurse's sense of justice seems defective. (These latter cases seem to involve not so much the inept exercise of a certain virtuous disposition, but rather are cases where one particular disposition influences the agent's actions excessively on a certain occasion at the expense of another virtuous disposition that is warranted on that occasion. Nevertheless, this sort of failure can also be characterised as a form of ineptitude, although of a different kind from the former.)

---

[56] Robert Veatch, 'The Danger of Virtue', *Journal of Medicine and Philosophy* 13, 1988, p. 445.

[57] See Tom L. Beauchamp and James F. Childress, *Principles of Biomedical Ethics*, 4th edn, New York, Oxford University Press, 1994, pp. 62–9; Julia Driver, 'Monkeying with Motives: Agent-Basing Virtue Ethics', *Utilitas* 7, 1995; Frankena, *Ethics*, pp. 63–71; R. M. Hare, 'Methods of Bioethics: Some Defective Proposals', in L. W. Sumner and Joseph Boyle (eds.), *Philosophical Perspectives on Bioethics*, Toronto, University of Toronto Press, 1996; Edmund Pellegrino and David Thomasma, *The Virtues in Medical Practice*, New York, Oxford University Press, 1993; and Rachels, *The Elements of Moral Philosophy*.

[58] See, e.g., Michael Slote, 'Agent-Basing Virtue Ethics', in P. French et al. (eds.), *Midwest Studies in Philosophy, Volume 20: Moral Concepts*, Notre Dame, University of Notre Dame Press, 1995.

Conceiving of virtues as regulative ideals helps virtue ethics meet this criticism, because it allows for the possibility that an action done out of good motives or good intentions may fail to reach the appropriate standard of excellence which one is normatively disposed to uphold. For example, in seeking to help a friend who is despairing of finding a suitable job, I might bring to his attention a certain weakness which I think may be impeding his chances. However, I might later come to realise that it was a mistake to do so at the time, because I failed sufficiently to appreciate the nature and depths of my friend's despair, and that such comments were contrary to what can reasonably be expected of a good friend in such circumstances. There is a variety of reasons – such as false beliefs, insufficient attention, care, energy, or simply bad luck – why a virtuous person may on a particular occasion fail to act as their regulative ideals would dictate, but the regulative ideals of virtue ethics nevertheless provide a standard for act evaluation which allows us to see that acting out of good motives or good intentions, while it may be necessary for right action,[59] is not sufficient for the rightness of one's action. So virtue ethics can recognise, as R. M. Hare reminds us, that 'it is possible for very virtuous people to do terrible things'.[60]

However, the critic might respond by insisting that the sorts of terrible things he was suggesting it is possible for very virtuous people to do are not actions that are due to the agent's having inadequately developed a particular virtuous character-trait, or to the agent's lacking some other virtuous character-trait appropriate to the situation – rather, the objection was based on examples where an agent who has inculcated the requisite virtues to a level of excellence nevertheless acts in a way that seems to be bad or wrong. But when we examine in more detail the sorts of examples which the critic seems to have in mind, we can see how extreme this objection really is. In doing so, we can see that it is far from obvious that the answer delivered by a virtue ethics approach in such cases is incorrect or implausible.

One sort of case where a person with adequately developed virtues might be said to do something terrible can be illustrated with H. J. McCloskey's well-known example – which he uses to attack act-utilitarianism – in which a sheriff in a town in the Wild West knows that he can prevent a destructive riot amongst the townspeople only by framing an

---

[59] Acting out of good motives is required for motive-dependent virtues, such as friendship and courage, but certain virtues, such as justice, may not have such a motive requirement. That is, while acting justly requires that one acts from a just *disposition*, it may not require that one acts out of certain *motives*.   [60] Hare, 'Methods of Bioethics: Some Defective Proposals', p. 27.

innocent person.[61] Suppose that this sheriff has properly inculcated the virtue of justice and, acting out of this virtue, decides not to frame the innocent person, thereby helping to bring about the destructive riot. According to the critic of virtue ethics, the sheriff acted wrongly here, even though he acted from the virtue of justice. However, if this is the sort of example which the critic has in mind, it is not clear that he has such a strong case against the virtue ethics criterion of rightness. For many who are presented with such an example find it far from obvious that the destructive riot which the sheriff's decision helped bring about makes the sheriff's decision here wrong. Indeed, there is disagreement even amongst utilitarians themselves about whether the sheriff's decision here is wrong – act-utilitarians will say that the sheriff acted wrongly, while rule-utilitarians are inclined to say that, despite the bad consequences he helped bring about on this occasion, the sheriff acted rightly because he acted from a disposition – a sense of justice – which, when had by everyone, maximises overall utility.[62]

Moreover, there is much dispute amongst ethicists who do not use virtue-based approaches about how the terrible consequences of an agent's acting from an estimable character-trait bear on the proper evaluation of the agent's action in such circumstances. In cases where the terrible consequences which resulted from the agent's acting from an estimable character-trait were neither foreseen by the agent nor foreseeable by a reasonable person in the agent's position, many ethicists reject the actualist claim that the terrible consequences which – actually, though unexpectedly – resulted make the agent's action wrong here.[63]

---

[61] See H. J. McCloskey, 'A Note on Utilitarian Punishment', *Mind* 72, 1963. McCloskey's example is discussed, in connection with the virtue of justice, by Roger Crisp, 'Utilitarianism and the Life of Virtue', *Philosophical Quarterly* 42, 1992, pp. 156–7.

[62] Some act-utilitarians and act-consequentialists, while maintaining that the sheriff acted wrongly here, would not necessarily hold that the sheriff ought to change his disposition to be just, merely because it results in the occasional wrong act, since they would argue that when determining what dispositions we ought to develop, we should consider which among the available dispositions is likely to result in the most utility in the long run. And they might argue that the sheriff's having a strong disposition to justice is more likely to maximise utility in the long run than would the sheriff's having a weaker disposition to justice. Thus, Roger Crisp argues (in 'Utilitarianism and the Life of Virtue', p. 156–7) that while it would be correct to say that what the sheriff did here was wrong, the outcome of his action here does not give the sheriff sufficient reason to change his disposition to act justly.

[63] On Roger Crisp's 'utilitarianism of the virtues' (p. 155), one upshot of what he calls 'living virtuously' (i.e. living in a way that provides the agent with the best chance of maximising utility over his life) is that one will be living in a way whereby some of one's actions will not maximise utility. Thus, actualists (or, for that matter, expectabilists) who tell us to focus primarily on maximising (or developing those dispositions which will allow us to maximise) utility *over one's life*, rather than necessarily in every individual *act*, will allow that very virtuous people (i.e. people

Thus, many consequentialists reject that claim because, as we mentioned earlier, they hold that the evaluation of the agent's action is determined by its *expected* consequences, rather than by its *actual* consequences.

Suppose, then, that the critic of virtue ethics puts their objection in terms of expectabilism, and points to examples where an agent acting from a virtuous (or at least, an estimable) character-trait might appear to stand condemned by the bad *expected* consequences of their act. Such examples, it seems, would not be plausibly put in terms of a *subjectivist* form of expectabilism – where, as we noted earlier, the consequences which bear on the evaluation of the agent's act are those which the agent *believes* the act is likely to result in – for a virtuous agent is not apt to be moved by their virtuous character-traits to perform actions which they *believe* are likely to have terrible consequences overall. However, what if the examples are put by the critic in terms of an *objectivist* form of expectabilism, where the consequences which matter are those which are correctly judged (for example, by some ideal observer of probabilities), at the time the agent acted, as likely to result from the agent's action (whether or not the agent themselves judged those probabilities correctly or incorrectly)? That is, what if an agent is moved by a well-developed virtuous character-trait to perform an act which is objectively likely to result in very bad consequences? For example, suppose that a generous person is deceived into donating money to someone he takes to be a beggar, when in fact the recipient is a member of a religious group which uses cruel means to systematically oppress women, but the 'beggar' succeeds in his deception because his façade is extremely convincing. Suppose further that, when the donation was made, it was objectively likely that the money would be used to continue the group's oppression of women. (We might even imagine that the generous person was in a foreign city, where he had heard that such a scam existed, but was given inaccurate advice by a local when he asked how he could avoid the area with the counterfeit beggars.) In this case, the objective expectabilist

---

with optimific dispositions) will *on occasion* do things which fall well short of maximising utility (and indeed, perhaps even 'terrible things'), when those things are considered by themselves.

On actualism, see Jackson, 'Decision-Theoretic Consequentialism'; Philip Pettit, 'The Consequentialist Perspective', in Marcia W. Baron, Philip Pettit, and Michael Slote, *Three Methods of Ethics: A Debate*, Oxford, Blackwell, 1997, p. 128; and Slote, *From Morality to Virtue*, chapter 15. See also discussions of 'moral luck', where many wish to resist the idea that unlucky bad outcomes of an agent's act can redound to the agent's discredit. Contemporary philosophical debate on this issue originates with Bernard Williams' paper 'Moral Luck' (in Bernard Williams, *Moral Luck*, Cambridge, Cambridge University Press, 1981), and Thomas Nagel's response, also titled 'Moral Luck' (in Thomas Nagel, *Mortal Questions*, Cambridge, Cambridge University Press, 1979).

would claim that the generous person was moved by his generosity to act wrongly,[64] and that the virtue ethics criterion of rightness is therefore mistaken. However, it seems far from clear that the generous person *does* act wrongly in donating the money to the counterfeit beggar here. Indeed, generally speaking, where an agent acts from a virtuous character-trait but, because of his non-culpably having false beliefs, brings about bad consequences, we think that it is far from clear that the agent has acted wrongly.

These sorts of examples help to bring out how extreme the critic's objection really is – for it would be an objection to *any* criterion of rightness which places importance on something other than the actual or expected consequences of the agent's act. It would therefore be an objection not only to virtue ethics, but also to Kantianism and, for that matter, to rule-utilitarianism and rule-consequentialism. Given that this is a very general objection, which could be made to a whole range of ethical theories, and given how many would find counterintuitive the critic's judgements about the above examples, we do not take it as incumbent on us to continue our rejoinder to it any further here.

---

[64] It might be noted that while the objective expectabilist would judge the generous person as acting wrongly in giving the money to the counterfeit beggar, the objective expectabilist need not regard the generous person as *blameworthy* for doing this (insofar as the generous person was non-culpably ignorant of how his donation was to be used).

CHAPTER 2

The regulative ideals of morality and the problem of friendship

Our main concern in this chapter is to argue that consequentialist and Kantian ethical theories are unable to recognise the nature and value of friendship.[1] As we mentioned in the introduction to the book, the plausibility of any ethical theory rests importantly on its capacity to recognise great human goods, such as friendship, and the problems which impartialist theories like consequentialism and Kantianism have in accommodating friendship may provide important insights into the capacity of these theories to accommodate the value and normative force of various professional roles. For not only have both friendship and professional roles been thought to license departures from what impartialist ethical theory would ordinarily require of us, but friendship has been appealed to as a model to explain how such departures might be justified in professional life.

We do not think – as some writers have – that the independent value of friendship and the departures it might license from Kantian and consequentialist moralities provide (at least, in any straightforward way) a justification for such independence of value and departures in various cases of professional morality. As should become clear from our later discussions in this chapter and in chapter 4, we think that there are some important disanalogies between friendship and professional life with respect to the challenge each might be thought to pose for impartialist ethical theory. In any case, our discussion of the ways in which consequentialism and Kantianism might or might not be properly criticised for the ways in which they seek to accommodate friendship will, we hope, be instructive – in terms of both similarities and differences – for

[1] Earlier versions of this chapter were read at the Australasian Association of Philosophy Annual Conference, University of Queensland, and at the University of Western Australia. We are grateful to the audiences for their comments on those occasions. We are also indebted to John Campbell, Owen Flanagan, Michael Smith, David Sosa, and the editors of *Ethics*, along with numerous others, all of whom provided extensive and very helpful comments on earlier versions.

our later discussion of how consequentialist and Kantian moralities might be thought to govern professional roles.

We focus in what follows on the relation between an ethical theory's criterion of rightness and its account of moral deliberation. We will examine this relation in the context of some influential contemporary consequentialist and Kantian attempts to capture the nature and value of love and friendship, through the modifications they have introduced into their respective accounts of the relation between rightness and moral deliberation. In doing so, we develop the notion of a 'regulative ideal' (introduced in chapter 1), as a way of explicating this relation. We will argue that the regulative ideals posited either by an ethics of Kantian side-constraints or by a consequentialist ethic concerned with maximisation of agent-neutral value fail adequately to capture the nature and value of love and friendship.[2] In doing so, we will also suggest that our account of virtue ethics (as detailed in chapter 1) is better placed to provide a regulative ideal which will adequately capture the nature and value of these goods, and so to provide appropriate resolutions to problems of right action involving these goods.

I SOPHISTICATED CONSEQUENTIALISTS, GOOD KANTIANS, AND THEIR REGULATIVE IDEALS

The move to indirect consequentialism has become a standard manoeuvre in response to those who criticise consequentialism as alienating us from ourselves and from those who are special to us. One version of this criticism claims that consequentialism has problems with friendship because of the *purposes* which a consequentialist agent would have. According to this version, a consequentialist agent would aim at maximising the good, but to act with such an aim would preclude one from having goods like friendship, since achieving friendship seems to require, in certain contexts, that one does *not* aim at promoting the abstract good itself, but rather that one focuses on the good of the friend themselves.[3] Another, perhaps more influential, version of this criticism holds that consequentialism has a problem with friendship because of the *motives*

---

[2] We should make clear that, in rejecting a consequentialism concerned with maximising *agent-neutral* value, we are not thereby necessarily rejecting consequentialism as such. Our arguments in this chapter are not targeted at, e.g., a decision-theoretic consequentialism, where rightness requires us to do what we have most reason to do, such that we ought to maximise *whatever* it is that is valuable.

[3] See, e.g., Bernard Williams, 'A Critique of Utilitarianism', in J. J. C. Smart and Bernard Williams, *Utilitarianism: For and Against*, Cambridge, Cambridge University Press, 1973, p. 128.

which a consequentialist agent would have. According to this version, a consequentialist agent would act from a desire to maximise the good, but one who took maximisation of the good as their *motive* in engaging in personal relationships would thereby be prevented from having genuine friendships, because genuine friendship conceptually requires that one act from motives other than the desire to maximise the good.[4]

Consequentialists now widely reject such criticisms as resting on a misunderstanding of how good moral agents are to be guided by a consequentialist standard of right action. In rejecting such criticisms, consequentialists have typically argued, along with Sidgwick, that a consequentialist agent need be committed to maximisation of the good only as an objective *criterion of rightness* by which their actions can be assessed, rather than as directly providing a motive or a purpose which such an agent is consciously to adopt in performing any action.[5] The commitment of the consequentialist agent here, then, operates in an indirect way, to realise in the agent a disposition to lead the objectively consequentialist life.

Indirect consequentialists seem right to stress that a consequentialist moral agent need not *aim at* maximising the good, or be motivated directly by the desire to maximise the good. And so, to the extent that critics' arguments have focused on consequentialist moral agents who do have such a purpose or motive, those attacks have not been well directed. But while the consequentialist criterion of rightness need not serve as a moral agent's purpose or motive in acting, this does not necessarily mean

---

[4] See, e.g., Michael Stocker, 'The Schizophrenia of Modern Ethical Theories', *Journal of Philosophy* 73, 1976, pp. 458–61.

[5] See Henry Sidgwick, *The Methods of Ethics*, 7th edn, Indianapolis, Hackett, 1981, p. 413: 'The doctrine that Universal Happiness is the ultimate *standard* must not be understood to imply that Universal Benevolence is the only right or always best *motive* of action. For . . . it is not necessary that the end which gives the criterion of rightness should always be the end at which we consciously aim: and if experience shows that the general happiness will be more satisfactorily attained if men frequently act from other motives than pure universal philanthropy, it is obvious that these other motives are reasonably to be preferred on Utilitarian principles.' This distinction, and the claim that consequentialism is best interpreted primarily as giving a criterion of rightness, is also made by, for example, Robert M. Adams, 'Motive Utilitarianism', *Journal of Philosophy* 73, 1976; David O. Brink, 'Utilitarian Morality and the Personal Point of View', *Journal of Philosophy* 83, 1986; Derek Parfit, *Reasons and Persons*, Oxford, Clarendon Press, 1984, chapter 1; and Peter Railton, 'Alienation, Consequentialism, and the Demands of Morality', in Samuel Scheffler (ed.), *Consequentialism and its Critics*, Oxford, Oxford University Press, 1988. See also Owen Flanagan, *Varieties of Moral Personality*, Cambridge, MA, Harvard University Press, 1991, pp. 34–5: 'One can be an act utilitarian when it comes to assessing the rightness of any action without requiring that individual agents operate with an act-utilitarian psychology'. This distinction is also employed by R. M. Hare (in *Moral Thinking*, Oxford, Clarendon Press, 1981), in justifying our everyday functioning at what he calls the 'intuitive level' of thinking.

that consequentialism is able to overcome the problem of alienation. For the underlying worry which the problem of alienation poses for consequentialism might be due to something other than the consequentialist agent's motives or purposes.

In this chapter, we argue first that worries about whether a consequentialist agent will be alienated from those who are special to them go deeper than has so far been appreciated. Rather than pointing to a problem with the consequentialist agent's motives or purposes, we argue that the problem facing a consequentialist agent in the case of friendship concerns the nature of the *psychological disposition* which such an agent would have, and how this kind of disposition sits with those which are commonly thought proper to relations of friendship. To the extent that we are right, then, the rejoinders which indirect consequentialists have offered to the problem of alienation are ill directed, and so do not succeed in meeting the real problem. In articulating what we see as the source of the alienation problem which friendship poses for consequentialism, we also hope to clarify the general distinction between dispositions and motives, and to show how certain kinds of guiding internalised normative dispositions – which we characterise in terms of our account of regulative ideals – help us to define and therefore distinguish between various types of relationships. Undertaking this task will help to identify some of the crucial issues for an adequate moral psychology of friendship, and the nature of its relation to ethical theory.

Second, we argue that the regulative ideals of the good Kantian agent also seem unable to accommodate the nature of the good of friendship. Here, on the basis of some account of the nature and value of the good of friendship and of the guiding normative dispositions that seem proper to it, we argue that it does not seem reasonable that one should have one's life governed, specifically one's friendships, by an overriding commitment to Kantian moral value. To have one's life so governed would, on our account, be to forgo a significant and commonplace part of the good of friendship.

The indirect consequentialist rejoinder to the problem of alienation

Peter Railton says that 'Objective Consequentialism' is the view that 'the criterion of the rightness of an act or course of action is whether it in fact would most promote the good of those acts available to the agent'.[6]

---

[6] Railton, p. 113 (page references in the text are to that essay).

Drawing on the distinction between this consequentialist criterion of rightness and the picture of deliberation and motivation with which it is compatible, Railton suggests that the consequentialist agent need not be motivationally guided by consequentialism in a *direct* way – i.e. by having the commitment to consequentialism as their motive or purpose. Instead, Railton suggests a psychological picture of the moral agent who leads the objectively consequentialist life in an *indirect* way. This agent, says Railton, is someone 'who has a standing commitment to leading an objectively consequentialist life, but who need not set special stock in any particular form of decision making and therefore does not necessarily seek to lead a subjectively consequentialist life [whereby a consequentialist calculus would, prior to acting, be consciously brought to bear by an agent on his every act]' (p. 114). Such an agent, whom Railton calls the *sophisticated* consequentialist, would not, he argues, be alienated from friendship in the way that the direct consequentialist agent has been thought to be. On this alternative psychological model of how the disposition to lead the objectively consequentialist life might be realised, an agent may be both a good consequentialist and a true and good friend.

In appealing to the distinction between a criterion of rightness and the psychological model of a good moral agent, consequentialists such as Railton do not typically argue for a *total* severance between an ethical theory's criterion of rightness and an agent's moral psyche. That is, they do not argue for a total severance in the sense that the criteria to determine what ought to be done are to play *no* psychologically significant role in guiding and justifying an agent's deliberation and motivation about what they ought to do. What Railton suggests is that the sophisticated consequentialist's motivational structure should be guided by the concern to meet a *counterfactual condition*: i.e. while they ordinarily do not do what they do simply for the sake of doing what is right, they would nevertheless alter their dispositions and the course of their life if they thought that these did not most promote the good (see pp. 105, 111). An agent whose psyche is guided by the concern to meet this counterfactual condition, Railton claims, is someone who could act from a wide variety of dispositions and modes of deliberation; and so a sophisticated consequentialist may satisfy this counterfactual condition while acting from any of a whole range of motives, dispositions, commitments, or deliberative frameworks. As Railton puts it: 'On an objective consequentialist account . . . [one should try] to lead one's life in such a way that an objective consequentialist criterion of rightness is met as nearly as possible. In a given instance, this criterion might be met by acting out of a deeply felt emotion or an entrenched trait of character, without consulting morality or even directly in the face of it' (p.132 n. 42).[7]

What Railton has in mind, in describing the sophisticated consequentialist's moral psyche, is that such a person will regulate their dispositions and their conduct so that their lives maximise the good. In some cases this may require aiming at promoting the good, while in other cases (for example, where having such an aim will be inimical to maximising the good) it will require an agent to have other aims instead. A helpful way of putting the sophisticated consequentialist's position is by saying that maximisation of agent-neutral value will be their *regulative ideal*. As we saw in chapter 1, to say that an agent has a regulative ideal is to say that they have internalised a certain conception of correctness or excellence, in such a way that they are able to adjust their motivation and conduct so that it conforms, or at least does not conflict, with that standard. Regulative ideals operate as guiding background conditions on our motivation, and so they can direct us to act rightly, even when we do not consciously formulate them or aim at them. So, for instance, my actions towards my son can be guided and governed by a certain conception of what it is to be a good father, even though I am thoroughly engaged in playing with him rather than thinking about what it is to be a good father. Likewise, my speaking Greek as a second language will be informed and regulated by the principles of Greek grammar, even though I am not consciously formulating the principles of Greek grammar before carrying on a conversation in that language. My disposition to speak Greek is guided by my meeting a counterfactual condition: while I do not ordinarily speak Greek for the sake of exemplifying my grasp of the principles of Greek grammar, I would nevertheless alter what I say if I thought that it contravened those principles. Thus, a regulative ideal can guide us in our actions, without becoming one of our *purposes* in acting. Also, a regulative ideal can govern our behaviour, without becoming one of our *motives* in acting – I might, in speaking

---

[7] For the most part, we interpret Railton's sophisticate as someone who is guided in a psychologically significant sense by the concern to maximise the good, since this is how Railton himself understands the sophisticate (see our note 16). As we discuss later, however, an indirect consequentialist agent need not be guided in this way. For the indirect consequentialist's commitment to objective consequentialism need not itself endorse any particular view of the psychology required to realise a disposition to maximise the good. We thank an editor for *Ethics* for helping to clarify this. The *sophisticated* indirect consequentialist agent that we, following Railton, *do* take to be guided by their consequentialist commitment is not, however, someone who thereby leads the *subjectively* consequentialist life (or not, at least, as Railton describes the latter – that is, as someone who is concerned to maximise the good as their aim or purpose, or who would be an incessant consequentialist calculator).

Greek to a Greek person, be motivated here by my affection for them as one of my friends. A regulative ideal is thus an internalised normative disposition to direct one's actions in certain ways. And the good consequentialist's life, as Railton sees it, will be guided by a general regulative ideal, as exemplified in their normative disposition to maximise agent-neutral value.

Now, this move to indirect consequentialism is, of course, well known as a standard manoeuvre in responding to various criticisms of consequentialism as somehow alienating us from ourselves and those who are special to us. For consequentialism has been thought problematic by many writers on the grounds that if it requires us to *aim at* maximising the good, we shall in the case of certain goods (such as friendship) thereby actually undermine or defeat our achieving those very goods.[8] It is now widely accepted as a matter of empirical and conceptual fact that the proper achievement of many valuable goods, such as friendship, sometimes requires our *not* aiming at promoting the abstract good itself, but rather focusing on, for example, the good of the friend themselves. This is precisely the point Sidgwick was addressing when he said that 'if experience shows that the general happiness would be more satisfactorily attained if men frequently act from other motives than pure universal philanthropy, it is obvious that these other motives are reasonably to be preferred on Utilitarian principles'.[9]

The Kantian strategy

A similar strategy of indirection has been developed by recent Kantians, in response to correlative worries about Kantian ethics' denial of moral value to special relationships and affective connections such as love and friendship. Barbara Herman, for example, has argued in a series of papers that the Kantian Categorical Imperative should not be interpreted as providing an explicit decision-procedure to be engaged in by agents prior to everything they propose to do. Rather, according to Herman, we should understand the CI as providing only the standard of rightness by which actions can be judged:

Normal moral agents do not question the permissibility of everything they propose to do (having lunch, going to the movies, etc.). We expect moral agents to have acquired knowledge of the sorts of actions it is generally not permissible

---

[8] See, e.g., Williams, 'A Critique of Utilitarianism', esp. p. 128.
[9] Sidgwick, *The Methods of Ethics*, p. 413.

to do and of the sorts of actions which, in the normal course of things, have no moral import . . . we do not imagine normal moral agents bringing maxims of grossly immoral acts to the CI procedure routinely, only to discover (to their surprise?) that these acts are forbidden . . . It is useful to think of the moral knowledge needed by Kantian agents (prior to making moral judgments) as knowledge of a kind of moral rule. Let us call these 'rules of moral salience'. Acquired as elements in a moral education, they structure an agent's perception of his situation so that what he perceives is a world with moral features. They enable him to pick out those elements of his circumstances or of his proposed actions which require moral attention . . . Typically they are acquired in childhood, as part of socialization; they provide a practical framework within which people act. When the rules of moral salience are well internalized, they cause the agent to be aware of and attentive to the significance of 'moral danger'.[10]

In other words, in the good moral agent the CI operates as a kind of 'limiting condition' or *regulative ideal*, which sets the conditions on which we can act on other motives, so that we avoid acting impermissibly. As Herman explains, 'Kantian ethics does not block the satisfaction of certain obligations from motives of connection as they are available and/or appropriate, so long as the agent's volition (her maxim) is regulated by the motive of duty functioning as a secondary motive or limiting condition. That is to say: in acting from a motive of connection I must . . . act only on the condition that the particular action I am moved to take is permissible.'[11] Thus, the motivational structure of a good moral agent, on this account, should meet a parallel *counterfactual condition* to the sophisticated consequentialist: while he ordinarily does not do what he does simply for the sake of doing his duty, he would nevertheless alter his dispositions and the course of his life if he thought that they led him to do what is impermissible. We can put this, then, by saying that the good Kantian agent's regulative ideal is informed by *duty-based side-constraints*, while the sophisticated consequentialist's regulative ideal is the *maximisation of agent-neutral value*.

[10] Barbara Herman, 'The Practice of Moral Judgment', *Journal of Philosophy* 82, 1985, pp. 417–19. See also Barbara Herman, 'Integrity and Impartiality', *The Monist* 66, 1983, p. 236. Other writers who have argued for a similar construal of the Categorical Imperative and the motive of duty are: Marcia Baron, 'The Alleged Moral Repugnance of Acting from Duty', *Journal of Philosophy* 81, 1984; Marcia Baron, 'Kantian Ethics and Supererogation', *Journal of Philosophy* 84, 1987, esp. pp. 252–3; Paul Benson, 'Moral Worth', *Philosophical Studies* 51, 1987, pp. 377–9; Robert B. Louden, 'Kant's Virtue Ethics', *Philosophy* 61, 1986, esp. pp. 478–9, 484–9; Adrian M. S. Piper, 'Moral Theory and Moral Alienation', *Journal of Philosophy* 84, 1987; and W. E. Schaller, 'Kant on Virtue and Moral Worth', *Southern Journal of Philosophy* 25, 1987, esp. pp. 569–70. Earlier suggestions of this understanding of the duty motive can be found in A. C. Ewing, *Ethics*, London, English Universities Press, 1953, pp. 147–8; and W. D. Ross, *The Right and the Good*, Oxford, Clarendon Press, 1930, pp. 172–3.

[11] Barbara Herman, 'Agency, Attachment, and Difference', *Ethics* 101, 1991, p. 777.

Thus, in response to the criticism that Kantian and consequentialist ethics fail to capture the nature and value of our special relations, both Kantians and consequentialists alike have argued that their respective criteria of rightness ought to be understood as regulative ideals operating on the agent's psyche. The claim is then made that the Kantian and consequentialist criteria of rightness, when construed as regulative ideals, are able to accommodate the nature and value of our special relations.

Now, insofar as recent criticisms of Kantianism and consequentialism have been claiming that, with respect to various goods such as love and friendship, an agent's *aiming at* what is right will be self-defeating, we do not think that those attacks have been well directed. Indeed, insofar as those criticisms of, for example, a consequentialist criterion of rightness have been concerned with inadequacies of consequentialist content in a person's dispositions and motives, they have, we believe, missed their target in at least two ways. First, the indirect move seems to us right to stress that, for example, the consequentialist moral agent need not be too deliberative in consequentialist terms, or *aim at* promoting values, conceived in consequentialist terms. And second, it does not in any case seem a requirement of a correct criterion of rightness that it allow us to achieve various valuable goods – which it therefore might be right to pursue – by *aiming at* attaining these goods, or these goods qua their rightness. It is after all a quite general feature of various activities, both moral and non-moral, that, as a matter of empirical fact or probability, or even as a matter of conceptual fact, to *aim* at attaining them in a certain situation will undermine our actually attaining them in that situation. For example, as is well appreciated, *aiming at* relaxing will, as a matter of empirical fact, itself sometimes undermine our achieving the goal of relaxation. Yet, it might nevertheless still be true that to relax in various circumstances will be the right thing to do because to do so will most promote the good. Or, to give a clear non-moral case, a complex mathematical theorem may be true, but one may not best or even possibly at all be able to learn or glean this truth by *aiming at* doing so (just as one may not best or even at all be able to *act out* the consequentialist dictum by aiming at doing so). This comparison might be resisted since it could be said, and quite correctly, that moral theories are, of course, concerned to guide us as to how we ought to live – that is, they are meant to be practical – whereas mathematical thereoms may not be concerned to do this. But then meeting a requirement of practical guidance upon a moral theory is achieved by the move to a counterfactual regulating condition. Promoting the most good in Railton's case, for example, guides the agent in their actions. If a certain course of action would conflict with this regulative ideal, then the agent would drop this course of action. It therefore remains puzzling, if being able to learn a theoretical axiom by aiming at it is not itself considered a requirement of the correctness of that axiom, why we should expect of a moral practical truth that we be able to aim at it in order for it to be true.

What we want to argue is that objective consequentialism and its Kantian correlative are, in important ways, parasitic on establishing other claims about moral deliberation and motivation. Of course, this is obviously true in the sense that they need to be supplemented with an account of what kinds of deliberative and motivational structures they would permit us to have. However, we want to make a more penetrating claim. We want to argue that the *plausibility* of these consequentialist and Kantian regulative ideals is crucially parasitic on the plausibility of the deliberative and motivational structures with which they are compatible, and on the substantive account of the good which those structures embody. In our view, these regulative ideals are, in fact, *not* compatible with a substantive account of the good of *friendship*, or at least, not if they are to remain faithful to the sort of value they champion as overriding. On a substantive account of the good of friendship, the nature of this good is importantly informed by the sort of interest and attention characteristic of the friendly disposition and intentions a person has for another. And in our view, as we will argue, it is conceptually a part of this interest and attention that a friend would not give you up or override their interest from friendship just in any case of conflict with promoting the good of agent-neutral consequentialism or a duty-based morality. This is not to endorse a romanticism that would say one could never give up a friend or loved one for some other value, or indeed, even for another friend. Rather, it is to hold a *plural values* view that charts a middle course between the claims of overridingness made on behalf of the regulative ideals of either Kantian or consequentialist morality. Whilst sometimes Kantian duty or the claim of agent-neutral value may trump love and friendship, so too love and friendship may sometimes trump these other moral values.

2 CONSEQUENTIALIST DISPOSITIONS, AND THE ROLE OF GOVERNING CONDITIONS IN DIFFERENTIATING RELATIONSHIPS

How might the sophisticated consequentialist's underlying commitment to maximising agent-neutral value be thought compatible with their

having relationships of friendship? On Railton's account, the sophisticated consequentialist's standing commitment to maximising the good
need not (or not often) interfere with their commitment to acting for the
sake of their friends. Railton gives an example of such a person – Juan
– who believes that his love for his wife is not impaired by his commitment to maximisation as a regulative ideal. In justifying his love for his
wife Linda, Juan explains that it is a better world where people can have
a relationship like theirs. Further, Railton's Juan points out that we are
not all equipped to save the world, and that in any case, those who might
do so still need special relationships to sustain them. Thus, 'what Juan
recognizes to be morally required is not by its nature incompatible with
acting directly for the sake of another. It is important to Juan to subject
his life to moral scrutiny . . . His love is not a romantic submersion in the
other to the exclusion of worldly responsibilities.'[12] Rather Juan remains
committed to upholding those responsibilities to the extent that his life
is regulated by the principle of maximisation of agent-neutral value – a
principle which might, depending on the empirical circumstances,
require him to abandon his relationship with Linda.

However, it is far from clear why a relationship like that which a consequentialist agent such as Juan has with Linda should qualify as one of
love or friendship. Railton may be correct to claim that a person such as
Juan, whose life is governed by an agent-neutral consequentialist regulative ideal, would be capable of having certain kinds of relationships,
in that he can permissibly devote more time, attention, and resources to
a particular person. But why should we call such relationships love or
friendship? In answer to this, Railton might point to the fact that Juan
acts *for the sake of* Linda. However, there are many different kinds of relationships where we can favour others with our time and attention, and
moreover, act for their sake, but which would not thereby necessarily
qualify as friendships. For example, a good doctor–patient relationship,
or a good teacher–student relationship, would be compatible with those
characterisations, yet clearly those relationships are not typically conceived of as friendships.[13] A good doctor may see it as part of her role
to give special attention to *her* patients over others, even where those
others may sometimes stand to gain more from her care, and she might

---

[12] Railton, pp. 111–12.
[13] See, for example, Patricia M. L. Illingworth, 'The Friendship Model of Physician/Patient
Relationship and Patient Autonomy', *Bioethics* 2, no. 1, January 1988; and Robert Veatch, 'The
Physician as Stranger: The Ethics of the Anonymous Patient–Physician Relationship', in Earl
Shelp (ed.), *The Clinical Encounter*, Dordrecht, Reidel, 1985.

provide care for her patients for their own sake, rather than, say, for the sake of meeting her job requirements, and yet we would not necessarily regard her relationships with her patients as friendships. So the fact that Juan favours Linda with his time, attention, and resources, and can act for her sake, does not entail that an agent-neutral consequentialist such as Juan can have a *friendship*, still less a *good* friendship.

Another way a consequentialist might seek to demonstrate that a person such as Juan is capable of relationships of love and friendship is by pointing to the fact that his acting for Linda's sake is motivated by deeply felt care and interest towards her. Indeed, it is partly to allow for an agent's being motivated by such immediate emotional concern that the move to an indirect consequentialism like Railton's was made by many writers in the first place. However, it does not follow from the fact of being motivated to act for the other's sake out of deeply felt emotion that one is thereby a *friend* of the other, for there are many instances where agents act out of such motivation towards others, but yet those others do not stand in relationships of friendship towards the agent. Again, a good doctor or a good teacher may act for the sake of their patient or their student out of a heartfelt concern for and interest in their welfare, without thereby being a *friend* of their patient or their student.

One important reason why these therapeutic and pedagogical relationships would not count as friendships is that they are grounded in quite different motivational and dispositional structures from friendship. To see this, consider, for example, the sort of motivational and dispositional structures which would be appropriate to a good teacher. Lawrence Blum illustrates this well, with an example from secondary-school teacher Herbert Kohl's account of providing special extra-curricular tutoring to an illiterate fourteen-year-old boy. This example is instructive for our purposes, because it demonstrates the distinctive way in which Kohl *as a teacher* was guided in the nature of his interest and concern to teach the boy. It was as an agent with the particular sort of motivational and dispositional concerns proper to being a good teacher that Kohl was moved by and perceived the educational disadvantage which the boy would have were he to grow up without being able to read. Kohl was not moved to help the illiterate boy as a friend – indeed, he did not even *like* the boy.[14] And so the point we want to bring out is that a person can act out of deeply felt concern, and for the sake

---

[14] Lawrence A. Blum, 'Vocation, Friendship, and Community: Limitations of the Personal/Impersonal Framework', in Owen Flanagan and Amélie O. Rorty (eds.), *Identity, Character, and Morality: Essays in Moral Psychology*, Cambridge, MA, MIT Press, 1990, pp. 176–9.

of a particular other, as Kohl did, without this yet telling us terribly much about the distinctive sort of relationship which the person has with the other. The relationship the person may have with the other may be as their teacher, their doctor, their friend, or as something else. To capture the distinctive nature of the relationship which the person has with the other would require an account which recognises the distinctive ways in which the motivations and dispositions that govern their relationship with the other are guided.

An important and hitherto neglected way of capturing this difference between, for example, teacher–student and doctor–patient relationships, on the one hand, and those of friendship, on the other hand, would be to highlight how these relationships are conditional upon certain features which, whilst importantly informing the guiding psychological dispositions of the former relationships, would be irrelevant to or incompatible with those of good and true friendships. For example, therapeutic and pedagogical relationships are conditional upon the fact that the other is someone in need of care or instruction. Thus, Kohl's developing a relationship with the illiterate boy was conditional upon the boy's needing to learn how to read. Let us call such features of a relationship its 'acceptance conditions'. Correlatively, such concerns can function as the conditions under which one would cease a certain relationship. So, for example, where a patient is no longer in need of treatment, it is appropriate for the doctor to terminate the relationship with the patient. Let us call the conditions under which a relationship would be withdrawn its 'terminating conditions'. What we want to emphasise is that these acceptance and terminating conditions importantly inform the distinctive nature and value of different relationships. For example, a doctor who was disposed to cease her relationships with her patients when the patients were no longer in need of medical care would not be deficient as a doctor in that respect. This would be characteristic of the nature of her relationships with her patients and would also be entirely appropriate. By contrast, it is *not* part of the nature or the norms of friendship that the relationship is undertaken because one is in a position to provide a form of care that the other needs, or that it should cease simply because such care is no longer needed by one's friend. Moreover, someone who was *disposed to* undertake and give up his relationships of friendship with others under such conditions would be thought importantly lacking from the perspective of friendship. Indeed, there would be a serious doubt about whether such a relationship would qualify as one of friendship at all, were it conditional upon such a feature.

Now, given what we have said about the acceptance and terminating conditions of relationships, Railton may be seen as offering a distinctive and plausible consequentialist reply to some common formulations of the problem of alienation in the case of friendship. The good consequentialist agent, the reply would go, has as part of their regulative ideal the acceptance and terminating condition that their engaging in a particular relationship of love and friendship is best in agent-neutral terms, and if it were not, then they would end the relationship. However, this does not entail that the agent is thereby *moved* by their concern to maximise agent-neutral value in their loves or friendships. On Railton's view, the indirect consequentialist agent can be moved directly by their friendship with another, whilst their consequentialist acceptance and terminating condition both justifies and guides their relationship of friendship.[15] Thus, as Railton says, were their friendship the lesser of options, qua maximisation of agent-neutral value, then they would end the friendship.[16]

There is an important kernel of truth in this move concerning the relations between what we have called acceptance/terminating conditions, and motives. What seems to be correct is this. Whilst X may be an acceptance condition (or not-X a terminating condition) of my relationship with Y, this does not entail that X (or not-X) is therefore a *motivating* reason for my being in the relationship with Y. So, for example, suppose that it was one of the terminating conditions of my relationship with you that I would be prepared to break it off if you were ever to lie to me. My being disposed to terminate my relationship with you under those circumstances does not entail that it is one of my *motivating* reasons for being in the relationship with you that you do not lie to me. My motivating reason for being in the relationship may rather be that you are a good

---

[15] It is by now common for consequentialists to justify friendship by appealing to the claim that, as a matter of empirical fact, such relationships will be for the best in agent-neutral terms (see, e.g., Frank Jackson, 'Decision-Theoretic Consequentialism and the Nearest and Dearest Objection', *Ethics* 101, no. 3, April 1991. We think that the appeal to this empirical claim is implausible. It is hard to believe, for example, that often one would not do more agent-neutral good by devoting one's resources to famine-relief than to friendship. (Things may have been different in the distant past, when a lack of relevant services and organisations would have made it extraordinarily difficult to devote one's life to famine-relief.) Nevertheless, our line in this chapter is that even if one were to suppose that pursuing friendship can in typical cases be for the best in agent-neutral terms, there is still good reason to think that the indirect consequentialist agent, on account of their distinctive motivational dispositions, will be unable to have true or good friendships.

[16] It is not just that it is counterfactually true of the agent that they will in some cases *actually* choose some greater good, at the expense of the friend. It is also that the agent's motivational disposition to be in a relationship with the other is *guided* by their view that it is consequentially for the best that they are in such a relationship with the other.

teacher, or simply that you are good fun. At least, this is what we believe.[17] And so in our view Railton may correctly say that whilst an agent may have maximisation of agent-neutral value as an acceptance or terminating condition upon their relationship with another, this does not entail that such an agent must have this as their motivating reason for being in the relationship with the other.

Nevertheless, it is an unjustified leap for consequentialists to think that appealing to this distinction between acceptance/terminating conditions (hereafter 'governing conditions') and motives establishes their claim that being governed in these ways by the condition of the maximisation of agent-neutral value is compatible with the motivational disposition proper to relationships of *friendship and love*. For whilst it might be true that the maximisation of agent-neutral value operating as a governing condition on a person's relationship does not entail that they are *moved* by this concern, and even if these conditions were consistent with an agent's being moved by a particularistic care and concern for another, these facts would by no means establish that the agent can be motivationally disposed as a friend or lover. We can see the gap which Railton's argument fails to bridge when we recall how in the cases of the good doctor and the good teacher, agents can be engaged in a relationship where they are governed by conditions which also allow them to be moved by quite distinct concerns – and indeed, by particularistic care and concern for another. For we saw in these examples that the governing conditions applicable to the teacher and the doctor in these relationships were *not* compatible with these relationships being ones of friendship or love. Similarly, then, it might well be true that an agent such as Juan, who is governed by the consequentialist condition of maximising agent-neutral value, can be moved by quite distinct concerns – perhaps, for example, by particularistic care and concern for another – but that would not suggest that being governed in these ways is compatible with friendship or love. So, although Railton might be able to avoid the common criticisms of consequentialism mentioned above, he does

[17] It is unclear and controversial exactly how one is to account for the relationship between motives and governing conditions. For example, Barbara Herman, in her writings on Kantian ethics, seems to think that having a certain concern as a governing condition would make this concern part of one's motive. See Barbara Herman, 'On the Value of Acting from the Motive of Duty', *Philosophical Review* 90, no. 3, 1981; Herman, 'The Practice of Moral Judgment'; and Herman, *The Practice of Moral Judgment*, Cambridge, MA, Harvard University Press, 1993. We do not think that this view is correct. However, whether one thinks that Herman's or our view is correct here is immaterial to our purposes. For all we are claiming is that the governing conditions of a relationship importantly inform the dispositions and motivations of that relationship. And that claim is not affected by *this* dispute about how governing conditions are to be related to motives.

not establish that the more sophisticated indirect consequentialist agent which he offers can consistently have friendship and love.

3 INDIRECT CONSEQUENTIALISM AND THE NATURE OF FRIENDSHIP

Indeed, there are good reasons for thinking that indirect consequentialism may *not* be able consistently to recognise the nature and value of friendship and love. For the fact that a relationship is governed by the consequentialist acceptance/terminating conditions of maximising agent-neutral value does not leave open the range of possible characterisations of that relationship which Railton seems to think that it does, and may well rule out the possibility that such a relationship can be true or good love or friendship. To see this, take Railton's contrasting cases of John and Anne, and Juan and Linda. Railton describes John as a *direct* consequentialist, who deliberates about and is motivated directly in his relationship with Anne by the consequentialist concern to maximise agent-neutral value. He also feels great affection for her, and this affection is also part of his motivational disposition towards her. Juan, on the other hand, is described as an *indirect* consequentialist, whose motivational dispositions of friendly affection are justified and guided by the consequentialist regulative ideal. Now, Railton says that this difference in how we can understand the motivational dispositions of the direct and indirect consequentialist marks a difference in the capacity of the consequentialist story consistently to recognise relationships of friendship and love. So, for example, he says that whilst we might well imagine that Anne felt alienated from John and was saddened by how he viewed his relationship with her, we need not imagine that Linda would feel the same with respect to Juan's view of his relationship with her. But why should a person in Linda's position feel any less alienated from a love with Juan than a person in Anne's position would feel from a love with John? After all, the 'friendly' motivational dispositions of both John and Juan are justified and guided by the same consequentialist regulative ideal, so that both accept and are prepared to terminate their relationships with their spouses under the same conditions.

The alienation which Railton finds in people like Anne on account of their having direct consequentialist partners like John should not be regarded as merely a concern with the consequentialist motives or purposes of agents like John, for it is importantly due to the consequentialist governing conditions which justify and guide the motivational dispositions of a person like John. As demonstrated above, a crucial factor in defining certain specific sorts of relationships is that they are informed by certain kinds of governing conditions. We now want to show that it seems just as clear that these governing conditions remain definitive of a relationship, *whether or not* the concern they embody *also* operates directly as part of the agent's motives or purposes in the relationship. And so the alienation and incapacity for friendship which Railton and the many others who have gone indirect on account of objections from friendship accept to be a feature of the direct consequentialist agent should be regarded as just as much a feature of the indirect consequentialist agent.

To see this, imagine a case which is structurally similar to the case of John and Anne. An ambitious philosopher 'befriends' an influential professor. The ambitious philosopher has particularistic care and concern for the professor; however, in his relationship with the professor, he aims at or is moved by his concern that the professor can provide his career with the promotion and assistance that he needs to become successful. He also, of course, justifies and is guided in his relationship with the professor by this concern. It seems plausible to think that, as Railton says of Anne, the professor would, on being told the truth about how the ambitious one is motivationally disposed toward him, properly regard their relationship as something other than a true or good friendship. Now imagine that the ambitious philosopher, perhaps after reading about Juan, takes a leaf out of Juan's book and reshapes his motivational dispositions so that he now no longer *aims directly* at achieving success. As in Juan's case, his guiding concern now functions solely as a governing condition upon his 'friendly' motives and dispositions toward the professor. So, whilst he does not now pursue his relationship with the other *aiming at* the achievement of success, this concern still justifies and guides his pursuing the relationship in the sense that he is motivationally disposed to engage in the relationship in the light of its contribution to his achieving this success, and he would abandon it were it to conflict with his achieving this success. On being told the truth about how the 'friendly' motivational disposition of the ambitious one is guided and justified, would it now be appropriate for the professor to be less inclined to regard their relationship as something other than a true or good friendship, merely on account of the fact that ambition does not *also* operate as a motive or a purpose in the psyche of his colleague? It is hard to see why it would be. After all, the pivotal justificatory and guiding role in the motivational disposition of the ambitious one's relationship to him is still the ambition to be successful. The ambitious one still accepts and would give up the relationship *on the grounds* of how doing so would serve his ambition. The fact that he is governed in this way, it seems clear, suffices to disqualify the relationship from being one of friendship. The professor might find the other's guiding concern with ambition less *obtrusive* in the indirect case. But it seems far-fetched to suppose that *this* difference would lead him to redefine the relationship as one of friendship. And so, similarly, whilst Linda might properly regard Juan's consequentialist guiding concern as less *obtrusive* than Anne would find John's, it is hard to see why Linda, on account of *this* difference, should find friendship where, as Railton has conceded, Anne would not.[18]

It might be objected that there is an important disanalogy between these two cases. In our ambitious philosopher case, the agent pursues a *self-serving* interest, whereas in Railton's cases, John and Juan pursue the other-regarding interest of the greater good. And so, the objection might go, whilst the absence of self-interest in one's motives or in the objects of one's motives might not render the moral psychological role played by a guiding concern of self-interest more able consistently to recognise friendship, this conclusion need not be transmitted to an *other-regarding* guiding concern.

However, this objection fails, for the incompatibility of certain guiding concerns with friendship is not due to their being self-regarding or other-regarding. The point that a certain guiding concern is equally incompatible with friendship, whether it operates as a motive, a purpose, or a governing condition, also applies in cases where the agent's guiding concern is other-regarding. For example, the doctor's concern to heal his patients is other-regarding, yet this guiding concern is no more compatible with friendship on account of its operating solely as a governing condition rather than additionally as a motive or as something aimed at directly. It might be claimed that where the doctor's concern operates directly as a motive, there is less motivational 'room' for other concerns,

---

[18] We are arguing that if you accept that the direct consequentialist agent is alienating and incapable of friendship, then on account of the importance of governing conditions in defining the nature of one's relationships, you should also think that the indirect consequentialist agent is similarly lacking. In reply, one might deny that the direct consequentialist agent is alienating and incapable of friendship. For reasons of space we do not here deal with the direct consequentialist who would bite the bullet on this issue, and in any case, this debate has been widely covered elsewhere. We accept that this omission in our presentation here may, to that extent, limit the scope of our argument. But since the move to indirect consequentialism has been such a widespread and influential response to the problem of alienation in the case of friendship, this omission should not, we believe, be taken *seriously* to limit the scope of our argument here.

such as a particularistic care and concern. And so taking out a guiding concern from an agent's motives might seem to provide more motivational room for other concerns that the agent might have. But as the doctor and teacher cases clearly show, this does not suffice to provide an account of a motivational disposition that can consistently recognise friendship. For it is clearly the distinctive governing conditions of doctor–patient and teacher–student relationships, rather than anything about the motivational 'space' available to those agents, which rule out their capacity to act from the motivational dispositions proper to friendship.

We have argued that there is good reason to believe that both the direct and the indirect consequentialist agent would be incapable of friendship, since they are both disposed to engage in and terminate their relationships with their partners under the same conditions, and it is this which their partners find alienating. In arguing for this, we have had in mind a certain picture of the sophisticated indirect consequentialist agent's psyche that would realise this disposition.

A different objection, returning us to the concern about how a disposition to maximise the good might be realised psychologically, is that we have loaded our case against the indirect consequentialist by our very use of a psychological model involving the consequentialist *regulative ideal* as our target. For it might be said that the agent who is disposed to meet Railton's counterfactual condition as a result of complex unconscious psychological processes need not be guided to do so by the consequentialist regulative ideal at all. After all, the indirect consequentialist might say, the fact that objective consequentialism requires that we maximise the good is simply to state a *criterion of rightness*.[19] Thus, in the absence of an empirical story about what kinds of dispositions would maximise the good, the indirect consequentialist's commitment to objective consequentialism would be utterly silent on the question of what dispositions should be endorsed. It need only be modally true for the indirect consequentialist agent that such an agent's psychology realises a disposition that meets the criterion of rightness put forward by objective consequentialism. If, then, indirect consequentialism is committed only to the idea

---

[19] This view of all that is required by indirect consequentialism has been put to us by David Sosa. See also his article 'Consequences of Consequentialism', *Mind* 102, 1993. We thank him and an anonymous editor for *Ethics* for clarifying the point that the standing commitment of the indirect consequentialist agent to leading the objectively consequentialist life need only function as a counterfactual condition on their dispositions, and so need not involve their being *guided by* this in any psychologically significant sense.

that it must be true of an agent that their behaviour meets the consequentialist counterfactual condition, how does our attack show that the indirect consequentialist agent cannot have friends?

Whether this type of indirect consequentialist agent is capable of having friends depends upon the empirical circumstances. We hope to have shown that there is good reason to believe that the indirect consequentialist agent who is guided by the consequentialist regulative ideal in the different ways we have discussed above would face the same problem of alienation which has been widely thought to afflict the direct consequentialist agent. If we are right, then insofar as empirical circumstances *are* such that the psychology required to meet the consequentialist counterfactual condition is a psychology which is guided by the consequentialist regulative ideal in the ways we have described, indirect consequentialism would still fail to overcome the problem of alienation. But of course, empirical circumstances need not be like this. Indeed, as some consequentialists have pointed out, circumstances might be such that a person who has never heard of or has altogether forgotten about consequentialism might in fact be disposed to lead the objectively consequentialist life.[20] Thus, we might imagine someone who was disposed to meet the consequentialist counterfactual condition by some complex unconscious psychological process that does not involve any concern to maximise the good whatsoever, or just as well, someone disposed from simple conscious psychological processes not involving any concern to maximise the good who nevertheless meets the consequentialist counterfactual condition. Since our objection from alienation is directed at psychological dispositions that are guided by the consequentialist regulative ideal, we would not be attacking indirect consequentialism in these cases. We are not arguing that if the maximisation of the good is simply a counterfactual condition upon an agent's dispositions, this would necessarily be inconsistent with good and true friendships.[21]

At this point it might be accepted that there are certain relationships which agents cannot have insofar as they are guided in some

---

[20] See Parfit, *Reasons and Persons*, pp. 40–3; and Sidgwick, *The Methods of Ethics*, pp. 489–90 on the idea that consequentialism might turn out to be an 'esoteric' morality.

[21] Moreover, it is hard to see how anyone could possibly argue this. After all, there might be a person who is governed only by the regulative ideal of friendship, but for whom circumstances are such that she nevertheless, as it happens, always maximises the good – that is, the conditionality of her dispositions, as it turns out, happens to track precisely what is required by objective consequentialism. It would not be out of any consequentialist concern, either conscious or unconscious, that she maximises the good, but would simply be a modal fact about her psychological disposition, which, in this case, is to be an excellent friend.

psychologically significant sense by the consequentialist regulative ideal, but it may then be questioned whether such relationships are realistically characterised as friendships. The sort of relationships we have in mind, it might be objected, involve excessively romanticised and unrealistic ideals of friendship. On a more plausible and realistic conception of friendship, it might be thought, there need be no incompatibility between friendship and a life guided by consequentialism.[22]

In response, let us first notice that this objection may be taken in a moderate or a more radical way. The moderate form of the objection would see ideals of friendship as generated from certain social norms and practices, and so would judge the appropriateness of certain conceptions of what friendship is and what dispositions it involves according to how well they fit what those norms or practices are generally taken to be. The dispositions of a consequentialist agent would then be compared with the dispositions characteristic of friendship, on that conception, to determine the extent, if any, of their compatibility with each other. Broadly speaking, this is the kind of approach we have taken here. The moderate reading of the objection, then, alleges that our argument depends on a conception of friendship and its proper dispositions which exaggerates the kind of commitment which such relationships are generally taken to involve. The more radical form of the objection, on the other hand, sees appropriate conceptions of friendship and its proper dispositions not as socially derived, but as generated directly from the relevant ethical theory itself – here consequentialism. On this more radical approach, then, an agent's conceptions and dispositions of friendship will be plausible and realistic only to the extent that they are consistent with the demands of, for example, consequentialism. There would be no defensible conception of friendship which arose independently of the theory itself. It is worth noting that Railton himself does not seem to favour the radical approach, as he states that

We must recognize that loving relationships, friendships, group loyalties, and spontaneous actions are among the most important contributors to whatever it is that makes life worthwhile; any moral theory deserving serious consideration must itself give them serious consideration . . . If we were to find that adopting a particular kind of morality led to irreconcilable conflict with central types of human well-being [such as love and friendship] . . . then this surely would give us good reason to doubt its claims.[23]

---

[22] We would like to thank Owen Flanagan for making this objection.

[23] Railton, 'Alienation', pp. 98–9.

In any case, since the radical is, in effect, rejecting the very possibility of even having the kind of debate in which this chapter is engaged, it seems more promising to interpret and respond to the objection in its moderate form.

Does our argument depend on an excessively idealised conception of friendship and its governing conditions which is not faithful to the norms we commonly take such relationships to involve? Clearly, were our argument to presuppose an implausibly strong conception of friendship, then we could hardly regard consequentialism's inability consistently to recognise such a conception as a fault with the theory. However, what we have said does not trade on an unrealistic conception of friendship. And perhaps more significantly, it seems clear that our target here, namely, the indirect consequentialist, also does not think that the problem of alienation brought by the case of friendship depends upon an unrealistic conception of friendship. The reply from the indirect consequentialist has not been to suggest that, for example, an agent such as Anne, who feels alienated from John, ought to adopt a more realistic conception of friendship. The reply has been, rather, that whilst the friendship between agents such as Anne and John *would* be violated if one of them had consequentialist motives or purposes, good consequentialist agents can be governed by the maximisation of agent-neutral value as their regulative ideal, and yet not take this as their motive or purpose in acting. And so being a consequentialist agent need not preclude one from being a friend. Now, our reply has not been to up the ante, so to speak, regarding the conception of friendship that is at stake. That is, we have not rested our case, for example, on a conception of friendship which involves a more demanding commitment (or, even stronger, a conception of friendship as involving an *unconditional* commitment), which would then be precluded by an agent's being governed by the consequentialist regulative ideal. Rather, we have argued that when one looks at the import of acceptance and terminating conditions for defining the nature and value of various relationships, there is good reason to believe that the source of the problem of alienation lies in the consequentialist agent's dispositions, as informed by these governing conditions, rather than in their motives or purposes. And so there is good reason to believe that the alienation which is commonly thought to characterise the direct consequentialist's relationships would be just as much a feature of the indirect consequentialist's relationships. In the light of this, then, the suggestion that our argument relies on an unrealistic conception of friendship would be both a misreading of our argument and somewhat against the spirit of the debate itself. Nevertheless, one might in any case think that the debate itself is misguided, since it is premised upon an unrealistic conception of friendship. While it is beyond our scope here to provide a full account of friendship and its varieties, let us say a little to redress this worry that the alienation pointed to in the debate, both by us and our opponents, rests on an unrealistic conception of friendship.

There are many cases where a person's feelings of alienation or disillusionment with another do not show that the other is not a friend. So to claim in these cases that on account of the feeling of alienation the other was not a true and good friend would be to make the mistake of invoking an unrealistic conception of friendship. For example, suppose Sue discovers that Paul is prepared to terminate his relationship with her if it becomes unenjoyable and deeply unfulfilling to him. If, upon realising this, Sue feels saddened, disappointed, and perhaps even alienated from Paul, this does not mean that Sue's feelings here show that Paul is not a friend to her. Rather, Sue might simply have an unrealistic view of what a relationship of friendship requires. Similarly, suppose that Sue felt alienated at discovering Paul's preparedness to terminate their relationship were she *seriously* to betray his trust. Again, Sue's feelings bespeak unrealistic expectations about forgiveness in relationships, rather than disqualify the relationship's claim to be one of friendship.[24] Indeed, sometimes we think it more appropriate to correct the negative feelings we have towards another on account of their dispositions, rather than taking those feelings as indicating a lack of friendship between us. For example, suppose that Kate finds herself disappointed and angry at Helen's tendency to behave tactlessly on certain occasions. Here Kate herself might be inclined to view her disappointment and anger at Helen as misplaced, if Helen's tactlessness was the result of nonculpable ignorance, or as inappropriate, if Helen immediately attempts to make amends for her tactlessness.

But why should we think that the sadness and alienation Linda might be thought to feel towards Juan on account of his consequentialist governing conditions on their relationship are like those in any of the above kinds of cases? In the first two cases, the agents feel alienated by dispositions of the other, even though those dispositions do seem to be part of our ordinary conceptions of the norms of friendship, and that is why such alienation seems premised upon unrealistic conceptions of friendship.

---

[24] On the other hand, if Paul were disposed to terminate their relationship on account of *minor* betrayals, then Sue might rightly regard Paul's preparedness here as bespeaking an unrealistic expectation on *his* part of the sort of commitment appropriate to friendship.

Thus, a friend who is prepared to end their relationship with another if it becomes empty and unfulfilling, or if their trust in the other is *seriously* damaged, seems to be no less a friend on those accounts. But on the other hand, being disposed to terminate one's relationships with others whenever these relationships do not maximise the good is a disposition which does *not* seem to be a part of our ordinary conceptions of friendship, and so unlike the cases mentioned above, it does not seem excessively romanticised or unrealistic to suppose that an agent like Linda would feel alienated from a person such as Juan, who is guided by such dispositions in his relationship with her.[25]

4 INDIRECT CONSEQUENTIALISM AND THE VALUE OF FRIENDSHIP

We have argued that there is good reason to think that the concern to maximise agent-neutral value operating as a governing condition on an agent's relationships may not be compatible with the motivational dispositions proper to friendship. In arguing in this way, we have been assuming that an important source of the *value* of friendly acts is the distinctive motivational dispositions from which such acts are performed.[26] To support this in the case of friendly acts, consider a comparison between being consoled by a friend and being consoled by a professional counsellor about the loss of our partner. Assume that both the friend and the counsellor are acting out of sympathy towards us, and that both are acting for our sake. Further, both the counsellor and the friend say things to us which we find very helpful. Nevertheless, the contrasting motivational dispositions of the counsellor and the friend are clearly the sources of quite different sorts of value. Again, this difference in value can, we believe, be helpfully illuminated by considering the contrasting governing conditions appropriate to these different relations, since the contrasting conditions of these relations entail quite distinct sorts of

---

[25] Moreover, unlike Helen, Juan does not view his consequentialist dispositions as flaws in his character, and so we may not think that Linda ought to overcome her alienation and forgive him instead.

[26] We take this to be a natural and straightforward way of accounting for much of the value in friendly acts, and many writers have given similar accounts of a variety of other valuable acts and relations. See, for example, Lawrence Blum, *Friendship, Altruism and Morality*, London, Routledge & Kegan Paul, 1980; Julie Inness, *Privacy, Intimacy, and Isolation*, New York, Oxford University Press, 1992; Stocker, 'The Schizophrenia of Modern Ethical Theories'; Michael Stocker, 'Values and Purposes: The Limits of Teleology and the Ends of Friendship', *Journal of Philosophy* 78, 1981; and Laurence Thomas, *Living Morally: A Psychology of Moral Character*, Philadelphia, Temple University Press, 1989.

commitments. Being consoled by the counsellor expresses a quite different kind of commitment from that expressed by the friend's action. For
the counsellor is committed to us qua client in need of care and support,
and the nature of the help they provide is importantly governed by and
conditional upon my being in such a plight. Thus, once I have resolved
my feelings about the loss (or if, without having completely resolved my
feelings about it, I just feel better able to deal with the loss), the counsellor can quite properly terminate the relationship, and indeed, would be
expected to terminate the relationship. However, the care and support
offered us in being consoled by a friend is of quite a different nature. For
unlike what happens in a counsellor–client relationship, what is distinctive about the care and support given us by a friend is that it expresses
a commitment to us that is not conditional upon our being in such a
plight – it is a commitment which is not based on the condition that we
are in a certain plight, and will not be terminated just on account of our
having resolved things. And were we to discover that the other had been
acting towards us in a way which expressed, say, the kind of commitment to us shown by the counsellor, then we would naturally feel that
an important part of the value of such an act would be lost. In short,
what we are arguing is that the kind of value expressed in the commitment one has to another is significantly informed by the governing conditions of one's relationship with them, and by the way in which these
conditions shape the motivational dispositions of one's relationship.
And since we have already argued that there is good reason to think that
indirect consequentialism may not be able consistently to recognise the
motivational disposition of friendship, then *a fortiori*, there is good reason
to think that indirect consequentialism may not be able consistently to
recognise the *value* of the kind of commitments found in friendship.

We have argued that there is good reason to believe that a motivational disposition governed by a consequentialist governing condition
may not be compatible with the nature and value of friendship, and so
with the commitment found in friendship. It follows, then, that we have
good reason to believe that, while sometimes agent-neutral value will
trump friendship, the nature and value of friendship are such that, in
other cases, friendship will trump the claim of maximisation of agent-
neutral value. True and good friends, that is, will have a motivational disposition which involves a preparedness to act for the friend, such that the
claims of friendship will sometimes trump the maximisation of agent-
neutral value. Now, this is not to endorse a romanticism which holds that
one could *never* give up a friend or loved one for some other value, or

indeed, even for another friend. Rather, it is to hold a *plural values* view which sees friendship as one intrinsically valuable agent-relative good, and so charts a middle course between the idea that considerations of friendship are always overriding and the claims of overridingness made on behalf of the regulative ideal of agent-neutral consequentialist morality.[27]

Despite what we have said, indirect consequentialism might still be thought to have sufficient resources to defend itself from the charges we have made against it. What our examples might be thought to suggest is wrong with the consequentialist is that the latter treats their relationships with others as of merely *instrumental* worth, as valuable only as a means, say, to promoting happiness. And while this might be conceded as posing a problem for a consequentialist who holds a *monistic* account of value (where friendship itself is not accorded intrinsic value), it might not be thought problematic for a *pluralistic* consequentialism, which posited friendship itself as one of the intrinsic values a consequentialist will have a standing commitment to maximise.[28]

However, our argument was not that consequentialists must regard their friendships as only instrumentally valuable, but rather that the conditions governing the relationships of a good consequentialist agent give us good reason to believe that such agents are incapable of friendships. Our argument would therefore also tell against pluralistic consequentialists who include friendship among the intrinsic goods an agent is committed to maximising. To see this, let us modify the governing conditions guiding the indirect consequentialist agent's relationships, so that their disposition to engage in and terminate their relationships with others is conditional upon those relationships being the best the agent is capable of promoting. On this view of Juan, then, if he could produce more of the good of friendship (i.e. more friendships) by leaving his wife Linda and putting all his energies into setting up a match-making service, he

---

[27] Similarly, we think that whilst Kantian duty may sometimes trump love and friendship, so too, may the claims of love and friendship trump that of duty.

[28] In some places, Railton writes as if he holds a view like this about the value of friendship. See pp. 109–10: 'Knowledge or friendship may promote happiness, but is it a fair characterisation of our commitment to these goals to say that this is the only sense in which they are ultimately valuable? . . . [I favour] a pluralistic approach in which several goods are viewed as intrinsically non-morally valuable – such as happiness, knowledge, purposeful activity, autonomy, solidarity, respect, and beauty. These goods need not be ranked lexically, but may be attributed weights, and the criterion of rightness for an act would be that it most contribute to the weighted sum of these values in the long run.' See also G. E. Moore's 'Ideal Utilitarianism' (in his *Ethics*, London, Oxford University Press, 1978), and what Parfit, *Reasons and Persons*, p. 4, describes as 'Objective List' theories.

would be obliged to do so. Indeed, according to maximisation, he would be irrational not to do so. But it seems implausible to suppose that engaging in and maintaining relationships on those conditions is compatible with those relationships being good and true friendships. Indeed, why should Linda feel any less alienated from Juan simply because it is in order to maximise friendships in general, rather than to maximise agent-neutral good as such, that he is prepared to be with her or leave her?[29]

It has been put to us that a pluralistic consequentialist who regarded friendship as one of the intrinsic values they were committed to promoting might object that the idea of someone abandoning their own friendships in order to promote friendships elsewhere is psychologically implausible. That is, it might be suggested that one cannot maximise friendships unless one has friendships oneself, since, as Yeats reminds us, too long a sacrifice makes a stone of the heart. Maybe it is true of some people that a preparedness to abandon friendship for themselves would render them unfit to promote it in others. However, it seems just as plausible that this need not be true of some other people. A generalisation either way here seems to us to be very unconvincing. After all, we do not take it to be necessarily true that abstaining from *other* sorts of relations with people must render a person incapable of effectively promoting those relations in others. To take just one case, presumably not *all*

---

[29] As Michael Stocker (*Plural and Conflicting Values*, Oxford: Clarendon Press, 1990, pp. 313–14) puts it: 'Friendship is . . . in opposition to maximisation. One can, of course, recognize that certain friends and friendships are better than others and that one could have more or better friends and friendships than one does. In certain cases, once such possibilities are seen, they should lead to action. However, if in general one will give up a friend and friendship because the other would be better – or if in general, one is even prepared to do this – then whatever the first relationship is, it is not a good or a true friendship. True and good friends and friendships involve a sort and strength of commitment that is importantly proof against the claims of betterment.' In our view, an important truth brought out by these sorts of cases is the conceptual claim to the effect that part of the nature and value of a true, real, or good friendship is that we have an attitude of irreplaceability both towards the particular person who is our friend and towards the particular relationship that is the friendship. This, we take it, is the sort of thing Stocker means in pointing to the kind and strength of commitment involved in true and good friendship, and how this is incompatible with the kind of preparedness for relinquishment which he adverts to. However, unlike Stocker, we do not take these sorts of cases to be anti-maximisation *as such*. We do not take this example to show the impossibility of a decision-theoretic consequentialism, where rightness requires us to do what we have most reason to do. For 'what we have most reason to do' could be filled out in a way which accords value to friendship construed as a relationship involving attachment to a particular person in a way that is resistant and indifferent to thinking about value as straightforwardly aggregative.

The claim that friendship (or 'end friendship') requires a recognition of the friend as irreplaceable is also made by Neera Badhwar Kapur, 'Why it is Wrong to be Always Guided by the Best: Consequentialism and Friendship', *Ethics* 101, 1991, who argues that because of this, a consequentialist agent cannot have friends, since for a consequentialist agent, others are essentially replaceable.

celibate priests who administer marital rites are ineffectual in promoting such relationships. In any case, even if one did believe that too long a sacrifice makes a stone of the heart, this would clearly not entail that we require *friendship* in order to maximise other friendships. For a person without friends is surely capable of contributing in many ways (for example, financially, organisationally, etc.) to the promotion of others' friendships.

Let us summarise our argument in this chapter so far. In attempting to overcome the problem of alienation which many have thought besets consequentialism in its direct forms, consequentialists have put forward an account of the sophisticated moral agent. The sophisticate, they have argued, does not have their consequentialist commitment as their motive or purpose, but rather is committed to the consequentialist criterion of rightness only as an internalised psychological normative disposition governing their relationships – or what we have characterised as their 'regulative ideal'. This psychological model of the indirect consequentialist agent, many have claimed, enables consequentialism to circumvent the problem of alienation and so give friendship its due. We have argued that this move does not succeed in overcoming the problem of alienation, because it mislocates the underlying source of the problem. Closer attention to the importance of the governing conditions of an agent's regulative ideals for defining the nature and value of their relationships suggests that it is this aspect of the consequentialist agent's psyche which is most significantly responsible for the problem of alienation. The sophisticate, then, does not avoid the problem of alienation, and like the direct consequentialist agent, remains unable to have true and good friendships.

5 DUTY-BASED APPROACHES TO ACCOMMODATING FRIENDSHIP

In explaining how a moral agent will regulate their life according to the principle of impartiality, Barbara Herman has argued that having this underlying commitment to impartiality need not be at the expense of other commitments, concerns, and relationships with those to whom we have special affective attachments. We can see how a commitment to impartiality is compatible with these other attachments, Herman argues, when we understand that a commitment to impartiality is essentially a *formal* commitment: 'Impartiality per se is the requirement that like cases be treated alike. As a requirement on justification, it is not trivial. Differential treatment or judgment requires the demonstration of relevant difference. But as a substantive moral requirement, impartiality by itself demands little.'[30] On this conception, the commitment to impartiality allows us to pursue commitments to other ends, such as promoting our friends' and family's well-being, to the extent that we are not thereby led to violate impartiality. And, according to Herman, a good moral agent recognises this condition when setting ends in a 'deliberative field':

> According to this deliberative field model, the practical self does not have as its major task negotiating a settlement among independent competing claims. Insofar as one has interests and commitments, one is a (human) self. But a human life is not the resultant of a 'bundle' of competing interests (among which is an interest in morality). One's interests are present on a deliberative field that contains everything that gives one reasons. Thus, in addition to interests and attachments, there are also grounds of obligation, principles of prudential rationality, and, depending on the individual, a more or less complex conception of the Good . . . An agent with a deliberative field constructed by [Kantian] moral principles recognizes from the outset, in the adoption of ends, that pursuit of important goals [for example my friendship with you] may unforeseeably lead one to means that are morally inappropriate (not permissible). The commitment to pursue an end is always conditional.[31]

Thus, a particular friendship can help shape and figure in one's deliberative field, but in a good moral agent this field must itself be regulated or conditioned by an underlying commitment to impartiality.

The concept of impartiality here is given an essentially formal interpretation: treat like cases alike.[32] Kantian impartiality thus construed may well be able to accommodate friendship. However, with impartiality drained as it is of any substantive content, this would be a rather hollow victory. As a notion of impartiality it is uninteresting and empty, and the question of whether Kantian impartiality yields a plausible morality becomes idle. What, for instance, are to count as relevant similarities and differences between cases? And why?

Suppose, then, a view of Kantian impartiality that involves an overriding commitment to a regulative ideal which does have some substantive account of the good of a familiar Kantian sort – such as one's moral duty not to tell lies, break one's commitments, or cheat on others.

---

[30] Herman, 'Agency, Attachment, and Difference', p. 776.   [31] Ibid., p. 784.
[32] This principle, that we treat like cases alike, is, of course, itself an Aristotelian principle. See Aristotle, *Nicomachean Ethics* v.3; Aristotle, *Politics* III.13, v.1. See also Will Kymlicka, *Contemporary Political Philosophy*, Oxford, Clarendon Press, 1990, p. 4.

Even if such a commitment might in some cases allow one to be *moved by* concerns proper to friendship, this does not at all suggest that being so governed is compatible with friendship. Similar to what we saw in discussing Railton's account of a sophisticated consequentialist, what matters for a Kantian account will be whether or not it is compatible with close friendship that one would be disposed to pursue the attachment and interest proper to it conditional upon the commitment to a Kantian regulative ideal.

Imagine, then, one of your own closest friends or loved ones. Surely it is a proper part of the nature of your attachment to and interest in them that (at least, in some circumstances) where they need your help or support you would be prepared to break a conflicting moral commitment – say, to lie or cover for them. Perhaps you would not be prepared to do so in any old circumstances, or to do so where the moral cost far exceeded any cost to your friend. But clearly, if we bring to mind those dearest to us, it seems an obvious and commonplace truism of the nature of our attachment to them that we would, say, lie or cover for them to help them out of some trouble or difficulty. To deny that it is a proper part of close friendship that one is disposed to take on such moral burdens for the other, at least in some circumstances, suggests a 'fair-weather-friend' account of one's intimate attachments that is fancifully aloof from the realities of persons and their circumstances. Those dearest to us are persons who will occasionally act badly or make mistakes, or fall victim to unfortunate circumstance. As such, the goods of mutual deep affection and partiality towards one another's interests and well-being that are widely accepted to characterise close friendship between persons are properly located in such realities of persons and their circumstances. And so, for instance, one may be moved to tell a lie in order to help a friend in trouble – say, pay the rent for a friend who has suffered a loss at the races and support his 'cover' story to his partner about the late rent (and perhaps lie to your own partner about what you did with the money since she has little time for your friend or his gambling extravagances). The pursuit of friendship between persons in such ways, while involving certain wrongdoings, seems a natural and commonplace expression of our attachment to and interest in our friends and of the value we associate with these. As such, it provides good reason to believe that our pursuit of friendship and the value attached to it are not conditional upon an overriding commitment to duty-based morality.

Kantians have tried to capture the force of such reasons we might have on account of friendship by appealing to special duties of friendship, which would render our acting for a friend and against some conflicting moral demand permissible (or even obligatory).[33] So, for example, Ross would say that cases such as telling a lie in order to avoid hurting the friend's feelings pose no real problems for the duty-theorist, since all such cases do is point to a conflict that is entirely *within* a duty-based morality. That is, this kind of case could be construed simply as one involving a conflict between one's prima facie duties themselves, rather than as showing a conflict between a duty-based morality, on the one hand, and some *other* moral or non-moral value.[34] On a view like Ross's, then, this conflict between prima facie duties might be resolved in favour of *either* friendship or truth-telling, depending on what the agent's intuitions tell the agent about the circumstances of the particular case. And so, if the agent's intuition is that their duty to their friend is here more important than their duty not to tell a lie, then according to a view like Ross's, the duty to the friend here wins out. In any event, in these kinds of conflict cases, it is *duty* that always wins.

In this way, a prima facie duty view might appear to have some initial plausibility in capturing the nature of the conflicting values in such cases, and offer further support to the project to accommodate friendship within an overriding commitment to a Kantian regulative ideal based in duty. It may do so since it can allow a guiding force to the reasons of friendship not only in those cases where friendship is co-operative with duty but also in cases where friendship conflicts with some other duty.

In reply, it might be thought that whether or not it is accurate to cast all such cases of acting to help a friend against some conflicting duty as cases of fulfilling special duties of friendship, it is clear that in many such

[33] See Barbara Herman, 'Rules, Motives, and Helping Actions', *Philosophical Studies* 45. See also Ewing, *Ethics*, pp. 147–8; H. J. Paton, 'Kant on Friendship', *Proceedings of the British Academy* 42, 1956; and Ross, *The Right and the Good*, chapter 7. Another typical way in which Kantians have tried to accommodate the value of friendship is by regarding friendship (or our capacity for such relationships) as a 'necessary natural predisposition' for an agent's appreciation of their special duties. For this account, see Herman, 'The Practice of Moral Judgment'; Immanuel Kant, *The Metaphysics of Morals – Part II: The Doctrine of Virtue*, trans M. J. Gregor, Cambridge, Cambridge University Press, 1991, Ak. pp. 399–400, 456–7; and Paton, 'Kant on Friendship'. However, in accommodating friendship in this way, Kantians would not grant moral value, much less any guiding or regulative force, to the affective states proper to friendship. So, for example, a duty of care for a friend, in a Kantian view, might have as a precondition that we are beings who can have feelings of friendly care and concern. But as others have argued, it seems false that friendly feelings of care and concern cannot themselves have moral value. See for example, Blum, *Friendship, Altruism and Morality*. [34] See Ross, *The Right and the Good*, chapter 7.

cases it is not the disposition to do one's special duty that guides one. Typically, it is the concerns proper to one's friendship – say, one's affection for the friend – that guide one. And so taken generally as an account of the nature of the values in cases of conflict between friendship and duty, the Kantian view will in many cases miss the affective grounding which importantly confers value on relations of friendship.[35] A Kantian, such as Herman, however, can accept that in many cases it is the guiding disposition proper to friendship and not to duty that the friend will act on, and so deny that she is 'missing' the value of the former or substituting the value of the latter for the former. For her claim is that friendship does have non-instrumental value, so long as it is governed by the overriding commitment to duty. This account may not tell us much, if anything at all, about the nature and value of friendship. But it does, at least formally, provide an account of how the nature and value of the good of friendship pointed to in our conflict cases might be accommodated by the duty theorist.

However, even if our pursuit of friendship against other conflicting moral demands could in many cases be properly cast as a conflict between duties, it seems clear that often it cannot. For often where we pursue friendship against some conflicting moral claim (in ways which nevertheless seem proper to and well within the nature and value of close friendship), it is not plausible to think of our pursuit here as accommodated by a governing commitment to duty, much less as a requirement of duty. So, for instance, out of friendship I might lend or simply give my friend some money to indulge his gambling extravagances, but lie to my partner, who has little time for my friend or his gambling, about where the money went. Perhaps I would not do so at great financial cost to myself or my partner, or I would not do so where I think that his gambling has become an addiction that is destroying his life (or maybe I would also do other things here – say, try to convince him to get some counselling help). But surely it is a commonplace part of the affection and interest we have in our close friends that at times we are inclined to indulge, at some moral cost, some such vices. So, for instance, we might not just provide a cover for our friend's infidelity on a given occasion but

---

[35] To be sure, in the case of telling a small lie in order to avoid breaking a friend's heart, the prima facie duty not to cause such avoidable suffering may itself suffice as a justification for telling the lie. And so, the affection and interest which we have in the friend may not themselves be doing any justificatory work here. Indeed, this can be seen to follow from the perfectly general point that this duty would plausibly suffice to justify telling a small lie in cases where this is necessary in order to avoid breaking the heart of a complete stranger.

take some amusement in it – as we might of her particularly crude, but nevertheless hilarious, sense of humour. Thus, while it seems plausible to regard such expressions of the affection and interest we have in our friends as part of the nature and value of the good of close friendship, it is not plausible to suppose that we could construe such pursuits of friendship (against other conflicting moral demands) as governed by one's overriding commitment to Kantian moral duty. Certainly, one is hardly required by any Kantian moral duty to indulge a friend's gambling extravagances, say, or her crude sense of humour, at the expense of some conflicting moral duty.

Thus, while an appeal to the special duties of friendship might seem able to accommodate the conflict between friendship and duty-based morality in some cases, it fails to do so for a commonplace class of everyday cases of such conflict, and fails to provide the desired support to the Kantian, such as Herman, who seeks to allow the pursuit of friendship conditional upon governance by an overriding commitment to one's moral duties.

On our view of the good of friendship, therefore, a close friend might not act like, or display the character of, an agent governed by an overriding commitment to duty when, say, she covers for the infidelity of her friend. Nevertheless she may be acting like, and displaying the character of, a perfectly good friend. Moreover, it seems plausible to think that one acts with good reason in pursuing one's friend or her interests in such cases. Thus, one may sensibly point to the force of reasons given by one's friendship – say, one's affection and interest – to provide explanation and justification for one's pursuit of friendship over conflicting moral demands in some cases. For instance, on being found out by one's partner about indulging the friend's gambling and lying about where the money went, one could point to one's affection for the friend and his risk-taking exploits and to the partner's intolerance of this, rather than plead excuses or any lack of choice and control of one's affection, to account for one's actions. The partner here may not share this particular reason – she may not share an affection for such risk-taking or for the risk-taking of this friend – but she can, at least for *her* friends, share relevantly similar reasons. She may, for example, have much affection for the naughty or slightly outrageous character-trait of her friend who has the crude sense of humour, and this may, on occasion, lead her to cover for this friend – say, to you, since you have always shown disdain for this person or this aspect of her character. And likewise, she may, on being exposed, explain and justify her actions by pointing to the force of reasons given by her friendship.[36]

The account of the nature and value of friendship to which we appeal here[37] diverges from standard philosophical accounts of friendship which characterise the good of friendship wholly in terms of the moral virtue it may exhibit, such as the revealing or developing of some key morally good character-traits in the friends. Certainly our view diverges from traditional Aristotelian accounts which not only locate the good of friendship within this kind of moral framework, but locate the very *nature* of friendship within an explicitly moral disposition.[38] On our account of a virtue ethics approach, the overarching regulative ideal of the virtuous person is not given by commitment to any particular kind of moral

---

[36] We are not, of course, claiming that such reasons of friendship can rightly trump conflicting duties in any such cases. One may not, for instance, justify the decision to employ a friend instead of a better-qualified applicant just by appeal to the force of reasons given by one's affection and interest.

Significantly, and sometimes decisively, what confers value on an act of love or friendship is the sort of affection, interest, desire, or feeling that one has in performing the act, and, at least sometimes, these provide good reason to act even if to do so would be at the expense of a conflicting duty.

Typically, Kantians have something like contempt for this sort of suggestion. In their view, it sounds as if one is endorsing moral scepticism – that is, some view which is asking: 'Why do what you ought to when you feel like doing something else?' Or, following Paton, who instructs us that 'in spite of the views and behaviour sometimes reported in the Sunday newspapers . . . [it might be held that] Friendship is an added grace . . . it gives no one a right to cheat or assault or murder' (Paton, 'Kant on Friendship', p. 52). Of course, it would be absurd to think that how one felt in friendship could be the *sole* regulative constraint on right action. And Paton's comments *would* be an adequate reply to the view that friendship is morally good wherever it is exemplified: i.e. that it has *unconditional* value. But then who holds this view? This view would hardly follow from the claim that friendship has *intrinsic* value. To claim, as we do, that friendship has intrinsic value is to claim that friendship is valuable not merely extrinsically – i.e. insofar as it is governed by some other value, say, duty (much less that it is merely instrumentally valuable, i.e. valuable only as a means to realising some other value) – but rather has value in and of itself. And as Shelly Kagan ('The Additive Fallacy', *Ethics* 99, October 1988), Jonathan Dancy ('The Role of Imaginary Cases in Ethics', *Pacific Philosophical Quarterly* 66, 1985), and others (e.g. Michael Stocker, 'Some Problems with Counter Examples in Ethics', *Synthese* 72, 1987) have pointed out, to claim that something such as friendship is good in and of itself is not yet to claim that it is good wherever it is exemplified.

[37] For further defence of the view that it can be reasonable to favour a friend in certain cases, even where this would not gain support from, and would be in conflict with, what Kantian duty would require, see Dean Cocking and Jeanette Kennett, 'Friendship and Moral Danger', *Journal of Philosophy* 97, no. 5, May 2000.

[38] On classical Aristotelian accounts, the nature and value of friendship and the trust and intimacy that it involves are marked by the mutual recognition of one another's virtue and the opportunity for moral self-examination and improvement this affords. See, for instance, Aristotle, *Nicomachean Ethics* 1159a35; Thomas, *Living Morally*, pp. 153–5; and Nancy Sherman, 'Aristotle on the Shared Life', in Neera K. Badhwar (ed.), *Friendship: A Philosophical Reader*, Ithaca, Cornell University Press, 1993, pp. 105–6. For a detailed critical discussion of such views see Dean Cocking and Jeanette Kennett, 'Friendship and the Self', *Ethics* 108, no. 3, April 1998.

value, such as to the maximisation of good consequences or to those moral concerns that may plausibly be conceived of as one's moral duties. Rather, as we explained in chapter 1, it is informed by the governing concerns that define the various goods that contribute to a flourishing human life. Hence, if, as we believe, part of the good of friendship involves being governed by attachment, the nature of which will be to lead one, in some circumstances, to act (with justifiable reason) against conflicting demands to promote good consequences or fulfil a moral duty, then the pursuit of friendship in such cases may be licensed by an overarching regulative ideal of virtue.

CONCLUSION

The prominence which Herman and Railton give to character stems partly from their concern to improve earlier accounts of Kantianism and consequentialism, by showing how a good agent would internalise what those theories hold to be the appropriate criteria of rightness, while nevertheless accommodating the value distinctive of particular activities, relations, and roles. However, while something might be said in favour of Kantian impartiality or consequentialist maximisation as purely *formal* criteria of rightness, when we try to embody them in our lives as regulative ideals, they fail to capture adequately the value of certain fundamental human goods, such as love and friendship. And, since Kantians and consequentialists have recognised the demand that an acceptable morality must accommodate central types of human well-being, such as love and friendship, this failure, by their very own lights, provides good reason to doubt the plausibility of the Kantian and consequentialist regulative ideals.

CHAPTER 3

A virtue ethics approach to professional roles

Now that we have a better understanding of the nature of a virtue ethics approach, and of its distinctiveness and plausibility by comparison with its consequentialist and Kantian rivals, let us consider how this approach could be applied to the specific case of professional roles. In this chapter, we demonstrate how virtue ethics can provide a useful account of the nature and moral significance of professional roles. We begin by outlining briefly a general framework which indicates the conditions under which a person could be regarded, on our virtue ethics approach, as performing a good professional role, after which we present an account of some of the distinctive strengths of this general approach to professional roles.

Broadly speaking, what counts as acting well in the context of a professional role is in our view importantly determined by how well that role functions in serving the goals of the profession, and by how those goals are connected with characteristic human activities. That is, good professional roles must be part of a good profession, and a good profession, on our virtue ethics approach, is one which involves a commitment to a key human good, a good which plays a crucial role in enabling us to live a humanly flourishing life. Further, while a certain profession itself may meet these requirements, it must also be possible to demonstrate how the particular role under scrutiny contributes to the overall goal of that profession. So, for example, if (as many suggest) it is appropriate to take serving *health* as the central goal of medicine, then given the importance of health for human flourishing, medicine would clearly count as a good profession on this approach.[1] And, for example, given a general practitioner's concern with the broad health needs of their patients, the general practitioner's role within medicine would seem to count as a good professional role. Similarly, if (as many suggest) it is appropriate to

---

[1] See also Aristotle, *Nicomachean Ethics* I.i.1094a8: 'the end of the medical art is health'.

take achieving *justice* (in some sense) as a central goal of lawyering, then the importance of justice in human flourishing would clearly enable the legal profession to qualify as a good profession. And, given the importance that achieving justice plays for, say, a state prosecutor, such a role would count as a good professional role on this approach. Thus, in order to generate a defensible professional ethic, the norms of the profession in question cannot simply be taken as given; rather they must be shown to reflect a commitment to an important substantive human good that contributes to our living a flourishing human life.

We are claiming that an appropriately action-guiding professional ethic cannot be generated without specifying what the appropriate orientation and essential guiding concerns of the particular profession ought to be.[2] Thus, the content of the regulative ideals of a good doctor must be determined by reference to some model of what doctoring purports to be. That is, those regulative ideals will be informed by an account of the proper goals of medicine as a *practice* – a *philosophy* of medicine – and an account of what sorts of doctor–patient relationships are appropriate in such a practice. This approach should then tell us how the proper goals of medicine will figure in the character and actions of a good doctor, and should thereby deliver an account of the virtues that are appropriate to medical practice (or to legal practice, and so on). Once one had articulated what the ends of medicine are, and shown how these ends contribute to human flourishing, a fully developed virtue ethics approach to medical practice would then need to demonstrate how the different branches of medicine serve the *general* ends of medicine. (One would need to allow that certain branches of medicine might serve the general ends of medicine better than other branches of medicine do.) We do not seek to provide a comprehensive virtue ethics approach to medical practice.[3] Nevertheless, to give our approach to professional roles more content, let us say a little more by way of example about the notion of *health* that we take doctors as entrusted to serve.

There are long-standing controversies about how the concept of health is to be understood. Some writers define health in purely negative terms, as the absence of disease, and then proceed to analyse health

---

[2] Note that we are not here referring to any current example of a specific profession in a particular country; rather, we are talking about 'the profession of (eg.) medicine', generally, as a practice.

[3] One such account is given by Edmund Pellegrino and David Thomasma, *The Virtues in Medical Practice*, New York, Oxford University Press, 1993. See also Edmund Pellegrino and David Thomasma, *A Philosophical Basis of Medical Practice*, New York, Oxford University Press, 1981.

by developing an account of what a disease is. Others argue that health is not merely the absence of disease, but has certain positive elements also. One example of a positive account is the well-known statement by the World Health Organisation which defines health very broadly as 'a state of complete mental, physical, and social well-being'. As Ramsey points out, however, this definition seems to entail

> that professional medical judgments assume responsibility for the full range of human moral considerations. This would be to locate medical considerations in direct lineage with all of man's moral reflections upon the meaning of *eudaimonia . . .* since Aristotle![4]

Such an account of health would give doctors a very broad brief indeed, and would place upon them expectations that would far exceed their training. Without wishing to become embroiled in long-standing controversies about the appropriate definition of 'health', we should say that the accounts of health we think most plausibly characterise what the practice of medicine undertakes to serve are those which define health in terms of normal biological and psychological functioning – that is, biological and psychological functioning at a level within that which is typical of the species in question: here, human beings.[5] Very briefly, then, on this view a human being is healthy when its biological capacities are functioning normally, statistically speaking, for a human being of its sex and age group, and when its psychological capacities are functioning normally. Normal human functioning is here taken to include the absence of disease, as standardly conceived, and is distinct from the notion of *excellent* human functioning, where our human capacities would be developed to a high degree.[6] This sort of account, in our view, helps to refine and capture much of what is meant by those who explicate health in more metaphorical terms as 'wholeness'.[7] Thus, we under-

---

[4] Paul Ramsey, *The Patient as Person*, New Haven, Yale University Press, 1970, p. 123.

[5] For a defence of such an account, see Christopher Boorse, 'Health as a Theoretical Concept', *Philosophy of Science* 44, 1977; Christopher Boorse, 'What a Theory of Mental Health should be', *Journal for the Theory of Social Behaviour* 6, no. 1, 1976; and Christopher Boorse, 'On the Distinction Between Disease and Illness', *Philosophy and Public Affairs* 5, Fall 1975. For applications of Boorse's account to issues about justice in the allocation of health-care resources, see Norman Daniels, *Just Health Care*, Cambridge, Cambridge University Press, 1985.

[6] Of course, an individual whose psychophysical capacities are functioning at *high* levels would still count as healthy; it is just that such a high level of functioning is on this account not necessary for an individual to count as healthy. This notion of health is distinct from that of our everyday notion of 'fitness', which focuses more narrowly on the development of certain physical capacities. As Boorse notes, the account of health mentioned here is by no means without its difficulties; but we agree with him that these problems are less severe than are those facing the rival accounts that we know of.

[7] See, e.g., Leon Kass, 'Neither for Love nor Money: Why Doctors must not Kill', *The Public Interest* 94, Winter 1989.

stand the practice of medicine as having undertaken to serve health, construed as having biological and psychological dimensions, where there are human norms for each of these dimensions of our lives, but where health is not equated with *eudaimonia* itself. It is common to distinguish between health and the broader concept of 'well-being', and we would see certain explications of the latter concept as coming closer to the notion of *eudaimonia*.[8]

But while this notion of health, being narrower than a full bio-psycho-social model, does not go so far as equating health with *eudaimonia*, the account nevertheless portrays medicine as serving goals that are importantly linked with *eudaimonia*. Aristotle sees biological health as a significant good of fortune – along with friendship and other such goods that improve our lives.[9] And conceiving of health as having a psychological as well as a biological dimension would make it an even more important constituent of *eudaimonia*, since we cannot live well when our psychophysical functioning is significantly impaired.[10] This is not to deny that highly talented individuals with poor physical health can still have good lives.[11] But we would say that, other things being equal, the lives of most such individuals would be improved were they in better health. There have, of course, been individuals whose genius seems to have been intrinsically connected to their unhealthy condition, and whose lives would perhaps not have been improved overall had they been healthier (one thinks here of painters such as Claude Monet, Vincent Van Gogh, and the German Expressionist Egon Schiele). However, the fact that there are people whose lives might have been no better overall for the addition of health does not undermine the claim that normal psychophysical functioning is still a very significant *intrinsic* good (and, for most people, a great *instrumental* good also). For, as Michael Stocker and others have argued, sometimes the addition of an intrinsic good to a state of affairs leads to no overall improvement,

---

8 That is, Aristotle's conception of *eudaimonia* can be seen as providing us with one account of what human well-being consists in. For developments of the Aristotelian approach in the context of contemporary accounts of well-being, see the discussions of Amartya Sen and Martha Nussbaum's 'capability' approach to well-being, in Martha C. Nussbaum and Amartya Sen (eds.), *The Quality of Life*, Oxford, Clarendon Press, 1993.

9 See, e.g., *Nicomachean Ethics*, VII.13.1153b16–21. Note that we are not calling health itself a virtue.

10 Michael Stocker and Elizabeth Hegeman provide an illuminatingly detailed account of how impaired psychological functioning due to 'spiritual maladies' such as depression, detachment, and despair prevents us from living a good human life. See Michael Stocker with Elizabeth Hegeman, *Valuing Emotions*, Cambridge, Cambridge University Press, 1996. (In chapter 9, Stocker also discusses why such maladies seem to have been neglected by Aristotle and in classical Greek literature.)

11 See James Griffin, *Well-Being: Its Meaning, Measurement, and Moral Importance*, Oxford, Clarendon Press, 1986, pp. 46–7.

because of the nature and level of the intrinsic *bads* (or other values) which are present there.[12]

It is beyond the scope of this book to provide a detailed account of the concept of *health*.[13] Our focus here is on the broader question of how a virtue ethics approach could justify and give content to various professional roles, such as the role of the doctor. (In chapter 5 we discuss in more detail how the role of the lawyer is properly governed by the goal of justice.) Doctors serve the proper medical goal of health through their commitments to various subsidiary goals, such as healing the sick, the promotion of healthy behaviour, and the prevention of ill-health, and through effective palliative care. Thus, even when a patient cannot be *healed*, or have his health restored – say, because he has a chronic disease – often there are still many ways in which a doctor can serve health by assisting the patient: for example, by helping the patient to overcome or minimise various impairments to functioning resulting from his disease. Likewise, palliative care to alleviate the distressing symptoms of a patient with a terminal disease can also count as serving health. For providing a patient with, say, effective pain relief can be thought to make her less *unhealthy*, since being racked with uncontrolled pain would typically take one even further away from normal functioning than one would already be on account of one's condition. Although there are disputes about the meaning of *health*, the idea that doctors should serve the goal of health is not really controversial – just how the goal of serving health should govern the conduct of the ethical doctor, and how it is to be weighed against other values confronting a doctor, such as the autonomy of patients and the appropriate allocation of health-care resources, is the subject of continuing debate, and we shall say a little more about this topic shortly. Let us now, however, highlight some of the advantages of a virtue ethics approach, when applied to the morality of professional roles.

One of the strengths of an approach to professional roles which takes their moral status to depend importantly on their links with key human goods is that this sort of approach fits naturally with a central feature of

---

[12] See Michael Stocker, 'Some Problems with Counter-Examples in Ethics', *Synthese* 72, 1987; Michael Stocker, *Plural and Conflicting Values*, Oxford, Clarendon Press, 1990. See also G. E. Moore's discussion of 'organic wholes', in *Principia Ethica*, Cambridge, Cambridge University Press, 1903; Shelly Kagan, 'The Additive Fallacy', *Ethics* 99, October 1988; and Christine Korsgaard, 'Two Distinctions in Goodness', *Philosophical Review* 92, 1983.

[13] For more, see debates by Boorse, 'Health as a Theoretical Concept'; R. M. Hare, 'Health', in his *Essays on Bioethics*, Oxford, Clarendon Press, 1993; and H. R. Wulff, S. A. Pedersen, and R. Rosenberg, *Philosophy of Medicine: An Introduction*, Oxford, Blackwell Scientific Publications, 1990.

any occupation's claim to be a profession in the first place. That is, it is widely agreed that for an occupation justifiably to claim to be a profession, its practitioners must deal not simply with goods that many of us strongly *desire* to have; rather its practitioners must be able to help us attain certain goods that play a crucial *strategic* role in our living a flourishing life for a human being.[14] Indeed, it is because of this strategic nature of the goods professionals characteristically help us to secure that cases where a practitioner fails to uphold their *professional* role – compared with a non-professional who fails to fulfil their *occupational* role – gain such moral significance. To illustrate this, suppose that the medical profession decided to adopt a policy of withholding from low-income patients a service that is central to the doctor's role, on the grounds that providing this treatment for such patients was thought not profitable enough for individual doctors (say, because of the lengthy time such patients were taking to settle their accounts). For example, suppose that doctors decided not to prescribe antibiotics for low-income patients, in any case where a disease was not life-threatening. Part of the wrongness of this would consist in the fact that in adopting such a policy, the medical profession would be betraying the community which has entrusted it with a monopoly on the provision of certain goods. However, it is not only the fact that the profession has a monopoly on certain goods, but also *what sort of goods* the profession has been granted a monopoly on providing, that makes such a decision to withhold particularly immoral. For without access to antibiotics to treat whatever non-lethal diseases they may contract, the lives of the low-income patients in question will be seriously impaired by disease and illness, which no other occupational group has been permitted to develop the skills to treat adequately. By contrast, suppose that a community had granted its plumbers a monopoly on roofing repairs (by, for example, ensuring that the tools to make the repairs were unavailable to the general public), but plumbers as a group decided to adopt a policy of not providing a certain service which was central to their role – such as fixing

[14] See, e.g., Paul R. Camenisch, 'On Being a Professional, Morally Speaking', in Bernard Baumrin and Benjamin Freedman (eds.), *Moral Responsibility and the Professions*, New York, Haven Publications, 1983. Sometimes this is put in terms of the contrast between *needs* and (mere) *desires*. Instead of speaking of the role of these goods in a 'flourishing human life', or of 'needs', Michael Bayles puts this characteristic of professions by saying that they enable us to obtain 'basic social values': *Professional Ethics*, 2nd. edn, Belmont, Wadsworth, 1989, p. 12. For a good account of one way in which health has strategic importance for individuals – namely, in helping position them to capitalise on their share of the normal range of opportunities – see Daniels, *Just Health Care*, chapters 1 and 2.

leaking roofs – for people on low incomes, on the grounds that they could make a much greater profit by concentrating their efforts on fixing the roofs of those who are not on low incomes. While there is a betrayal of the monopoly plumbers have been entrusted with here, and it is wrong that people on low incomes cannot get their roofs fixed, it seems clear that the individuals who have adequate treatment withheld because of doctors' concerns about profitability are, relative to normal human functioning, more significantly impaired – and thereby, we want to say, more seriously wronged – than are the individuals whom the plumbers have left with leaking roofs.

Now, some might argue that while it is plausible to link the justifiability of a certain professional role to the moral status of the profession itself, as determined by the goals which it professes to serve, nevertheless the proposal to evaluate a profession – and thus the roles of its members – according to the relative importance which its goals have for characteristic human functioning takes an overmoralised approach to the status of a profession. It might be thought more defensible to require of a good profession only that its constitutive goals be morally *permissible*, rather than to require that they be key components of human flourishing. For, compared to the Aristotelian approach we have been advocating, the sort of approach presently being suggested might be thought better to accommodate newer professions such as architecture, accountancy, and journalism, whose goals are arguably less central to human flourishing than are the goals of the medical and legal professions.

However, we consider it an important strength of our virtue ethics approach that it reflects a crucial distinguishing feature of professions, compared to other occupations. After all, it is partly because they deal with what are unequivocally key human goods that medicine and law are two of the traditional professions, and are commonly taken as having significant characteristics against which occupations aspiring to professional status measure themselves. Indeed, many of the arguments put by various occupational groups to support their aspirations to professional status seem to presuppose that (other things being equal) the more an occupation's body of special expertise deals with a *key* human good, the greater claim that occupation has to be properly regarded as a *profession*.[15] In any case, while the goals of, say, architecture may be less central

---

[15] It is important to acknowledge another point here, which bears on the complaint by members of a profession that people who criticise professionals (eg. doctors) for withholding their services on prudential or conscientious grounds whenever the practitioner sees fit to do so are engaging in a sort of 'de-professionalisation' of the practitioner. That is, it is important for practitioners

to human flourishing than the goals of medicine or law, it is not difficult to see how living in aesthetically pleasing and functional dwellings could still contribute importantly to a flourishing life for a human being.

But while it might well be agreed that a good professional role must in some sense be directed towards a key human good, it may be objected that this teleological approach to professional roles is too broad or general to provide us with much guidance about which specific role demands are morally justifiable and which are not. For instance, the notion of health we think the practice of medicine aims to serve might seem too open-ended to tell us much about what content good medical roles would have. However, reflection on some examples of how the goal of health is commonly seen as properly governing medical practice suggests that the teleological approach we propose can yield more determinate results than is alleged in this objection. Consider, for instance, the notion of *betrayal* in medicine. Amongst the most egregious examples of medical betrayal are the experiments carried out on concentration camp inmates by the Nazi doctors, such as Josef Mengele and Eduard Wirths. The horrific nature of these experiments and the fact that the inmates were coerced to participate make these experiments morally repellent. But, as Robert Jay Lifton brings out well, the fact that the people who perpetrated these atrocities were *doctors* magnifies the outrageousness of what they did, since their actions were so contrary to the healing ethic to which they professed to be committed.[16] Another example of medical betrayal, though on a different scale, is having sex with a patient. A doctor who has sex with a patient betrays her, even in the unlikely event that he is thereby acting on the patient's autonomous request. Such an action is seen as 'perverse', in that it elevates the doctor's sexual gratification above meeting the health needs of the patient. This example also suggests that 'serving patient autonomy' is not itself a proper goal of medicine (a point we shall return to shortly). Less dramatically, in an age of scarce medical resources and declining idealism, many doctors look upon colleagues who have adopted the achievement of efficiency or the

who make such a complaint to appreciate that the greater claim which the particular good which one's profession serves has to being a *key* human good (and the more that ministering to that good requires *specialist* knowledge, thereby making the monopoly granted to its practitioners less easily replaceable), the greater claim the social demand for that good will have to be a *right* (to that particular good). And thus, such professionals will need stronger grounds (than will other occupational groups) for withholding their services (in circumstances where another doctor is unqualified or unavailable to provide that service).

[16] See Robert Jay Lifton, *The Nazi Doctors: Medical Killing and the Psychology of Genocide*, New York, Basic Books, 1986.

maximisation of personal wealth as their overriding goals in practising medicine as having betrayed their profession.[17] Thus, what sorts of things are counted as a betrayal of one's patients or one's profession can help bring out not only that it is constitutive of good doctoring that doctors have (implicitly or explicitly) pledged themselves to serve certain goals like health and to forswear certain others, but also that those goals are of a certain determinate kind.

Closer examination of professionals withholding their services for reasons either of conscience or of professional integrity can also illuminate how virtue ethics' teleological approach to professional roles helps to delineate the proper boundaries of professional practice. A number of writers have recently highlighted how appeals to some notion of 'professional integrity' as a reason for withholding one's services are importantly distinct from a refusal to provide services on conscientious grounds. In medicine, for example, the idea of a doctor maintaining their professional integrity has been characterised in terms of their practising in ways that honour their commitment to the proper goals of medicine, as distinct from practising medicine in ways that do not violate their own *personal* – for example, religious – values.[18] This distinction has helpfully broadened discussions of refusals to treat beyond familiar debates about conscientious objection. However, a connection between these two grounds for withholding one's services has gone unnoticed, and focusing on this connection provides another way of showing the determinate content given to the role of the doctor by medicine's distinctive goal(s). That is, in discussions of the sorts of things which doctors might legitimately refuse to do on grounds of their personal *conscience*, there is an implicit assumption in play that what is being permissibly refused is towards the periphery of the practice of medicine, and is not part of its core business. Consider, for example, how doctors would regard a colleague who, because of some personal 'vitalist' opposition to using antibiotics, refused to administer antibiotics to otherwise healthy babies struck down with some life-threatening disease, such as bacterial meningitis. The fact that many within a profession would balk at a doctor who refused, on 'conscientious' grounds, to provide such treatment indicates

---

[17] We have learnt a great deal about the notion of medical betrayal from Dr David Macintosh, and his Ph.D. thesis, 'Trust and Betrayal in the Physician–Patient Relationship', Centre for Human Bioethics, Monash University, 2000.

[18] See, e.g., Jeffrey Blustein, 'Doing what the Patient Orders: Maintaining Integrity in the Doctor–Patient Relationship', *Bioethics* 7, no. 4, 1993; and Franklin G. Miller and Howard Brody, 'Professional Integrity and Physician-Assisted Death', *Hastings Center Report* 25, no. 3, May–June 1995.

that, while there may be disagreement on the periphery, there are nevertheless certain specific practices which are taken as part of the core business of being a doctor. And those core activities are all fairly evidently connected with the goal of serving health.

Another strength of the virtue ethics approach to professional role morality provided here is that compared to certain other accounts, it better captures the distinctiveness of each profession, which in turn enables us to make better sense of debates about whether (for example) it is justifiable for a doctor to act on a patient's voluntary request to be killed, and whether it is justifiable for lawyers to fulfil a client's request in cases where doing so would violate broad-based justice. For, characterising the goal of a profession in terms of the substantive good it undertakes to serve helps us better understand appeals to a notion of professional integrity as a reason for refusing to carry out certain requests from patients or clients. It brings out, for example, why a substantial number of doctors feel that they cannot, *qua doctors*, act on a patient's autonomous request to be killed. For even in cases where it is clear that death would not be a harm to a patient, many doctors nevertheless feel that to kill such a patient at their autonomous request is to betray the goal of serving health which fundamentally defines their profession of medicine. Indeed, some of these doctors do *not* think that it is immoral for a person with a life of irremediable suffering and lacking even in basic goods to be killed at this person's autonomous request – say, by a loving spouse; nevertheless, they think that it is unjustifiable for them to act on the request *as doctors*, given the professional goals to which they are committed. We are not here endorsing the claim that it is unethical for doctors to perform active voluntary euthanasia (though we should say that we would have no in principle objection to a doctor who carried out active voluntary euthanasia with, as it were, 'her doctor's hat off' – say, at the request of her terminally ill spouse). Some argue that killing a patient for whom death would be a 'good' at his autonomous request is reconcilable with the proper goals of medicine because this can itself be a 'healing act', or at least, can be in the patient's overall best interests. (Consider here how forcibly depriving someone of the sort of death they had authentically requested and envisaged is sometimes regarded as a terrible violation or rupture of 'wholeness'.[19]) Certainly, mercifully to fulfil a terminally ill patient's autonomous request to end

---

[19] As Ronald Dworkin puts it, 'making someone die in a way that others approve, but he regards as a horrifying contradiction of his life, is a devastating, odious form of tyranny' (*Life's Dominion: An Argument about Abortion, Euthanasia and Individual Freedom*, New York, Knopf, 1993, p. 217).

his life of irremediable suffering and distress does not seem so clearly to
constitute a perversion of the notion of good medical practice as what
the Nazi doctors did in betraying their profession (and we are sceptical
of the assumption, which seems to be implicit in arguments against
doctors carrying out voluntary euthanasia, that death is always a harm
– or at least, can never be a good – to the person who dies). But whether
or not doctors performing active voluntary euthanasia is in the end
regarded as morally permissible, virtue ethics' teleological approach to
professional roles reinforces the relevance of a consideration which
many doctors see as crucial – namely, the nature of the profession's
goal(s) and its bearing on the conduct in question. This approach to professional role morality is thus illuminating, in enabling us to see analo-
gies between doctors refusing to carry out voluntary euthanasia and, for
example, lawyers refusing to act for a client in ways which would clearly
violate the value of justice which the legal profession undertakes to serve.

The ethical significance of the distinctive goals of different professions is often ignored by contemporary approaches to professional
ethics, in their understandable eagerness to highlight to professionals
the importance of honouring client autonomy. Indeed, contemporary
texts in both medical ethics and legal ethics often appeal to the notion
of autonomy in ways which suggest that respecting or upholding
patient or client autonomy, *simpliciter*, should be the overarching goal of
the medical and legal professions, respectively. For example, Charles
Fried advises that '[T]he doctor must see himself as the servant, not of
life in the abstract, but of the life plans of his patients.'[20] However,
according patient or client autonomy this sort of sovereignty over other
values in professional practice leaves it unclear when and why health
and legal professionals can justifiably refuse certain autonomous
requests made by patients or clients, since such refusals tend to be por-
trayed by medical and legal ethicists as failing adequately to serve the
life-plans of patients or clients. Thus, doctors who, for example, refuse
to act on a patient's voluntary request to be killed, or who limit a
patient's access to costly but futile treatment, are sometimes criticised
as violating or failing to respect patient autonomy. Such criticisms,
however, misconstrue the relevance of patient autonomy to a doctor's

---

[20] Charles Fried, *Medical Experimentation: Personal Integrity and Social Policy*, Amsterdam, North
Holland Publishing Co., 1974, p. 99. See also, e.g., Tom L. Beauchamp and James F. Childress,
Principles of Biomedical Ethics, 4th edn, New York, Oxford University Press, 1994. (This book is
regarded as the most widely used and influential text on medical ethics.) In legal ethics, see again
Charles Fried, 'The Lawyer as Friend: The Moral Foundations of the Lawyer–Client Relation',
Yale Law Journal 85, no. 8, July 1976.

properly fulfilling the doctor's professional role. For while doctors who refuse to meet certain patient requests will probably restrict or fail to promote patient autonomy, they clearly need not be *violating* or failing to respect the autonomy of the patient whose request they refuse to meet. For violating and failing to respect a patient's autonomy involve interfering with their self-determination in ways that are unjustifiable, and in refusing to act on a patient's autonomous request to be killed, or to be provided with costly but futile treatment, a doctor need not be restricting the patient's autonomy *unjustifiably*. Refraining from unjustifiably interfering with the autonomous decisions and actions of patients is an important *side-constraint* on what doctors can legitimately do in their role, just as refraining from such interventions is an important side-constraint on any professional in their legitimate dealings with their clients. (And, of course, the demand to respect the autonomy of one's client or patient assumes particular importance in medicine, because ill people are especially vulnerable to their capacity for autonomous decision-making being undermined.) However, it is misleading to suggest that the promotion of personal autonomy *simpliciter* is the appropriate overarching *goal* of a profession.[21]

Our virtue ethics approach to professional roles highlights the importance of seeing such roles as governed teleologically, by the proper ends of the profession in question. However, some who also emphasise the importance of seeing professional roles as teleologically governed play into the hands of critics by talking as though the goals of each profession somehow inhere in the nature of things. For example, Leon Kass claims that

[M]edicine . . . [is] an inherently ethical activity, in which technique and conduct are both ordered in relation to an overarching good, the naturally given end of health.[22]

But in response to such a construal of the teleology in medical practice, Richard Momeyer argues that

The ends medicine serves are of human invention, not 'naturally given' activities deriving from the structure of the natural order. Medicine as an activity of human devising serving human purposes is just what we make it to be, not what nature decrees it must be. Consequently, for instance, an absolute ban on medical practitioners assisting in the suicides of patients is a matter of human

---

[21] This is not to deny that a profession might appropriately have as part of its goal the aim of assisting people to determine the course of their lives in a relevantly specified domain – e.g. part of the goal of lawyering might be to assist people to determine the course of their lives by helping them to obtain their legal rights.   [22] Kass, 'Neither for Love nor Money', p. 29.

choice about value systems, not a naturally given inescapable imperative. Choosing such a value requires moral argument and justification, not appeal to the 'nature of things'.[23]

Momeyer is right to reject any suggestion that the goals of medicine (or of any profession) are given by nature, and his comments also serve as a salutary warning against an over-reliance on traditional conceptions of the doctor's role. But contrary to Momeyer, none of this entails that we can allocate to medicine whatever ends we choose (within the bounds of broad-based morality). As John Cottingham has argued, just because something is a human practice, it does not follow that we are now free to define it as we please.[24] For the proper roles of doctors are constrained by the characteristic features of medicine as a practice, and what could qualify as proper goals of medicine will be constrained by what those characteristic features of medicine are.[25] That is, like any profession, medicine has characteristic ends that define and set limits on what sorts of actions it is coherent to describe as practising 'medicine'. Similarly, there are limits to what things a dentist could do and still plausibly claim to be acting *as a dentist*, and likewise, it is partly constitutive of our notion of a teacher that they are committed to the goal of helping their students learn. These are not claims about the content of such roles being somehow 'naturally given', but rather are conceptual claims about the nature of certain practices.

That the practice of medicine has a determinate content and is governed by distinctive goals is also suggested by many doctors' reactions to pressures by government policies and health administrators to take efficiency in the allocation of health-care resources as their guiding aim. For some doctors wonder whether, if they took the achievement of efficiency as their overriding goal, they would still, properly speaking, be practising medicine. Of course, it would not be plausible for a doctor to claim that allowing anything other than a commitment to *health* to govern his professional conduct would rule out his actions as 'practising medicine'. After all, actions in the context of professional roles are not immune from broad-based moral values, such as justice and respect for personal autonomy, which are side-constraints on the legitimate pursuit of any

---

[23] Richard Momeyer, 'Does Physician-Assisted Suicide Violate the Integrity of Medicine?', *Journal of Medicine and Philosophy* 20, 1995, p. 17.

[24] See John Cottingham, 'Medicine, Virtues and Consequences', in David S. Oderberg and Jacqueline A. Laing (eds.), *Human Lives: Critical Essays on Consequentialist Bioethics*, Basingstoke, Macmillan, 1997, p. 129.

[25] On the notion of a 'practice' employed here, see Alasdair MacIntyre, *After Virtue*, 2nd edn, Notre Dame, University of Notre Dame Press, 1984, chapter 14.

professional goal. So, where efficiency in one's allocation of health-care resources is a value that results from the application of a plausible notion of justice to health-care practice, then it would be excessive for a doctor to regard his being *governed* by the side-constraint of efficiency as redefining his practice as something other than medicine. Nevertheless, were efficiency – or some other value external to medicine – to become an overriding guiding ideal for a doctor in the way he used his skills, there would be a real question about whether this doctor had now ceased to 'practise medicine' (regardless of what other characterisation of his actions would be appropriate).

But whether or not such a person is appropriately characterised as 'practising medicine', these sorts of examples bring out the significance of the distinction between guiding ideals and governing constraints, and help show that properly occupying a professional role depends not only on the sorts of actions one performs or is disposed to perform, but also, and importantly, on the sorts of guiding ideals that one has internalised. So, for instance, 'making money' could play an appropriate *governing* role in what one does as a doctor – someone who is prepared to continue serving patients' health only provided he earns enough money to subsidise his passion for the opera could still be a very admirable doctor (volunteering for 'médecins sans frontières' is not the only way of being a virtuous doctor). However, a doctor who takes 'making money' as his overarching *guiding* aim or ideal in practising medicine is a morally flawed occupant of the role of doctor – and not only because taking such a goal as paramount is likely to lead to morally problematic actions, such as over-servicing (and other actions which are not warranted on valid health grounds), but also because the professional character of such a doctor is, literally speaking, *mis-guided*.[26] The nature of the guiding ideals

---

[26] ('Over-servicing' occurs when doctors provide excessive and unwarranted medical attention and resources to patients, usually in order to boost the doctor's income.) Also, consider here the somewhat disdainful attitude with which doctors often regard those practitioners who carry out elective cosmetic surgery, and simply act on (and cultivate) demand. The reputation of such surgeons is not helped by advertisements such as the following, which appeared in the Melbourne *Age* newspaper, on 9 January 1999 (p. 4):

World leading cosmetic surgery clinic [invites applications for a] Patient Advisor: Working closely with the principal surgeon and other team members, you will develop long term relationships with patients *to ensure repeat business* . . . Essential to success in this role is the ability to instantly put people at ease and gain their trust. Persuasiveness, high level organisational skills, professionalism, and a commercial orientation are also necessary [our italics].

We do not cite this to make a wholesale condemnation of elective cosmetic surgery as a profession, but rather as a reminder of how far removed from the values constitutive of the practice of *medicine* are those cosmetic surgeons who regard making money as their overriding goal. (We are indebted to Beth Bennett for pointing out this advertisement.)

and governing conditions that constitute a given professional's overall regulative ideal also help to determine what counts as acting within that professional's role and what would constitute acting outside the role. That is, in saying of an individual that he is responding and acting *qua doctor*, we are not only referring to the fact that he is using his medical skills in dealing with another, but we are also taking his responses and conduct to be regulated by certain guiding ideals and governing conditions. Indeed, when we speak of someone 'taking his doctor's hat off', we are not necessarily saying that he is leaving his medical skills out of the situation – we are saying that he is (temporarily) to suspend the guiding ideals or governing conditions he is to have in his regulative ideal as a doctor here. For example, a man who helps his wife deal with her long-term illness need not here be acting towards her *qua doctor*, because the governing conditions of his helping her here could be those appropriate for a spouse, rather than those for a patient (with whom one's relationship could properly be terminated when the patient is cured), even though serving (here, his wife's) health might well be his guiding ideal, and he would certainly still be utilising his medical skills. (As we argued in chapter 2, the nature of the governing conditions and guiding values in a person's regulative ideal play a crucial role – more crucial than immediate motives of, say, affection – in differentiating among the types of relationships they are engaging in.)

However, Arthur Applbaum argues that little of moral import depends on whether it is appropriate to label as a 'doctor' a person who took some value external to medicine – such as efficiency – as their over-riding goal in the use of their medical skills. For Applbaum says that such individuals would still be engaged in a 'practice' of some kind, and if that is sufficiently different from 'doctoring' then we can give it some other label, such as 'schmoctoring'. Applbaum claims that this is unproblematic, so long the clients of such a practice are aware of what is being offered, and the goals of this practice are permissible by broader moral standards.[27] So those medically trained individuals who now take

---

[27] See Arthur Applbaum, *Ethics for Adversaries: The Morality of Roles in Public and Professional Life*, Princeton, Princeton University Press, 1999, chapter 3. Applbaum defends what he calls 'practice positivism', which holds that 'the concept of a practice does not impose any general content requirements or restrictions on the rules of all practices. The rules of a practice simply are what they are, not what they ought to be [according to broad-based moral standards] or what we want them to be' (p. 51). Thus, Applbaum argues that while a 'practice' has its constitutive goals (and so the notion of 'malpractice' still makes sense), a practice which evolved whereby, e.g., some medically trained individuals used their skills in the ultimate service of efficiency (as a socially valued goal) can still count as a 'practice', and could still have its own guiding ends and norms. Also, Applbaum explains that practice positivism allows that a coherent social practice with its

efficiency as their overriding aim would not necessarily thereby do anything *wrong*, just because they depart from the traditional norms and goals of 'doctoring':

[C]onventions and shared understandings are changing, and if enough doctors act like schmoctors, the time will soon come when it cannot be supposed that most of those with medical training have agreed to the role of doctor, not schmoctor. Once this happens – once medical practitioners fail to identify with and endorse the goods and virtues and commitments internal to the standard practice of doctoring – they indeed are morally free from the collective judgments of a social practice that is not their own and that does not apply to them.[28]

We agree that where the line is drawn about when an individual ceases to act 'qua doctor' does not *by itself* decide the overall moral status of what that individual thereby does (since, for all we know, some other worthy goal might be being served). But our point is not that there *couldn't be* a practice whereby medically trained individuals took the achievement of efficiency, or even maximising personal wealth, as their overriding goal (though at some point, such a practice might lose touch with the idea of serving the public interest to the extent that the practice could no longer be credibly regarded as a 'profession'). The proper application of the label 'doctor' cannot be resolved by mere stipulation, or by appeals to traditions alone. Rather, the issue is whether members of a certain profession (whatever label we use to refer to them) who profess to serve goal X can, in that same professional capacity, legitimately do not-X. That is, we are looking at cases involving individuals *professing* to be overridingly guided by the goal of health (whether we call them 'doctor' or 'healer' or whatever), and mercifully killing patients; and we can still ask whether there is any incompatibility here. Further, because the regulative ideals of an individual practitioner are to a significant extent *private*, it can be difficult for a patient to identify when they are attending a practitioner who is, by the lights of his own profession, *mis*guided. But patients should be given the means whereby they are able to tell whether the medically trained individual whose services they are engaging is a doctor, or is really a 'schmoctor'. Also, while the goals and practice of medicine, and thus various conceptions of the doctor's role, are indeed human inventions, just as Applbaum and

---

own set of rules, roles, and ends would not lose its claim to be a *practice*, were its ends or rules to be immoral (and so, as Applbaum says, the roles of executioner and torturer can still refer to practices). We see no reason to dispute *these* claims about what can count as a 'practice'.

[28] Ibid., p. 59.

Momeyer are right in saying that we should not take our familiarity with the traditional conception of the doctor as a reason for thinking that individuals with medical training act wrongly if they now decide to use their skills for different ends, so too the social construction of roles should not lead us to overlook the fact that some roles serve worthier goals than others – so it would become a particular cause for concern if a large group of individuals (and very socially powerful and influential individuals) who professed to have an overriding commitment to very worthy goals decided to abandon those goals and pursue ends that are entirely different.

We should note that, in arguing that the regulative ideals of good doctors should include a commitment to serving health as a central goal of medicine, we are not thereby ceding control of the medical profession to the profession itself. A variety of factors (both extra- and intra-professional) sometimes lead professions and their governing bodies to neglect or ignore the moral constraints that respect for patient or client autonomy imposes on the proper pursuit of professional goals, or, conversely, to lose sight of the importance of their constitutive guiding ideals, and devote themselves unquestioningly to meeting the autonomous requests of their patients and clients. Professions must remain open to broader social influences, to remind each profession of its constitutive ideals that it has been entrusted to serve, and of the importance of not violating various side-constraints and broad-based moral values in its pursuit of those professional ideals. Nevertheless, this does not entail that all of the specific demands of professional roles will or should necessarily remain rigidly fixed throughout the ages. For example, at times when health-care resources are especially scarce or in particularly high demand, the constraint upon doctors to allocate their resources *justly* might properly require doctors to be even more accountable for their use of such resources than might be warranted in periods where there is more to go around.

Further, the emphasis our virtue ethics approach places on determining role demands by reference to the proper *ends* of the profession in question should not be thought to imply that the approach is indifferent to the *means* chosen by practitioners to serve those ends. Side-constraints like respect for patient autonomy must be taken seriously in professional practice, and because of the characteristic weightiness of the goods whose jeopardising prompts people to seek professional help, there is a wide range of factors against which professionals must guard if they are to respect autonomy in their practice. Since we have defended as a guiding ideal of medicine a relatively *broad* notion of health as normal psychophysical functioning, this might be thought to heighten the risks of unjustified infringements of personal autonomy in the name of serving an appropriate professional goal. Let us therefore illustrate how a guiding ideal might on our approach be weighed against the constraint not to violate personal autonomy, by saying a little about how this constraint might be observed in the context of medical practice.

One limit imposed upon medical practice by our approach is that, to the extent that a problem experienced by an individual does not involve an impairment of normal psychophysical functioning, a doctor does not, *qua doctor*, have an ethical demand to deal with it. Of course, departures from normal psychophysical functioning will be very wide-ranging, and will bring many sorts of problems within the proper ambit of medicine, but doctors are not ethically required to help someone deal with problems of living that do not impair normal functioning. For example, a doctor would not act wrongly if she declined to see a patient who came in for social reasons – say, because he was unhappy that his friend had not come to visit that day, and he simply wanted to have a chat. Indeed, even where the focus of an individual's unhappiness is something about her *body*, on our approach there would still be nothing unethical about a doctor refusing to treat this individual, if her normal psychophysical functioning is not impaired. Thus, on our view a doctor would not act wrongly if, for example, she declined to provide fertility treatment for a post-menopausal woman, since infertility is not a departure from normal functioning for such women. By contrast, a pre-menopausal woman who wished to have an earlier tubal ligation reversed is requesting something that would clearly be within the proper purview of medicine, since infertility at that stage of life – whether or not her condition is properly seen as a 'disease' – is clearly an impairment of women's normal functions prior to menopause. Sometimes, however, a patient clearly does have a problem with their *health*, properly conceived, but they autonomously wish to pursue a course of action that is less likely to promote or restore their health than the action that the doctor favours. For example, people sometimes value sexual spontaneity, an active social life, relaxation through cigarette smoking, or productivity at work more highly than they value good health. What sorts of things may a doctor legitimately do in such cases to serve the goal of health, while observing the constraint against violating patient autonomy? In our view, part of a doctor's understanding the notion of health as a proper goal of medicine entails that she realise that patients have interests which are broader than their health interests, and she ought also to realise that to intervene paternalistically in a patient's autonomous decision to give a non-health-related interest higher priority than health would be an unjustified breach of the constraint against violating patient autonomy. Nevertheless, a doctor who expresses her commitment to the goal of health in such situations by informing the patient that his course of action is likely to be detrimental to his health in the long term, and by attempting through the use of reasoned discussion to persuade the patient to take these effects on his health seriously, would not breach the constraint against violating patient autonomy.[29] In medical practice, however, the line between permissible and impermissible beneficence can at times be difficult to see, because it can sometimes be unclear when attempts at persuasion become excessive, and because it can be difficult to disentangle what is a health problem from what is, rather, a patient's unhappiness with his personal circumstances. Generally speaking, we would argue that the closer a patient's problem is to the periphery of what is included in the notion of health, the less directive the doctor, *qua doctor*, is entitled to be with him.

But being a good doctor, on our account, involves having appropriate dispositions, emotions, and sensitivities in a medical context, as well as performing appropriate actions, and those elements of a doctor's character have ethical value in their own right, apart from the virtuous actions they issue in.[30] (This sort of claim, we would hold, could well be made about other professions also.) Which character-traits count as medical virtues is determined by looking at what sorts of dispositions help a doctor meet the goal of serving psychophysical health, with regard to the constraints of justice and respect for patient autonomy, as explained above. Thus, in our view, the character-traits that would count as virtues in the role of a doctor include the following. To begin with, a virtuous doctor would have medical *beneficence* – a disposition to focus on

---

[29] Our position on the manner in which respect for autonomy should constrain the pursuit of beneficence in patient care results in a view of good doctor–patient relationships that is akin to what Ezekiel and Linda Emanuel have called the 'deliberative model'. See Ezekiel J. Emanuel and Linda L. Emanuel, 'Four Models of the Physician–Patient Relationship', *Journal of the American Medical Association* 267, no. 16, 22–9 April 1992. For an illuminating and sensitive discussion of these ethical complexities in the context of general practice, see Ronald J. Christie and C. Barry Hoffmaster, *Ethical Issues in Family Medicine*, New York, Oxford University Press, 1986, especially chapters 8 and 9.

[30] For further discussion of how a professional's dispositions and attitudes can reflect on them morally, quite apart from the actions thereby prompted, see Mark H. Moore and Malcolm K. Sparrow, *Ethics in Government: The Moral Challenge of Public Leadership*, Englewood Cliffs, Prentice-Hall, 1990. See also our discussion of professional detachment and moral character, in chapter 6, section 3.

the patient's own psychophysical needs, and to distinguish which procedures are genuinely necessary for the patient's health and which would
be excessive (and so to avoid 'defensive medicine'), and to desire the
removal of the patient's impairment, for the patient's own sake, along
with a sensitivity and tactfulness in dealing with the vulnerabilities
common to sick people. The virtue of medical beneficence would also
include a well-developed capacity for compassion, heightening a
doctor's awareness and appreciation of the nature of their patients'
needs, and assuring patients that they are regarded as a fellow human
being (as distinct from, say, medical pity, where the sorrow a doctor feels
involves an element of condescension towards the patient). *Truthfulness*
would be another medical virtue, as such a disposition has been amply
demonstrated to serve patients' health,[31] and clearly enables doctors to
meet the constraint of respect for patient autonomy, in providing
patients with accurate and adequate information relevant to their condition. A virtuous doctor would also be *trustworthy*, since this helps
patients feel comfortable about making full, frank, and timely disclosures
of the sorts of intimate details that are necessary for effective diagnosis
and treatment, and helps give patients an assurance that their welfare is
important to the doctor. It is also important that doctors are not too
easily deterred from treating serious infectious diseases, yet do not rashly
fail to take adequate precautions against becoming infected themselves,
and so medical *courage* is an important virtue for doctors, along with
medical *humility*, or a preparedness to concede, when sincere and com-
petent efforts at diagnosis or treatment are unsuccessful, that one has
failed, and so not to subject the patient to a battery of further tests and
treatment, out of misplaced pride. Such humility is also an appropriate
acknowledgement of the limits of human influence over health, as a
good affected by a variety of factors beyond the control of doctors and
patients. A virtuous doctor would also have a robust disposition to *justice*
in the provision of their care, to see that morally irrelevant grounds do
not determine (for example) who receives their treatment and care.
These are some of the most important virtues that we see as relevant to
medical practice. Closer analysis of the different sorts of medical roles
that doctors can occupy could, of course, provide a finer-grained
account of many other virtues that would be specific to certain medical
roles.

In counterpoint to our positive case here, of the ways in which virtue

[31] See the extensive empirical evidence summarised in Lee Ross and Richard Nisbett, *The Person and the Situation: Perspectives of Social Psychology*, New York, McGraw-Hill, 1991, pp. 238–43.

ethics accommodates the practice of medicine, we shall now move in chapter 4 to provide a critique of how some rival ethical accounts have and might be thought to accommodate medical practice – in particular, the practice of the good general practitioner.

CHAPTER 4

Ethical models of the good general practitioner[1]

Over the past few decades, similar concerns to those that have fueled the debate over whether or not friendship is compatible with a life governed by Kantian or consequentialist regulative ideals have also provoked debate as to whether universalist or impartialist ethical theories are able to accommodate various values thought distinctive of certain professional roles – in particular, professional roles within medical and legal practice. According to many writers, there are distinctive role-generated obligations and sensitivities that mark the proper performance of these roles which cannot be accommodated by universalist or impartialist ethical theories. So, for instance, many have thought that there are important agent-relative attachments and loyalties that develop towards one's patient as their general practitioner, or towards one's client in legal practice, and that these attachments and loyalties may license divergence from broadly accepted moral requirements in some conflict cases. We discuss various aspects of this general issue of conflict between professional life and broad-based ethical theory in the following two chapters.

In the present chapter, we begin by addressing one important way in which various writers have claimed to account for the alleged moral independence of certain professional behaviour, namely, by appealing to the model of personal relationships – in particular, friendship – and how our attachments here may sometimes guide us against conflicting moral demands, as a way to justify similar actions in professional life. In section 1, we show why this appeal to the model of friendship is mistaken. In section 2, we go on to argue that it is not at all clear how the distinctive nature and value attached to various roles, and the issue of

[1] Various predecessors of this chapter were presented at the Australian Bioethics Association Second Annual Conference, University of Sydney, the Monash University Centre for Human Bioethics one-day conference Bioethics: Approaches and Methods, the Australian Bioethics Association Third Annual Conference, University of Adelaide, and the Department of Philosophy, University of Auckland. We are grateful to those audiences, and especially to Lynn Gillam and Peter Singer, for their comments.

an agent's interest in fulfilling them well, are to be accommodated by the consequentialist criterion of right action – namely, the maximisation of agent-neutral value. Utilitarian calculations of the good might direct the consequentialist to endorse certain roles and reject others. So, for instance, the good manager may be a valued role, whereas the good torturer might not, on account of the success and failure of these roles, respectively, in maximising pleasure or preference-satisfaction. Nevertheless, it is not clear how the consequentialist account might be able to capture the nature and value commonly taken to mark various roles and to contribute to human good. We end our discussion here by indicating how our virtue ethics account of professional roles can accommodate the distinctive nature and value commonly taken to mark the professional role of medical practice – specifically, the case of general practice, or the good general practitioner.

I ETHICAL THEORY, ROLE MORALITY, AND FRIENDSHIP

On the traditional model of the doctor–patient relationship, the doctor was conceived as someone whose training and expertise conferred upon them a special authority to give and withhold diagnoses and treatment from patients in whatever ways the doctor regarded as necessary to heal them. Consider, for example, this passage from a recent article in a professional medical journal where an Australian doctor tells of his encounter with a certain patient:

There comes a point when questions to obtain information become insulting questions challenging professional competence. I recall making a diagnosis of otitis media and suggesting antibiotics. The mother questioned the diagnosis and suggested treatment at extreme length and finally asked, no demanded, to use my otoscope so she could confirm the diagnosis. (She had, after all, completed two years of nursing before ceasing the course to have her child.)

Even though I recognised the psychopathology behind the mother's attitude (the child had suffered recurrent otitis media as a result of the recurrent URTIs contracted from being left in a creche while the mother worked – there were strong overtones of guilt which we could have dealt with, if we managed to establish a more trusting relationship) I had to refuse, as I felt my professional competence was being challenged.

A variant of this is expressed in the adage: Beware ladies with lists.[2]

In recent years, this sort of insular and elitist approach of a traditional medical ethic, where doctors seem to regard themselves as being above

---

[2] Dr Paul Nisselle, 'Difficult Patients – The Games they Play', *Australian Doctor Weekly*, 7 July 1989, pp. 56–7. This article was reprinted as part of a handbook for first-year medical students.

or immune from general moral requirements, has been widely rejected. In its place, medical ethicists have appealed to broader-based universalist ethical theories, such as utilitarianism and Kantianism, to provide a more plausible and defensible account of how doctors ought to be guided in their relations with their patients. Thus Robert Veatch has argued that: 'The real problem is the use of professional ethical standards rather than those rooted in some more universally accessible source of morality. One is forced to conclude that the use of a professionally generated ethic . . . makes no sense in theory or in practice.'[3]

However, the move to these broader universalist ethical theories has itself been charged with riding roughshod over the distinctive nature and value specific to doctoring, and so to the doctor–patient relationship. For example, drawing on his own experience of teaching bioethics to medical students, Larry Churchill has argued that while universalist ethics such as utilitarianism and Kantianism may form a useful background to discussing the moral role of doctors, these theories themselves underdetermine how it is right for a doctor, *qua doctor*, to behave in clinical situations. According to Churchill, these universalist ethical theories have

led us to ask the question about a distinctive professional ethic in a thin and unproductive way, *viz.*, 'Do or should doctors justify their actions by appeal to the same rules as the rest of us?' or 'Are there special principles of medical ethics?' A more productive question would be 'Are there traditions that should inform the moral thinking of doctors in special ways?'; or 'Should the moral sensibilities of doctors be tuned to different nuances of situations than those of individuals who do not practice medicine?'[4]

On this view, then, there are irreducible role-generated standards of professional behaviour, sensitivities, and responsibilities by which good doctoring can be judged, and these cannot be captured by universalist ethical theories.

Now, we think that Churchill's stressing of, as he puts it, 'the importance of role-differentiated behaviour and distinctive standards to guide that behaviour'[5] is instructive, and that we *do* need a medical ethics which is informed by the special responsibilities and sensitivities which a good doctor, *qua* doctor, ought to have in their relations with patients. However, Churchill does not say very much about what these special responsibilities and sensitivities of a good doctor might be, or about how

[3] Robert M. Veatch, *A Theory of Medical Ethics*, New York, Basic Books, 1981, p. 106.
[4] Larry R. Churchill, 'Reviving a Distinctive Medical Ethic', *Hastings Center Report* 19, no. 3, May/June 1989, p. 33.　　[5] Ibid., p. 29.

they are ultimately to be justified morally. This omission leaves it unclear why such features of a distinctive medical ethic could not be accommodated by a sophisticated consequentialism or Kantianism, or even by a more straightforward form of those theories.

Charles Fried, in his critique of utilitarian and Kantian models of the doctor–patient relationship, claims that there is a particular sort of care and integrity that is distinctive of the doctor–patient relation, and that this is not reducible to the sort of relations depicted by universalist ethical theories. Both the Utilitarian/Efficiency model and a Kantian Distributive Justice account of how the doctor should be guided in their treatment of their patients, Fried says, conflict with the sort of particularistic and concrete value that is a feature of a doctor's relationship with their individual patients. As Fried puts it, 'the ethical life of human beings, the values they perceive and follow, inhere in the concrete actions they perform and the concrete relationships into which they enter. It is these which allow a man to live in the present and to give ultimate, intrinsic value to the things that he does.'[6] Fried's criticisms of universalist ethical theories hinge on a conceptual view of the value inherent in various human activities and relations. Of the doctor–patient relation, Fried says that it is analogous to the personal relations cases of friendship and love in that 'it has its own integrity, and it demands, at least within its more circumscribed ambit, complete and unstinting devotion'.[7] A similar model of the doctor–patient relationship is presented by James Drane, who argues that the best doctors are those who are prepared to become *friends* with their patients.[8]

Unfortunately, however, Fried provides little argument as to why the doctor–patient relationship *should* involve personal notions akin to friendship or love, or why the integrity specific to doctoring is grounded in this sort of value. In our view, understanding the doctor–patient relationship on a friendship model of relations between people and/or conflating the sort of integrity and care proper to the latter with the former is clearly a mistake. There are some obvious disanalogies. For example, it would be uncontroversial to claim that a conceptual connection exists

[6] Charles Fried, *Medical Experimentation: Personal Integrity and Social Policy*, Amsterdam, North Holland Publishing Co., 1974, p. 76.
[7] Ibid., p. 76. Fried also argues that the *lawyer–client* relationship should be thought of on the model of a friendship, where the lawyer, like a friend, 'adopt[s] the client's interests as his own'. See 'The Lawyer as Friend: The Moral Foundations of the Lawyer–Client Relation', *Yale Law Journal* 85, no. 8, July 1976.
[8] See James F. Drane, *Becoming a Good Doctor: The Place of Virtue and Character in Medical Ethics*, Kansas City, Sheed and Ward, 1988.

between a good friendship and *liking* the person who is one's friend. However, it seems false to say that a good doctor must *like* their patients, or that a good lawyer must like their clients. A doctor, for instance, might have a perfectly good relationship with their patient qua being their doctor, without even having a view about whether they like the patient in a personal way.[9] Nevertheless, as we go on to argue, like friendship, and unlike impersonal ethical models of relations between persons, we agree that there is an important input of *agent-relative* value into the regulative ideals that govern the good doctor (or lawyer). That is, the concern for the particular and concrete individuals a doctor treats, will, we believe, significantly shape the nature of the concern a good doctor has for their patients. Such agent-relative reasons or values, however, are best conceived as agent-relative to the agent *qua doctor*, and not to the agent *qua friend*. To see this more clearly, let us look at some apparent similarities and differences between how the distinctive features of one's professional role as a good doctor or lawyer might be thought to guide one against the broader dictates of morality and how reasons of friendship might do so.

In chapter 2, section 5, where we discussed the question of whether friendship is compatible with a life governed by a Kantian regulative ideal of commitment to moral duty, we presented some examples of how the reasons of friendship might move one to act against conflicting Kantian duties. In one such kind of case, an agent may be moved by concern for the good of her friend to help or support her in some way and in so doing act against some conflicting moral demand, such as not to tell lies. Here, since the agent may be accurately described as acting from an altruistic concern to promote her friend's well-being, it may be plausible to think that she acts with some moral justification in acting against the conflicting moral claim. Indeed, we suggested in chapter 2 that it might be plausible for the Kantian to claim that there are special duties of friendship operating in such cases, so that the conflicts presented are really only conflicts within a duty-based morality. The agent who pursues friendship in these conflict cases, therefore, might in fact be plausibly understood as a good Kantian agent governed by an overriding commitment to duty-based moral concerns. In a second kind of case, however, we claimed that reasons of friendship, such as one's affection for or interest in a friend, need not involve such altruistic concern to promote the friend's well-being (and so need not embody a concern that

---

[9] See Patricia Illingworth, 'The Friendship Model of Physician/Patient Relationship and Patient Autonomy', *Bioethics* 2, no. 1, January 1988, esp. p. 28.

might plausibly be thought to contain moral content or be cast as a moral duty), but nevertheless provide reasons which might plausibly be thought to compete favourably with conflicting moral demands in some cases. And so here we claimed that it may be reasonable to pursue the good of friendship, rather than the incompatible conflicting good of a life governed by the Kantian regulative ideal of commitment to one's moral duties.

Consider, however, how one's professional role – say as a general practitioner – might provide one with reason to pursue the interests of a patient at the expense of some conflicting moral claim. The doctor (as with other professionals, such as the lawyer) acts in the interest of those she serves through the prism provided by the governing commitments and understandings that define her professional role. Thus, she might choose to maintain the confidentiality of her patient at the expense of the legitimate claims of some other party, such as the sexual partner(s) of her patient, because she is governed by a concern to maintain the trust of her patients on such matters. Moreover, her acting against the conflicting moral claim here may be justified by the governing commitments and sensitivities that define her professional role – since, for example, maintaining trust through confidentiality in such matters may be a necessary and important part of how one promotes the good of human health in general practice.

Insofar as such an explanation as this is a plausible justification for a doctor favouring her own patients' medical good over a conflicting moral claim, it will be so because the justification for her carrying out her professional role in this way is shown to originate from the moral good which the proper performance of her professional role is supposed to serve – i.e. human health (a good which is also at least commensurate with the conflicting moral good involved in the case). One could not make a case seeking to justify the doctor's keeping patient confidentiality here (even if it were justified for her to do so) on the basis that she liked the patient a lot, or had great affection for her, since offering these sorts of reasons would not help to explain how the doctor's partiality towards her own patients might best serve the good of human health. Similarly, citing how the good of human health is best served by certain sorts of partiality towards one's own patients against some conflicting moral claims could not help explain – much less begin to justify – why the doctor chose to take a particular patient out for a romantic dinner or to the movies, rather than, say, keep her appointments with other patients. Thus, while the doctor may justifiably have and act on certain agent-relative attachments of concern and loyalty towards particular patients and may sometimes do so against other conflicting moral claims, her disposition and action here – unlike the friendship case – will instantiate profession-defining commitments and sensibilities that might plausibly be thought to serve the moral good served by her profession. Her partiality is, therefore, strictly role-governed by the moral good her profession serves. (Similarly, consider the lawyer who serves justice by zealously advocating her client's interests, but does so at the expense of compassion for the victim of the crime.)

Such conflicts, then, between the requirements of one's professional role, where these involve particularistic, agent-relative attachments, and, say, the legitimate moral claims of others represent conflicts between widely accepted key moral values. While the nature and value of the agent-relative attachments of one's professional role may be distinctive to and generated by the role, they are nevertheless governed by key moral goods, such as the promotion of human health in medicine or of justice in the legal profession. As such, they are goods that would be recognised by and important to any impartialist or universalist ethical theories admitting of plural values – such as the Kantian and consequentialist accounts we have focused on. And the moral conflicts that may occur in serving these goods on account of professional partiality would, on these ethical theories, be simply regarded as conflicts between some of the plural values that these theories admit. Moreover, unlike the friendship case, we are not in the above cases presented with conflicts where the reasons of partiality really do seem incompatible with, say, governance by a Kantian regulative ideal concerned to constrain one's actions under the overriding commitment to moral duty. The doctor (and the lawyer) mentioned above could, apparently quite plausibly, account for her favouring her patient (or the lawyer, his client) at the expense of some other moral claim, in terms of its being her moral duty. In our view, then, the appeal to the friendship case as a way to claim licence for violations of other moral demands in professional life, and to claim a moral independence from the universalist or impartialist ethical theories usually taken to be concerned with such other demands, is mistaken.

Nevertheless, we do think that there are significant problems facing the consequentialist who would claim to be able to accommodate the nature and value of the good attached to the role of the general practitioner, and we also think that there are worries about the general Kantian understanding of the moral self which impact on how we are supposed to accommodate certain aspects of our professional life. In the next section we present our case against the consequentialist. In chapter 6, section 3, we present our worries about the Kantian account of the moral self and its accommodation of the morality of professional life.

2 CONSEQUENTIALISM AND THE GOOD GENERAL PRACTITIONER

What, then, are the regulative ideals of a good general practitioner? There are several distinguishing characteristics of the norms guiding general practice, as compared to medical specialisms. General practice evolved as a 'reaction to the reductionistic biomedical model in medicine, which largely ignores the individual and social contexts of diseases',[10] and so, general practitioners are expected to have a strong commitment to the patient as a person, to provide continuing and comprehensive care, to embrace broad conceptions of health and disease, and to take an active interest in the prevention of ill-health.[11] But what is involved in having a strong commitment to the patient *as a person*? McWhinney puts it this way:

The physician will 'stay with' a person whatever his problem may be, and he will do so because his commitment is to people more than to a body of knowledge or a branch of technology. To such a physician, problems become interesting and important not only for their own sake but because they are Mr Smith's or Mrs Jones' problem. Very often in such relations there is not even a very clear distinction between a medical problem and a non-medical problem. The patient defines the problem.[12]

Thus, in treating his patients, a good general practitioner will be guided by a certain determinate conception of what general practice is about which marks it as distinct from other forms of medical practice under which the doctor might treat a patient, and a constitutive part of this mode of practice is the development of certain sensitivities, motivations, and skills in attending to their patients. So, for example, the general practitioner should have a preparedness to pursue their patients' health problems in ways which demand a significant length of time and breadth of engagement with particular individuals, even where this is at the cost of maximising overall medical utility. This agent-relative concern would

---

[10] Ronald J. Christie and C. Barry Hoffmaster, *Ethical Issues in Family Medicine*, New York, Oxford University Press, 1986, p. xiii.   [11] Ibid., pp. 4–13.
[12] I. R. McWhinney, 'General Practice as an Academic Discipline', *The Lancet* 1, 1966, p. 420, cited in Christie and Hoffmaster, *Ethical Issues in Family Medicine*, p. 4.

seem to fail to register in a consequentialist view which believes in the promotion only of agent-neutral value. In reply, however, the consequentialist might object that treating patients as persons does not require that a general practitioner sacrifice overall medical utility. After all, it might be said, to focus on *one's own* patients, at the expense of others who might be needier and who stand to benefit more from one's attention, is hardly to treat those others as persons.

It may be true that this would not be to treat those others as persons. However, if the general practitioner is to meet their own patients' needs, where meeting these needs demands an involvement with their patients (of their time, energy, and resources) which is *broader* than that which would be given by a strict medical conception, then their involvement may well come at the expense of the greater medical needs, more narrowly conceived, of others. Medical utility, then, more strictly conceived, would not play an all-governing role for the good general practitioner.

The consequentialist, though, might object to being saddled with a narrow view of what counts towards medical utility, and so how it would best be maximised. For they might accept this widely accepted sketch of part of the role of the general practitioner, but say that meeting the broader needs of patients in this way would be a legitimate and important part of what goes into maximising medical utility overall. There would then not be any conflict between the role of the general practitioner and the maximisation of medical utility. For example, indirect utilitarians might argue that the norms and ideals of general practice sketched above could guide doctors as 'rules of thumb', because this would, as things are, maximise utility. Thus R. M. Hare argues that

Another principle, especially relevant here, is that requiring a scrupulous devotion by doctors to their own patients. It is for the best that such a principle should be given a high priority by doctors . . . for otherwise patients will be less well looked after . . . The interests of the patient are likely to be more affected than those of any other single individual, and that is why they are so important. Doctors in general tend to give extra weight to the interests of their own patients, just as parents tend to give extra weight to those of their own children; and this is a good thing, for the same reason in both cases, namely that the acceptance of this principle by doctors and parents leads, all in all, to patients and children being looked after better.[13]

---

[13] R. M. Hare, 'Moral Problems about the Control of Behaviour', in R. M. Hare, *Essays on Bioethics*, Oxford, Clarendon Press, 1993, pp. 54–5. See also R. M. Hare, 'The Philosophical Basis of Psychiatric Ethics', in Hare, *Essays on Bioethics*, pp. 22–4; R. M. Hare, *Moral Thinking*, Oxford, Clarendon Press, 1981, pp. 135–40; and R. M. Hare, 'Methods of Bioethics: Some Defective Proposals', in L. W. Sumner and Joseph Boyle (eds.), *Philosophical Perspectives on Bioethics*, Toronto,

Now, this argument is premised on a rather large empirical claim, and we are entitled to be provided with some reasons why we should accept that claim. What reasons might be given to support the claim that the scrupulous devotion of doctors to their own patients' interests will maximise utility overall? Examining these reasons will help to bring out some differences between the conceptions and justifications of the good doctor offered by consequentialism and virtue ethics. So far as we can see, there are *three* reasons which might be given for the consequentialist claim that doctors being specially devoted to their own patients will maximise utility. First, one might appeal, as Hare does, to the deleterious consequences of an alternative policy:

> If they [doctors and parents] felt equal obligations to everybody else's patients and children, it is likely that the obligations would prove so daunting that none of them would be attended to and the patients and children would suffer from more neglect than they do now.[14]

The idea here is that doctors would be so overwhelmed by being expected to attend to the needs of their own patients, along with those of other people's patients, that such a policy would lead to doctors doing less good overall than they do under a policy allowing them to give priority to treating their own patients.

How plausible is this claim? Let us assume that Hare is referring to what would be too daunting for those who are already doctors, rather than for those contemplating a career in medicine. There are certainly doctors who do regard themselves as obligated to help all patients generally, and who, undaunted by this, have managed to do a great deal more good than they would have done had they devoted themselves specially to a more circumscribed group of patients. For example, in his account of practising medicine in the African jungle, Albert Schweitzer explains how he thought it proper that, as a doctor, he set up his practice

Footnote 13 (*cont.*)

University of Toronto Press, 1996, p. 31: 'A mother *should*, we think, give priority to the needs of her own children over those of other people's children. Doctors and nurses should devote themselves to their own patients more than to other people's patients. Partiality in caring is required by the intuitive principles that most of us have been taught, and probably these partial principles are sometimes innate . . . However, this is all at the intuitive level. Partial principles at the intuitive level can be justified by *impartial* thinking at the critical level. If we were concerned impartially for the good of all children, we should want mothers to behave partially toward their own children and have feelings which made them behave in this way. We should want this because, if mothers are like this, children will be better looked after than if mothers tried to feel the same about other people's children as about their own. The same applies to doctors and nurses.' See also Richard Wasserstrom, 'Roles and Morality', in David Luban (ed.), *The Good Lawyer: Lawyers' Roles and Lawyers' Ethics*, Totowa, Rowman and Allanheld, 1984, esp. pp. 30, 36–7, who discusses a similar argument in support of lawyers' partiality towards their clients.

[14] Hare, 'Moral Problems about the Control of Behaviour', p. 55.

at whatever location he could do most good in the world.[15] And in doing so, Schweitzer showed himself to be utterly impartial between those who sought his treatment. Thus, Schweitzer took himself to be equally obligated to treat natives from local tribes, natives from neighbouring tribes, foreign missionaries, and foreign sailors turned timber dealers. Further, when medicinal supplies ran short, he prioritised patients according to who he thought were the 'most urgent' – by which he meant those who, no matter where they came from, were in most dire need of his treatment.[16] But perhaps it is a bit much to expect that many doctors could become an Albert Schweitzer. So Hare might respond that while not *all*

[15] See Albert Schweitzer, *My Life and Thought: An Autobiography*, trans. C. T. Campion, London, Allen & Unwin, 1933, pp. 102–3, 114–15 (our italics): 'On October 13th, 1905 . . . I dropped into a letter-box . . . in Paris letters to my parents and to some of my most intimate acquaintants, telling them that at the beginning of the winter term I should enter myself as a medical student, in order to go later on to Equatorial Africa as a doctor . . . The plan which I meant now to put into execution had been in my mind for a long time, having been conceived so long ago as my student days. It struck me as incomprehensible that I should be allowed to lead such a happy life, while I saw so many people around me wrestling with care and suffering. Even at school I had felt stirred whenever I got a glimpse of the miserable home surroundings of some of my schoolfellows and compared them with the absolutely ideal conditions in which we children of the parsonage at Gunsbach lived. While at the University and enjoying the happiness of being able to study and even to produce some results in science and art, I could not help thinking continually of others who were denied that happiness by their material circumstances or their health. Then one brilliant summer morning . . . I settled with myself before I got up, that I would consider myself justified in living till I was thirty for science and art, in order to devote myself from that time forward to the direct service of humanity.

For years I had been giving myself out in words, and it was with joy that I had followed the calling of theological teacher and of preacher. But this new form of activity I could not represent to myself as being talking about the religion of love, but only as an actual putting it into practice. *Medical knowledge made it possible for me to carry out my intention in the best and most complete way, wherever the path of service might lead me.* In view of the plan for Equatorial Africa, the acquisition of such knowledge was especially indicated because in the district to which I thought of going a doctor was, according to the missionaries' reports, the most needed of all needed things.'

See also Albert Schweitzer, *On the Edge of the Primeval Forest*, trans. C. T. Campion, London, A. & C. Black, 1949, pp. 3–4: 'I had read about the physical miseries of the natives in the virgin forests; I had heard about them from missionaries, and the more I thought about it the stranger it seemed to me that we Europeans trouble ourselves so little about the great humanitarian task which offers itself to us in far-off lands . . . Just as Dives sinned against the poor man at his gate because for want of thought he never put himself in his place and let his heart and conscience tell him what he ought to do, so do we sin against the poor man at our gate . . . Society in general must recognise this work of humanity to be its task, and there must come a time when doctors go out into the world of their own free will, but sent and supported by society and in numbers corresponding to the need, to work for the benefit of the natives. Then only shall we be recognising and beginning to act upon the responsibility in respect of the coloured races which lies upon us as inheritors of the world's civilisation . . . I chose this locality [Lambarene] because some Alsatian missionaries in the service of the Paris Evangelical Mission had told me that a doctor was badly needed there on account of the constantly spreading sleeping-sickness.'

[16] See Schweitzer, *On the Edge of the Primeval Forest.* Of course, this is not the same as prioritising patients according to the *medical utility* (even *expected* medical utility) of treating them. Schweitzer did, nevertheless, take medical utility into account, particularly in regard to performing operations: 'As to operations, one undertakes, naturally, in the forest only such as are urgent and which promise a successful result' (p. 67).

doctors who regarded themselves as equally obligated to attend to the needs of all patients would be too overwhelmed to do much good, nevertheless the *great majority* of doctors would be.

However, this, even if true, would not suffice to justify the claim that those doctors are permitted to retain their 'scrupulous devotion' to their own patients. For while most doctors may, unlike Schweitzer, be overwhelmed by having equal obligations to all patients, it seems reasonable to think that many doctors might nevertheless produce more utility by at least *tempering* their scrupulous devotion to their own patients, in favour of meeting the needs of other patients. Given the dire widespread and yet treatable health problems of the sort Schweitzer concerned himself with, it would seem a rather surprising result if the precise level of devotion to one's own patients that is internal to the norms of the good general practitioner, happened to be exactly that which would also maximise utility. The claim to the contrary reminds one of Pangloss's blind faith, in Voltaire's *Candide*, that despite its vicissitudes and seemingly arbitrary changes, this world must still be (as Leibniz believed) the best of all possible worlds.

In discussing consequentialist arguments about lawyer's roles and lawyer–client relationships, Richard Wasserstrom says that

Many if not most of the arguments in defense of role-defined behavior of various sorts seem to insist that unless the role in question is preserved in just the form it has had to date, the results will clearly be worse, less justifiable overall.[17]

For example, Wasserstrom suggests that the expectation that a lawyer would not reveal to the opposition how they planned to conduct their case, which early in the twentieth century was considered part of the lawyer's role, was given a consequentialist justification in terms of maximising justice, while exactly the same justification is given for the current expectation that lawyers will make available such plans to the opposing side. It does not seem very plausible to assume that maximisation of utility must track such changes, especially when we keep in mind that they have occurred in response to a variety of political, economic, and institutional influences which have nothing to do with morality. The same point applies to doctors' roles and doctor–patient relationships. Hare cannot simply assume that the scrupulous devotion of general practitioners to their own patients will maximise utility. Indeed, as William May suggests, doctors may well maximise utility by returning to

---

[17] Wasserstrom, 'Roles and Morality' p. 36.

the old elitist tradition of the 'gentleman' professional with a very broad sense of public duty (given, of course, that this sense would be acted upon reliably and often), instead of retaining the idea of the doctor who specialises in a particular field of medicine:

> Some commentators have noted that [the] tradition of the 'gentleman' professional occasionally led to a more spacious sense of public duty than sometimes holds for the modern, scientifically trained, physician. Martin Pernick wryly notes that by 1920, '. . . the research scientist replaced the liberal gentleman as the archetype of medical professionalism' and, 'in its extreme form, bacteriological medicine seemed to imply that a physician no longer had a professional duty to combat poverty, hunger, or filth so long as the filth was germ free and the slum residents were all vaccinated'.[18]

It is often argued that since there is no necessary connection between a certain professional role and good outcomes, utilitarian justifications of professional roles are inherently unstable and therefore inadequate, because such roles thereby become, as it were, hostages to empirical fortune. This is indeed a serious problem for utilitarian justifications of professional roles, but we are making a different point here. Our point is more general. That is, when the same justification is given at one time for a certain policy and at another time for precisely the contrary policy, then that justification begins to look more like a rather arbitrary rationalisation than a sound argument.

In any case, consequentialism might actually require a great many general practitioners to abandon their practices for the jungles of Africa, since many general practitioners may feel daunted by impartial obligations when they shouldn't. There is no reason why a consequentialist should be complacent about such feelings of dauntedness. After all, these feelings might well be based, for example, on ignorance or on an underestimation of one's own capacity to meet such an impartial obligation. Schweitzer himself did not think that what he did was too daunting for others. Rather, he thought that many doctors could and ought to follow his lead and take up the call to become 'jungle-doctors':

> Let no one say: 'Suppose "the Fellowship of those who bear the Mark of Pain" does by way of beginning send one doctor here, another there, what is that to cope with the misery of the world?' From my own experience and from that of

---

[18] William May, 'The Beleaguered Rulers: The Public Obligation of the Professional', *Kennedy Institute of Ethics Journal* 2, no. 1, 1992, pp. 29–30. However, as May (p. 34) also notes: 'modern professionals wield a public power that vastly exceeds that of their predecessors. What they do fatefully affects the society at large. They have even less reason than their predecessors to construe their power in private, entrepreneurial terms [which is implied in the notion of a 'career'].'

all colonial doctors, I answer, that a single doctor out here with the most modest equipment means very much for very many. The good which he can accomplish surpasses a hundredfold what he gives of his own life and the cost of the material support which he must have. Just with quinine and arsenic for malaria, with novarseno-benzol for the various diseases which spread through ulcerating sores, with emetin for dysentery, and with sufficient skill and apparatus for the most necessary operations, he can in a single year free from the power of suffering and death hundreds of men who must otherwise have succumbed to their fate in despair. It is just exactly the advance of tropical medicine during the last fifteen years which gives us a power over the sufferings of the men of far-off lands that borders on the miraculous. Is not this really a call to us?[19]

A second reason consequentialists may give for the claim that doctors' special devotion to their own patients will maximise utility appeals not to the overwhelming burdens of alternative policies but to the idea of reliability. That is, they might claim that generally speaking, a patient's *own* doctor can more *reliably* diagnose and treat them than could another doctor, since a doctor is likely to have a better-developed *perception* and *understanding* of their own patients' needs than they would of other patients' needs. This, it might be argued, is a likely consequence of the continuity of care which (as we saw) is part of the philosophy of general practice. This kind of defence of partiality has been put by some consequentialists with respect to our favouring of friends and loved ones – namely, that generally speaking, the development of such relations better positions us to benefit others.[20]

We would make a two-part reply to this. First, it seems hard to believe that to spend time, energy, and resources in the way characteristic of a general practitioner rather than to devote one's time, energy, and resources to saving lives would actually maximise agent-neutral value. While it may be true that *some* good general practitioners might be doing the best they can by way of maximising agent-neutral value, it seems implausible to hold that this is true of *all* good general practitioners. For surely there would be good general practitioners who could have made a better contribution to maximising agent-neutral value by using their training in other ways. For example, many medical graduates who do excellent work as general practitioners may nevertheless have been better able to maximise agent-neutral value by deciding to train as specialists in intensive care or emergency medicine. Moreover, some may have done

---

[19] Schweitzer, *On the Edge of the Primeval Forest*, p. 127.
[20] See, for example, Frank Jackson, 'Decision-Theoretic Consequentialism and the Nearest and Dearest Objection', *Ethics* 101, no. 3, April 1991.

better for the world if they had not become doctors at all. Indeed, at one point even Schweitzer thought that he might have done more good for the world had he chosen a different path from becoming a doctor:

> A lady who was filled with the modern spirit proved to me that I could do much more by lecturing on behalf of medical help for natives than I could by the action I contemplated [i.e. training to become a doctor, in order to work in Africa].[21]

Second, however, even if one is to insist that the consequentialist empirical claim *is* to be taken seriously, it nevertheless gives a mistaken justification of this feature of the general practitioner's role. The point, after all, was that it was good for a general practitioner to engage with their patients in this way precisely because of the agent-relative features of such involvement with their own particular patients as persons. That is, such a manner of engaging with their patients was seen as a way of better treating the patient as a person. The guiding and justifying concern was not that to treat one's patients in this way might also, as it happens, be for the best in agent-neutral terms.

The final suggestion consequentialists might offer to defend doctors' special devotion or obligations to their own patients asks us to look not at the priorities of general practitioners in the course of their medical practice, but rather at the decision by an individual to undertake training to become a general practitioner in the first place. It has been suggested to us that while consequentialists might allow that there is a certain incompatibility between being a good general practitioner and having the maximisation of agent-neutral value as one's guiding and justifying concern in treating one's patients, *after* one has already chosen to become a general practitioner, consequentialists might nevertheless hold that there need be no such incompatibility at the earlier point when one is deciding whether or not to become a general practitioner.[22] For consequentialists might suggest that the maximisation of agent-neutral value should be what guides and justifies one's decision to become a general practitioner in the first place. That is, to be a good general practitioner, on this view, would require that, as a matter of empirical fact, my working as a general practitioner is the best contribution I can make to maximising agent-neutral value, given such things as my training, my character, and my opportunities.

---

[21] Schweitzer, *My Life and Thought*, p. 108.
[22] We would like to thank Peter Singer for this suggestion, and for general discussion of some of the points we have raised here.

There are several problems with this suggestion. We might begin by questioning the basic premise that we should choose a career according to whether we are making the best contribution to the world that we can. This view is held by Hastings Rashdall, who argues on Ideal Utilitarian grounds that 'it is a man's duty to choose the Vocation which, being what he is, he will contribute most to the social good'.[23] On the face of it, this might seem to entail that, as Norman Care has recently argued, we are all obligated to join the 'helping professions' involving service to others, and that we are living immorally if we have chosen otherwise.[24] However, Rashdall makes clear that he would not condemn those whose temperament leads them to forsake service careers for other fields, so long as their work in their chosen field itself still results in the good being maximised. For Rashdall, many service careers cannot be satisfactorily carried out unless they are done from a certain disposition, and so people who are incapable of having such a disposition ought not to choose those careers, but ought rather to find an alternative career (among those which contribute to the social good) which is within their capacities or temperament:

There are . . . certain departments of conduct in which a certain type of conduct only becomes right, as it is practically only possible, for persons of a certain temperament. There are duties peculiar to particular vocations – that is to say, not merely duties connected with particular offices or professions or classes, but duties incumbent on individuals of a certain temperament or certain capacities without being incumbent on all; and there are divergent types of intellectual and emotional constitution which qualify a man for one occupation or mode of life rather than for another, and make it his duty to adopt one rather than another.[25]

---

[23] Hastings Rashdall, *The Theory of Good and Evil*, vol. II, 2nd edn, London, Oxford University Press, 1924, p. vii (as paraphrased in his analytical table of contents). This view also seems to be held by Albert Schweitzer.

[24] See Norman Care, 'Career Choice', *Ethics* 94, no. 2, January 1984. Care argues that because of the radically unequal opportunities for self-realisation in today's world, 'morality requires that service to others be put before self-realization in the matter of career choice' (p. 285). Care argues for this from the implications of what he calls 'shared-fate individualism'. (Note, however, that as Care puts it, 'shared-fate individualism' seems to be a *political* view about the proper limits of state influence over our career choice, rather than a strictly *moral* view about what career choices are right or wrong; and so this seems to leave open the question of whether the state can legitimately discourage or prevent us from making immoral career choices. However, see Care's comments on this distinction at p. 298 n.32 of his article.)

[25] Rashdall, *The Theory of Good and Evil*, vol. II, p. 142. Moreover, Rashdall seems to be saying that if one is incapable of having the disposition proper to a certain service career, then one is not really able to perform it at all. In some remarks on 'vocation', Florence Nightingale seems to agree with both these claims of Rashdall's, especially in regard to nursing: 'What is it to feel a *calling* for anything? Is it not to do your work in it to satisfy your own high idea of what is the

But while Rashdall allows that different duties regarding career choice may apply to individuals with different temperaments and characters, he still justifies this in terms of how those differential obligations serve the common good. This is quite different from our role-based agent-relative permissions not to promote the agent-neutral good. For on our view, the exemption from promoting agent-neutral good stems from the nature of the commitment one is expressing in carrying out one's professional duties. Thus, even where an action expressing that professional commitment is *not* the best contribution that an individual can make to promoting the good – because an alternative action or profession which that individual could have carried out would have better promoted the good (for example, the forsaken profession of greater social utility has a 'disposition-requirement' which one's character *does* actually enable one to meet, but one chooses another profession instead; or the forsaken profession of greater social utility has no 'disposition-requirement', but one chooses another profession anyway) – it would still be justified on our view.

right, the *best*, and not because you will be "found out" if you don't do it? This is the "enthusiasm" which every one, from a shoemaker to a sculptor, must have, in order to follow his "calling" properly. Now the nurse has to do, not with shoes, or with chisel and marble, but with human beings; and if she, for her own satisfaction, does not look after her patients, no *telling* will make her capable of doing so' (Florence Nightingale, *Notes on Nursing: What it is and what it is not*, p. 99 in 1889 edition, quoted in Dorothy Emmet, *Function, Purpose and Powers*, 2nd edn, Philadelphia, Temple University Press, 1972, p. 260 n. 2).

Thus, Rashdall is saying just that certain actions or jobs promote the (social) good only when they are done from a certain disposition (which not all can produce at will): 'Common sense agrees with Roman Catholic Moral Theology in recognizing that it would be positively wrong for any one to enter upon certain careers which make great demands upon the moral nature, merely from a strong sense of duty, when they have no "internal vocation" for them. Th[is] principle, no doubt, requires to be extended to many careers beyond those afforded by the priesthood and the religious orders, or the modern equivalents of such orders; and the true ultimate ground of such a distinction must, from our point of view, be found in the social advantages (moral and hedonistic) which flow from its observance, and the social disadvantages which would be entailed by its neglect. The average sister of mercy is, no doubt, a more valuable member of Society than a Belgravian lady who is somewhat above the average; but a sister of mercy with no natural love or instinct for her work, with no natural love for the poor or the sick or the young to whom she ministered, would be far less useful to Society than the Belgravian lady who performs respectably the recognized duties of her station, even though she may devote what must in the abstract be considered a somewhat excessive amount of time to domestic trivialities and social dissipation' (*The Theory of Good and Evil* vol. ii, p. 123).

Rashdall then gives some further examples of careers with 'disposition-requirements': 'A man with a love of arbitrary power might be well advised in making himself an Indian civilian or a schoolmaster; a man in whom the passion of curiosity is strongly developed, a detective; a man with great distaste for regular work might justify his existence as an explorer; and so on. On the other hand, a man exceptionally sensitive to other people's sufferings would be disqualified for the profession of a soldier or criminal judge, while he might make a good clergyman' (*The Theory of Good and Evil*, vol. ii, p. 140).

3 DERIVING THE REGULATIVE IDEALS OF THE GOOD GENERAL PRACTITIONER

Let us now say a little more about how the regulative ideals of a good doctor differ from the regulative ideals of general impersonal morality, and also about how they inform the moral deliberations of the good doctor. This can be explained initially by an analogy with the regulative ideals of a good teacher. An excellent example of the regulative ideals of a good teacher is Herbert Kohl's account of teaching a young boy how to read, which we discussed in chapter 2. Lawrence Blum describes Kohl's experience as follows:

Kohl, then a secondary school teacher, was asked by some parents in a school in which he was teaching if he would give special tutoring to their son. The boy was 14 years old and did not know how to read. He was a large boy, angry, and defiant; his teachers did not know how to handle him. Kohl agreed to work with the boy two days a week after class.

Kohl worked with the boy for several months. Kohl found him extremely difficult and never grew to like him personally. But eventually he helped the boy to begin reading. Kohl describes how he came to take a personal interest in the boy's progress as a learner and to find satisfaction in what the boy was able to accomplish under his tutelage . . . [In deciding to help the boy] Kohl did not look at the situation in an impersonal way. He did not step back to adopt a standpoint reflecting a universal, impartial perspective, figuring out what that standpoint urged on anyone situated similarly to himself . . . Rather, Kohl's motivation was of a more particularistic nature. He responded to, was moved by, the particular boy's plight, namely his being 14 years old and unable to read. Kohl experienced this as a terrible condition for the boy himself and was aware how damaged the boy would be if the schools system continued to be unable to teach him to read.[26]

This example brings out well how universalist ethical theories may figure little in a person's moral deliberation and motivation. But what Blum wants to stress, in particular, is the influence which Kohl's conception of himself *as a teacher* had on his decision to tutor this boy. Kohl has a conception of what it is to be a good teacher, and it was *this* conception, rather than any universalist ethic, which operated as a guiding concern or regulative ideal in his deciding to take on the task of teaching this boy how to read. So too, we want to say, a good doctor is one whose motiva-

---

[26] Lawrence A. Blum, 'Vocation, Friendship, and Community: Limitations of the Personal–Impersonal Framework', in Owen Flanagan and Amélie O. Rorty (eds.), *Identity, Character, and Morality: Essays in Moral Psychology*, Cambridge, MA, MIT Press, 1990, p. 176.

tion, deliberation, and action towards their patients are guided by a certain conception of what the activity of doctoring involves, and it is to them *qua doctor* that they will quite correctly see certain commitments as applying specifically to them. Whilst we might not, contra Fried, want a *personal* relationship with our doctor,[27] or require of a good doctor their 'unstinting devotion', there are distinctive ways in which a good doctor would pursue what are the interests of a particular patient in a given case. So, for example, among what inform the regulative ideals of a good doctor would importantly be, as Fried suggests, a guiding concern to help in a person's adjustment to the threat which illness poses to their life-plans. That is, the doctor is to be guided by, in Fried's words, 'some conception of what kinds of life-plans persons actually have, what the capacities are that persons have for realising them, and what the realistic, inevitable constraints must be'.[28] A particular sensitivity central to the regulative ideal of good doctoring, therefore, is an awareness of a patient's vulnerability to the loss of control and self-direction which disease brings to their lives. Of course, as with teaching and the other professions, this conception of what being a doctor involves will be informed and given content by factors which are external to and independent of any particular doctor, such as the place of doctoring among other healing professions, and by accounts of the appropriate goals of patient care.

The renowned New Zealand ophthalmologist Professor Fred Hollows illustrates well how foreign the sorts of considerations emphasised by universalist ethical theories are to the motivations and deliberations of a good doctor. Until his death in 1993, Fred Hollows worked tirelessly on improving the health of indigenous people in Australia, Eritrea, Nepal, and several other countries. Many indigenous people in these countries had eye diseases which, often for want of relatively simply treatment, eventually resulted in their going blind. To counter this, in these countries Hollows set up advanced clinics to treat eye diseases, and established lens factories in these countries, run by local workers, to make eye treatment for their people more affordable. The esteem in which Fred Hollows was held by the communities he assisted is often remarked upon, and many have talked of his determination to prevent a person living in an impoverished community from going blind. As one of his co-workers observed:

[27] See Fried, *Medical Experimentation*, pp. 72–3. [28] Ibid., p. 98.

There is another thing about Fred's involvement in the Aboriginal scene . . . Fred was always very direct and, especially in the latter years, very critical of lots of aspects of Aboriginal leadership. Why then was he still so highly regarded and why did hundreds of blackfellas from all over the country get themselves from Bourke for his funeral? There are lots of reasons and probably most of all was the knowledge that he was absolutely serious and committed to the cause, he was a partisan. There is another important issue here. When Fred was sitting around talking or visiting a camp, he never did it as some sort of duty or self-sacrifice. Fred enjoyed being around blackfellas, he liked their company, found them interesting and enjoyed the time. This is not a characteristic that you can fake and I think people recognised it very clearly.[29]

In his autobiography, Hollows talks of his distress at being unable to help two Eritreans whose sight he could not restore:

That's the hardest thing in eye work, to have someone go blind or be unable to restore sight. There are lots of jokes about doctors burying their mistakes, but there is no such relief in ophthalmology. Every blind patient is a reproach and a cause of anguish.[30]

Thus, just as Herbert Kohl was moved by his conception of himself as a teacher to respond to the plight of the illiterate boy and teach him how to read, it was Fred Hollows' emotional grasp of the plight of patients going blind, and his conception of himself as a (very talented) ophthalmologist, rather than the adoption of a universalistic perspective, that moved him to restore sight to patients who were going blind from eye diseases.

To end our discussion here, let us sketch how the virtue ethics approach we detailed in chapter 3 would apply to the case of the general practitioner. In chapter 3, we argued that good professional roles must be part of a good profession, and that a good profession is one which involves a commitment to an important human good – such as health – without which humans cannot flourish. For the consequentialist, a doctor's doing X for a patient would be right, in the end, because doing X is expressive of a mode of practice which, when engaged in collectively, maximises utility. For the virtue ethicist, however, a doctor's doing X for a patient would be right because doing X is expressive of what the profession of doctoring (and thus, doctor–patient relationships) actually *is*, considered as an activity which is committed to one important substantive *human* good (health), which itself is partly constitutive of a

[29] Dr. Paul Torzillo, Aboriginal health worker, quoted in Pat Fiske and Michael Johnson, *Memories of Fred*, Sydney, ABC Books, 1995, pp. 111–12.
[30] Fred Hollows, *An Autobiography* (with Peter Corris), Melbourne, John Kerr, 1991, p. 215.

humanly flourishing life. For Aristotle, good human activity is analysed in terms of achieving excellence in performing various functions relevant to characteristically human activity. So, if we think of excellence in performing a function in terms of carrying out a role well, such as the personal roles of being a parent or a friend, or the professional roles of being a teacher or a doctor, then the project to capture appropriately the nature and value taken to mark such roles seems to sit well with the ethical framework provided by the Aristotelian account of good human activity. And on our story of a virtue ethics account of the connection between character and right action, virtue ethics promises a particularly appropriate ethical framework to accommodate the nature and value marking the professional role of the good general practitioner.

So, on our view it is the nature of that relationship relevant to the particular human good in question which determines the content of the domain-specific regulative ideal which governs the motivation and action of the virtuous agent in that context. Thus, it is not the broader regulative ideals of a good *moral agent* or a good *citizen* which detail the content of the regulative ideals of a good father, a good friend, or more to the point here, a good doctor. Rather, the content of the regulative ideal of a good doctor must be determined by reference to some model of what doctoring purports to be. That is, it will be informed by an account of the goals of medicine, and an account of what the doctor–patient relationship itself is supposed to be. This grounding of virtue ethics in practice makes the charge of impracticality, which is so often directed at virtue ethics by the proponents of universalist ethical theories, seem rather ironic. For on our account, the regulative ideal of a good doctor is informed by the appropriate conception of the doctor's role, and this must be derived in important ways from the *practice* of medicine itself. And indeed, other ethical theories, whose regulative ideals are distinctive by the prominence they give to universalist concerns, look decidedly impractical in their distance from the actual roles and concrete sensitivities of actual doctors.

CHAPTER 5

Professional virtues, ordinary vices[1]

I PROFESSIONAL ROLES AND BROAD-BASED ETHICAL THEORY

The development of systematic professional ethics in the 1970s saw the traditional norms and entrenched practices in many professions being scrutinised and revised in the light of general ethical theories such as utilitarianism and Kantianism, and more recently, virtue ethics has been employed in a similar way. So, in medicine, for example, doctors have been told that rather than paternalistically withholding treatment information from patients, they must inform patients about the risks of medical procedures, since doing so respects patients' rights, maximises utility, or is required by the virtue of honesty. As we noted in the previous chapter, various writers have argued in support of such uses of broad-based ethical theories, whereas other writers have criticised the idea that the legitimacy of professional norms and practices should be judged directly in terms of what broad-based ethical theories would require. On the latter approach, for instance, Michael Stocker has argued that the sort of specific, role-based criteria against which good administrators and good legislators are properly judged make virtue ethics' general conception of the virtuous agent a poor moral exemplar for those occupying such positions.[2] And, in rejecting appeals to ordinary virtues as an antidote to corruption in public life, Judith Shklar has

---

[1] Earlier versions of this chapter were read at the University of Reading; as part of a symposium on 'Virtue Ethics and Professional Roles' at the Australian Association of Applied Ethics Fourth National Conference, University of Melbourne; and at the University of Auckland. We would like to thank those audiences, along with our co-symposiast, Tim Dare, for helpful comments. We are also grateful to Bernadette McSherry and Jeannie Paterson, from the Monash University Faculty of Law, and to John Campbell and Jeanette Kennett, for their comments on a previous version of the chapter.

[2] See Michael Stocker, 'Emotional Identification, Closeness, and Size: Some Contributions to Virtue Ethics', in Daniel Statman (ed.), *Virtue Ethics*, Edinburgh, Edinburgh University Press, 1997. Here Stocker seems to have in mind (eg.) the sort of virtue ethics approach which Michael Slote applies to evaluating laws and legislators in 'Law in Virtue Ethics', *Law and Philosophy* 14, no. 1, February 1995.

argued that certain ordinary vices like dishonesty and hypocrisy can help public officials protect citizens' rights and national interests against internal and external threats. Shklar argues that 'we have no need for simple lists of vices and virtues', which she describes as 'aloof' from the complexities of institutional life, and she regards as 'naive' those who condemn public officials for having such vices without taking account of such institutional complexities.[3]

We agree with these critics that any general approach which evaluates all professional behaviour directly in terms of broad-based ethical requirements will fail to do justice to professional roles and sensitivities, and that any ethic adequate for a particular profession must take account of the specific roles and sensitivities which are appropriate to that profession. (We argued for these claims in chapter 4.) But whatever implications such criticisms might have for consequentialist and Kantian approaches to professional roles, we think that virtue ethics has the theoretical resources to meet such criticisms. A plausible virtue ethics approach to professional roles would not appeal directly to the general conception of the virtuous agent to evaluate all professional roles and their occupants. Rather, we would suggest that virtue ethics be applied to professional roles in a different way, which we outlined in chapter 3. That is, to begin with, good professional roles must be part of a good profession, and a good profession, on our virtue ethics approach, is one which involves a commitment to an important human good – such as health – without which humans cannot flourish. Further, one must also be able to demonstrate how one's particular role within that profession contributes to the overall goal of that profession. Thus, in order for a defensible professional ethic to be generated, the norms of the profession

---

[3] Judith N. Shklar, 'Bad Characters for Good Liberals', in her *Ordinary Vices*, Cambridge, MA, Harvard University Press, 1984, e.g. p. 249. See also Frank Anechiarico and James B. Jacobs, *The Pursuit of Absolute Integrity: How Corruption Control Makes Government Ineffective*, Chicago, University of Chicago Press, 1996. Shklar's argument might seem to recall Machiavelli's famous argument against rulers inculcating the virtues: 'a man who wants to act virtuously in every way necessarily comes to grief among so many who are not virtuous. Therefore if a prince wants to maintain his rule he must learn how not to be virtuous, and to make use of this or not according to need . . . A prince . . . must not flinch from being blamed for vices which are necessary for safeguarding the state. This is because, taking everything into account, he will find that some of the things that appear to be virtues will, if he practises them, ruin him, and some of the things that appear to be wicked will bring him security and prosperity' (Niccolò Machiavelli, *The Prince*, trans. George Bull, Harmondsworth, Penguin, 1975, pp. 91–2). However, Shklar does not see herself as endorsing Machiavelli's claims here, for she defends vices in public officials only insofar as such vices can be shown to be necessary to achieve morally good ends: see, e.g., p. 244. See further Thomas Nagel, 'Ruthlessness in Public Life', and Bernard Williams, 'Politics and Moral Character', both in Joan C. Callahan (ed.), *Ethical Issues in Professional Life*, New York, Oxford University Press, 1988.

cannot simply be taken as one finds them; rather, they must be shown to reflect a commitment to an important substantive human good which is partly constitutive of a flourishing human life. So, for example, given medicine's commitment to human health, and the importance of health for human flourishing, medicine clearly counts as a good profession on this approach. And, given a general practitioner's concern with the broad health needs of their patients, the general practitioner's role within medicine would count as a good professional role. This account may help explain how a morality of professional roles can be grounded in one particular broad-based ethic, in a way which renders those roles consistent with that ethic.

Now, perhaps broad-based consequentialist or Kantian ethical theories could be developed in ways which enable them consistently to accommodate the distinctive requirements and sensitivities appropriate to various professional roles. However, virtue ethics' teleological approach to right action in terms of good functioning relative to appropriate ends makes it especially well placed to capture the special roles and sensitivities of particular professions. For good functioning or performing a function well can be understood in terms of the good performance of a role, such as the personal roles of being a parent or a friend, or the professional roles of being a doctor or a lawyer, and virtue ethics can then assess the good performance of the role and the appropriateness of certain dispositions to a particular profession by how well those roles and dispositions serve the proper ends of that profession.[4] So, for example, if health and justice are taken as the appropriate ends of the medical and legal professions, respectively, then the proper roles and dispositions of doctors and lawyers will be determined according to how well those roles and dispositions serve health or justice, respectively. This account indicates how virtue ethics can deliver an approach to professional roles that fits well within a more familiar broad-based virtue ethics, and in chapter 4 we argued that this sort of approach offers a promising way to capture the distinctive roles and sensitivities of good general practitioners.

The move to develop familiar broad-based ethical theories in ways which deal more adequately with the distinctive characteristics of various professional roles acknowledges that professional roles carry their own specific requirements, which, once those roles are properly established, may have some degree of independence from what broad-based morality would ordinarily permit or require people to do in a non-professional context. So, for example, counsellors are required by their

---

[4] Indeed, Aristotle did this himself to some extent. See, e.g., *Politics* 1259b18–1260a14.

role to ask clients searching and intimate questions which would often be entirely inappropriate outside this professional context, and lawyers are sometimes required by their role to try to undermine the credibility of opposition witnesses, in ways which would be unacceptable outside the courtroom. Now, suppose that the roles of various professions had been properly derived and set up in ways which proceed clearly from some broad-based ethical theory. Various questions remain concerning how broad-based ethical theory is to be properly understood to govern the role-specific morality of a given profession. Would there be cases where the requirements of the broader ethical theory underpinning the role can legitimately be applied directly to the evaluation of an individual's behaviour within their professional role, in ways which override what their role might otherwise dictate? To what extent should the ordinary prohibitions and requirements of that broader ethical theory limit what an individual may be required to do by the individual's role within one such profession? Are the requirements of properly established professional roles always decisive in justifying what an individual should do within one such role, no matter which broad-based requirements they conflict with? Is the general conception of the virtuous agent always inappropriate for evaluating conduct within a professional role? We will not attempt to provide a general answer to such large questions here. Rather, in this chapter we are interested in examining how the sort of virtue ethics approach to professional roles outlined above might deal with such questions, and what limits ordinary virtue might impose on this functional account of professional roles. We will address these questions by taking the legal profession as our case study, and we develop our argument by focusing on the views of some writers who claim that lawyers' roles have a relatively high degree of independence from ordinary moral requirements.

How decisive are a lawyer's role requirements in determining what an individual lawyer should do when those requirements conflict with broad-based moral requirements? And what sort of answer might virtue ethics give to this question? Some writers on legal ethics have argued that once lawyers' roles are properly set up within a justifiable legal system, those role requirements are always – or nearly always – decisive in cases where they conflict with broader moral requirements.[5] So, for example,

---

[5] See, e.g., Monroe H. Freedman, 'Professional Responsibility of the Criminal Defense Lawyer: The Three Hardest Questions', *Michigan Law Review* 64, 1969; Monroe H. Freedman, *Lawyers' Ethics in an Adversary System*, Indianapolis, Bobbs-Merrill, 1975; and Tim Dare, '"The Secret Courts of Men's Hearts": Legal Ethics and Harper Lee's *To Kill a Mockingbird*', in Kim Economides (ed.), *Ethical Challenges to Legal Education and Conduct*, Oxford, Hart Publishing, 1998.

it is widely held that the professional role of the good lawyer would, at least importantly, be given by those rules and dispositions which best serve the value of justice. In our adversarial system, one of the more notable ways in which this role is supposed to serve justice is by the lawyer's zealous advocacy of their client's interests – as certain writers have put it, by their becoming the client's 'special purpose friend'.[6] However, as is also widely recognised, such zealous pursuit of one's own clients' interests may often lead a lawyer to act against certain basic, general moral values. Indeed, the violation here may in various ways go against the very value that is thought to govern the role itself – the value of justice. Some writers on legal ethics argue that even in cases where a lawyer's role would require them to do something which broad-based morality would regard as seriously unjust, the requirements of the role are still decisive. We argue that this takes things too far. We will argue that ordinary vices which might serve the goals of the relevant profession well do not always count as professional virtues in that context. Using the legal profession as our example, we first argue that certain ordinary vices which might on some construals of the lawyer's role serve lawyers' professional goals well do not always count as professional virtues in that context.

There are several reasons why *lawyers'* roles provide a particularly apt example for discussing conflicts between the requirements of a properly established professional role and broader moral prohibitions and requirements, and for examining what a virtue ethics approach would say about such conflicts. First, cases of such conflict where there is some plausibility in thinking that the requirements of the role hold sway seem to arise more commonly in legal practice than they do in other professions, and these sorts of cases have received much discussion in the relevant professional literature. Second, the systemic nature of law makes it a good candidate for evaluating the agent-focused approach of virtue ethics. For it might be thought that the lawmaker's proper focus on institutional design provides more reason why considerations of an individual's virtuousness as judged by ordinary moral standards should figure little in an account of what a good lawyer should do. And third, the particular nature of the institution that lawyers work within, as a procedure or mechanism designed to uphold certain rights of citizens or to deliver just outcomes, places considerable strain on the notion of lawyers as *professionals*, who are not simply cogs in that mechanism (as some

---

[6] This term was coined by Fried, in 'The Lawyer as Friend'.

bureaucrats might be more properly characterised).[7] Thus, if individual lawyers can make legitimate appeals to what broad-based virtues would require, in the face of the considerable institutional weight of their role requirements, then that might be thought to give us more reason for holding that broad-based virtues can justify a professional's repudiation of their role requirements in cases where those requirements have less institutional backing or weight than they do in the legal system.

In this chapter we will focus on the role of the lawyer to provide support for the general claim that the sort of virtue ethics approach to professional roles outlined above can allow professionals to act in accordance with the requirements of their (properly grounded) role, except in cases where to act in accordance with those role requirements would grossly violate the value upon which the profession itself is founded. So, for example, we argue that while recognising the distinctive value of the lawyer's role, virtue ethics would hold that a lawyer ought not to fulfil the requirements of their role in cases where fulfilling those requirements would involve gross violations of *justice*. We also argue that these exceptions can be allowed, without compromising the idea that those role requirements themselves have distinctive normative force (which is decisive, in many circumstances).

2 DOING JUSTICE TO LAWYERS' ROLES

Many writers on legal ethics argue that lawyers working within an adversarial system best serve their professional goal of justice by zealously advocating their clients' interests.[8] A famous statement of an extreme version of this sort of position was given by Lord Henry Brougham:

An advocate, in the discharge of his duty, knows but one person in all the world, and that person is his client. To save that client by all means and expedients, and at all hazards and costs to other persons, and, amongst them, to himself, is his first and only duty; and in performing this duty he must not regard the alarm, the torments, the destruction which he may bring upon others. Separating even the duties of a patriot from those of an advocate, and casting

---

[7] Indeed, Anthony Kronman has recently argued that the notion and values of professionalism are in decline amongst lawyers, many of whom now regard themselves essentially as technicians who can carry out various 'law jobs'. See Anthony Kronman, *The Lost Lawyer: Failing Ideals of the Legal Profession*, Cambridge, MA, Harvard University Press, 1993.

[8] Two of many writers who defend this claim are Freedman, 'Professional Responsibility of the Criminal Defense Lawyer' and Fried, 'The Lawyer as Friend'. William H. Simon calls this the 'principle of partisanship', which is one principle in what he refers to as the 'ideology of advocacy' dominating lawyers' conceptions of their role in an adversarial system (see 'The Ideology of Advocacy: Procedural Justice and Professional Ethics', *Wisconsin Law Review* 29, 1978).

them if need be to the wind, he must go on reckless of the consequences, if his fate it should unhappily be to involve his country in confusion for his client's protection.[9]

And while contemporary writers on legal ethics rule out wreaking certain kinds of destruction (such as murdering opposition witnesses) in the name of serving one's client, many of those writers nevertheless hold that lawyers' duties towards their clients require them to act in a variety of ways which clearly violate ordinary moral prohibitions. For example, Monroe Freedman has argued that a lawyer must allow their client to present to the court testimony which both lawyer and client know is perjurious, and that a lawyer defending an accused rapist must cross-examine the alleged victim in ways which make her appear promiscuous, even where the lawyer has strong reason to believe that she is not promiscuous (or has strong reason to doubt its relevance, even if she is promiscuous), and that the accused has actually committed the rape.[10] Now, it is well known that in zealously advocating their clients' interests, lawyers commonly do act in ways which are contrary to certain general moral values. Thus, to take a different sort of case, corporate and insurance company lawyers have notoriously engaged in stalling strategies, such as the use of discovery provisions, to delay court proceedings where this would be in the company's interests – for example where the plaintiff is too sick or poor to continue effective litigation.[11] Freedman defends the use of the tactics he describes on the grounds that they are required by respect for the client's autonomy. For without a lawyer energetically to pursue their interests, people's lack of knowledge of the law and its workings and their vulnerability when faced with litigation would often result in their interests not being adequately represented in legal proceedings. In linking the lawyer's role to values which would be endorsed by broad-based ethical theory, such as respect for autonomy,

---

[9] Lord Brougham made this statement before the House of Lords in 1820, in the context of his defence of Queen Caroline against the divorce proceedings initiated by King George IV. Brougham's statement was (among other things) a threat to reveal publicly the King's secret marriage (while heir apparent) to Mrs Fitzherbert, a Roman Catholic, which, under the Act of Settlement, would suffice to deprive the King of his crown (and so plunge his country into confusion). From J. Nightingale (ed.), *The Trial of Queen Caroline*, Vol. II, London, J. Robins & Co., Albion Press, 1821, p. 8; quoted in David Luban, *Lawyers and Justice: An Ethical Study*, Princeton, Princeton University Press, 1988, pp. 54–5. (The last sentence in the Brougham quotation is taken from the version quoted in Charles P. Curtis, 'The Ethics of Advocacy', *Stanford Law Review* 4, December 1951, p. 4.)

[10] See Freedman, 'Professional Responsibility of the Criminal Defense Lawyer'; and Freedman, *Lawyers' Ethics in an Adversary System*, chapter 4. For a discussion of Freedman's views here, see Luban, *Lawyers and Justice*, pp. 53–4.   [11] Thanks to Jeanette Kennett for this example.

Freedman is attempting to show how the lawyer's role can (despite appearances to the contrary) have a certain kind of moral integrity.

However, others who defend lawyers' zealous advocacy of their clients' interests argue that adequately to bring out how the role of the lawyer can have moral integrity, respect for client autonomy must be located within the context of a properly established institutional system of legal rights, which can be shown to serve appropriate ends. That is, the client's legal rights which a lawyer is zealously promoting must be shown to be part of a properly designed legal system whose requirements carry moral authority, and which aims to promote certain socially valued ends, such as the effective resolution of disputes.[12] This goal might be thought to rule out corporate lawyers advancing their clients' interests by taking advantage of discovery provisions to delay court proceedings. But while this sort of account shows the moral integrity of zealous advocacy (and the idea that a lawyer is a *professional*, rather than a mere 'functionary') more adequately than Freedman does, it shares the fundamental flaw in the sort of position defended by Freedman. For both accounts are still committed to the idea that, once the lawyer's role has been properly established, the requirements of that role have decisive weight in determining what an individual lawyer should do, in any case where those requirements conflict with broader moral prohibitions and requirements. Of course, certain excesses might be ruled out, in setting up the lawyer's role within such a system in the first place. Nevertheless, as we shall see, this approach still requires lawyers to carry out many ordinary injustices, in the name of (institutionally backed) zealous advocacy.

Before continuing, however, let us address an objection which might be raised to our argument at this point. That is, some would say that our discussion of the lawyer's role has so far focused too exclusively on the lawyer's duties to his client, and has neglected to consider a lawyer's broader duties to the court. For lawyers have various duties to the court, such as the duty not to make unsupported allegations and the duty not to mislead the court, and it might be argued that the actions of the insurance company lawyer and the defendant's lawyer in the rape case can be ruled out because they would violate those duties. But first, many legal writers have argued in support of a narrow interpretation of these duties

---

[12] See Jerome E. Bickenbach, 'The Redemption of the Moral Mandate of the Profession of Law', *Canadian Journal of Law and Jurisprudence* 9, 1996; and Jerome E. Bickenbach, 'Law and Morality', *Law and Philosophy* 8, no. 3, December 1989. This idea of a legal system derives from H. L. A. Hart, *The Concept of Law*, Oxford, Oxford University Press, 1961.

to the court that would not inhibit the lawyer's capacity to provide the most zealous advocacy of their client's interests. And second, even on a more generous interpretation of a lawyer's duties to the court, it is clear that lawyers' zealous advocacy of their clients' interests within the constraints imposed by such duties may still violate the concern to promote the value of justice. On the first point, for example, the Law Society and Bar Association codes of conduct in most Australian states instruct lawyers that their basic duty is to their client, and indeed, to serve their client 'without regard to any unpleasant consequences . . . to any other person'.[13] And as Justice David Ipp reports, some lawyers rely heavily in their practice on the distinction between fabricating evidence (which would be widely condemned) and not disclosing evidence (which some seem to regard as permissible).[14] As the Australian Law Reform Commission's recent discussion paper on lawyers' roles and legal training points out,

The consequences of this lack of candour in litigation can include:
* the deliberate suppression of relevant but unfavourable evidence
* the selective presentation of biased expert evidence
* the failure to admit the truth of the facts asserted by the opposition
* the use of tactical attacks on the credibility of witnesses to suggest that the witness cannot be believed on oath, even though their evidence is known to be true.[15]

Indeed, there are indications that lawyers are making increasing use of such tactics, and many believe that given the larger profits at stake for law firms in much current litigation, such useful flouting of ordinary moral concerns will become more widespread.[16]

Nevertheless, we might suppose that by reinstating the primacy of the lawyer's role obligations to administer justice via their duties to the court – such as not presenting unsupported and biased evidence – we will go some way to delivering a broader conception of the lawyer as a professional with moral integrity that would constrain the ideology of advocacy. Thus, while cross-examining for the purposes of discrediting the reliability or credibility of an adverse witness whom you know to be

---

[13] Victorian Bar *Rules of Conduct*, rule 3.1 (a). Similar provisions exist in Bar Rules in other Australian states.
[14] David Ipp, 'Reforms to the Adversarial Process in Civil Litigation – Part I', *Australian Law Journal* 69, 1995.
[15] Australian Law Reform Commission, *Review of the Adversarial System of Litigation: Rethinking Legal Education and Training*, ALRC Issues Paper no. 21, August 1997, p. 62.
[16] See Michael Kirby, 'Billable Hours in a Noble Calling?', *Alternative Law Journal* 21, no. 6, December 1996; and Kronman, *The Lost Lawyer*.

telling the truth might well help the defendant's chances of avoiding conviction, such conduct might be ruled out as contrary to the lawyer's duty
to the court, where this takes precedence over the lawyer's duty to their
client. However, lawyers' duties to the court will still in various ways fall
well short of providing a satisfactory constraint on the ideology of advocacy. This can be seen in a variety of cases. For instance, defence lawyers
in rape trials commonly take themselves to be entitled to subpoena and
present to the court records detailing any counselling sessions the plaintiff may have had after the alleged incident, if the lawyers think that such
records might diminish the damage done to their client by the plaintiff's
testimony. This practice has been very helpful for defence lawyers, and,
at least in some jurisdictions (such as Victoria), it has become very
common for defence lawyers to make use of it.[17] Presenting these counselling records to the court has helped defence lawyers overcome the
restrictions of rape shield laws, which many jurisdictions have introduced in order to prevent defence lawyers' common attacks on the credibility of the complainant's testimony through reference to her sexual
history. These counselling records have been useful to defence lawyers in
various ways. Most commonly they have enabled the lawyer to make the
complainant appear disturbed in some way, or even hysterical, or they
have just allowed the lawyer to make the complainant appear of dubious
character. Also quite commonly, victims of rape mistakenly believe that
they are in part to blame for the attack, and say so during these counselling sessions. By introducing these records, defence lawyers have been
able to cast doubt on the accuracy of the complainant's accusation of
rape. Now, there need be no reason why the lawyer's advocacy here must
violate their duties to the court. However, such conduct as preying on
feelings of victim-guilt on the complainant's part and portraying her as
disturbed in order to reduce her credibility, for the purpose of advocating one's client's interest and quite untempered by concern with relevant
issues of truth and justice, is clearly contrary to a broader conception of
these values.

Some writers think that there is something deeply misguided about

---

[17] See Simon Bronitt and Bernadette McSherry, 'The Use and Abuse of Counseling Records in
Sexual Assault Trials: Reconstructing the "Rape Shield"?' *Criminal Law Forum* 8, no. 2, 1997. See
also Virginia Trioli, 'Assault Victims not Protected, say Counsellors', *The Sunday Age*, Melbourne,
19 April 1998. Contrast this practice with the defence lawyer (played by Nick Nolte) in the rape
case at the centre of the recent film *Cape Fear*, who could not in good conscience allow a report
on the rape victim's chequered sexual history to be presented to the court, because he thought
that the report would lead the jury to wrongly acquit the accused, who he knew had committed
the rape.

using ordinary morality to attack the legitimacy of professional role obligations, and that the lawyer's role is significantly independent of the dictates of ordinary morality. But, given that a lawyer's role obligations are grounded in justice in a broad sense, how could one think that this broad sense of justice is irrelevant in all cases in which a professional's role obligations would lead them to *violate* that broader value? Whether one is a Kantian, a consequentialist, or a virtue ethicist, one should find this equally puzzling. As mentioned above, one common line of argument for why lawyers' roles, once set up within a well-founded legal system, must be independent of the injunctions of ordinary morality is that this independence is necessary to protect their clients' autonomy, which would be threatened if lawyers were allowed to sabotage their clients' case by moderating their zealous advocacy whenever this called for actions which would conflict with a lawyer's own conscience. After all, it might be asked, why think that a lawyer is particularly well positioned to judge the rightness or wrongness of their client's case, and anyway, who is a lawyer to decide what legal rights their clients are entitled to have advocated? Another argument claims that the independence of lawyers' roles is necessary to safeguard lawyers' promises to their clients, for allowing lawyers to modify their conduct on account of what they take to be its injustice would be seen by many lawyers as a licence to renege on their promise to put the best possible case for their clients.

However, we have not here been arguing that lawyers' role obligations to, for example, advocate their clients' interests zealously are justifiably overridden in cases where that role requires them to do something which they conscientiously object to doing. Whether or not this is true, our argument here is that lawyers' role obligations can be overridden in cases in which they would require a lawyer to carry out what ordinary morality would judge to be a serious *injustice*. And these role obligations are overridden in such cases of injustice, we would argue, whether or not the particular lawyer in question conscientiously objects to such injustice. (If they do not conscientiously object in such a case, we would argue that they *ought to*.)[18]

But while regarding ordinary injustices as overriding lawyers' role

---

[18] Further, there may be other values in ordinary morality apart from justice which would override a lawyer's role obligations in certain cases. If we are right that certain role obligations of lawyers can justifiably be trumped in cases where the role requires the lawyer to do something that is seriously *unjust*, that might give us some reason to think that those role obligations may be overridden in cases where they would require a lawyer to do something which would seriously violate some other value – such as altruism or compassion – which is uncontroversially external to the law.

obligations in certain cases might seem to pose less of a threat to client autonomy and promise-keeping than allowing lawyers conscientiously to object on any grounds they feel seriously enough about, it might still be thought that such an approach threatens seriously to jeopardise clients' interests. For it might be argued that allowing lawyers to modify or abandon certain role obligations towards their clients when those obligations would require them to carry out serious injustices runs a great risk of letting a lawyer with the wrong values prevail. To give some extreme examples, one might choose not to advocate a client's rights zealously under the law because they are black, or poor, or female. In fact, however, this seems to be another reason for accounts of role obligations to highlight and remain significantly governed by appropriate broad-based values, rather than to claim an independence from the influence of broad-based values. For what is wrong with such failures of zealous advocacy in the cases just mentioned is that the lawyer violates a founding value of their role – viz. justice – and this is just what is wrong in certain other cases where the lawyer single-mindedly pursues an ideology of advocacy. Moreover, it is mistaken to reason from the concern to guard against role departures on account of pernicious values to the claim that we should rule out role departures on account of legitimate appeals to relevant values. It may, for example, be wrong for a general practitioner to cancel an appointment with a patient because the patient is black. This, however, hardly suggests that he may not cancel an appointment for other, legitimate reasons, say, to be with his partner at the birth of their child.

It has been put to us, however, that there is a far more plausible account of the lawyer's role as exclusively governed by the concern to advocate one's own clients' legal rights as fully as possible.[19] On the more plausible account, the lawyers' role, conceived as governed by the concern to advocate their clients' legal rights, is thought of as already involving a deep moral commitment. It is so because the legal, institutional claims of clients before the courts are imagined to represent the rights that we as a community have determined that we should have before the law. Our legal rights before the courts represent the rule of public reason. They represent the result of a 'deliberative democracy', i.e. where the plural and conflicting reasonable views within the community are given due consideration, the result of which yields a compromise

---

[19] See Dare, '"The Secret Courts of Men's Hearts"'. This account is inspired by John Rawls, 'Two Concepts of Rules', *Philosophical Review* 64, 1955.

set of institutions, laws, procedures, and so forth, that enable us to sustain and live as a community.[20] On this picture, then, the lawyer as advocate of their clients' legal rights is pictured as engaged in a moral enterprise, since the lawyer is the advocate of rights resulting from and resting upon the moral framework of the rule of public reason. On this view, it remains true that the lawyer ought not to temper their advocacy of their clients' legal rights on account of the lawyer's own moral judgements about how these rights might in some cases violate other commensurate goods – however reasonable these judgements may be. For this would be to pervert the rule of public reason the lawyer ought to be committed to upholding. Likewise, however, various excesses of the ideology of advocacy, including some we have noted, such as the use of biased evidence or tactics to discredit testimony known to be true, would be ruled out since these too would involve the perversion of the rule of public reason.

As an account of how a legal system would ideally be set up and function, and of how the lawyer's role within such an ideal system would be governed, this account sounds plausible enough. And we might well not want lawyers exercising their own 'moral' judgements about the rights their client is entitled to have advocated, where such judgements would pervert or violate the proper functioning and rule of a just legal process. However, the sorts of cases where we have suggested that lawyers ought to exercise judgement based on broad-based moral standards not, in various ways, to advocate their clients' case within the legal means available in our less than ideal legal systems are not cases where the lawyers' exercise of such moral judgement would pervert or violate the proper functioning and just rule of public reason. In any case, the workings of legal systems in the actual world, in various, and plausibly ineliminable ways present a very different moral territory within which to understand how the role of the lawyer should be governed than does this liberal ideal of the rule of law. Thus, however appealing the latter goal might be, and however compelling a reason it might give us against licensing lawyers to exercise judgements – moral or otherwise – that conflict with the proper functioning and rule of a just legal process, it does not give support to the idea that in our much less than ideal world, where the use of legal process and the laws themselves may be manifestly unjust, lawyers are properly only concerned with advocating whatever legal rights their clients might actually have. Indeed, defending the overridingness of a

---

[20] See, e.g., Joshua Cohen, 'Deliberation and Democratic Legitimacy', in Alan Hamlin and Philip Pettit (eds.), *The Good Polity*, Oxford, Blackwell, 1989; and John Rawls, *Political Liberalism*, New York, Columbia University Press, 1993.

lawyer's role obligations by sketching an account of how that role should function in an ideal legal system may be dangerous, because it can give the lawyer a misplaced confidence that the dictates of their role as they currently happen to stand are the correct ones, and are to be followed unconditionally.

3 VIRTUE ETHICS, JUSTICE, AND LAWYERS' ROLES

Let us now develop and give some defence of how our virtue ethics approach might do justice to the lawyer's role. Virtue ethics holds that an action is right if and only if it is what a virtuous agent would do in the circumstances. On the Aristotelian approach, the character-traits of the virtuous agent are those which are constitutive of characteristic human functioning. This character-based criterion of right action is analogous to recent versions of consequentialism which hold that the rightness of actions is determined, not on a piecemeal basis according to whether they individually maximise the good (as in act-consequentialist theories, like Peter Railton's), but rather according to whether those actions would be done by an agent with a certain character.[21] For advocates of this sort of consequentialism (such as Richard Brandt and Brad Hooker), that character is one whose dispositions would maximise the good overall,[22] whereas for (Aristotelian) virtue ethics, that character is one who is disposed to live a characteristically human life. However, a virtue ethics criterion of right action in the context of a professional role is more specific than this, and would be directed towards the proper goal of the profession in question, as we explained earlier. For example, in a medical context, an action would be right if and only if it is what a virtuous doctor would do in the circumstances, and the character of the virtuous doctor would be constituted by dispositions which serve the goal of health in appropriate ways. Thus, on a virtue ethics approach to professional roles, something can be a virtue in professional life – such as a doctor's acute clinical judgement in making a correct diagnosis from a multitude of symptoms – which might be thought neutral in ordinary life.

---

[21] See Neera Kapur Badhwar, "Introduction" to Neera Kapur Badhwar (ed.), *Friendship: A Philosophical Reader*, Ithaca, NY, Cornell University Press, 1993, pp. 31–2; and Roger Crisp, 'Modern Moral Philosophy and the Virtues', in Roger Crisp (ed.), *How Should One Live? Essays on the Virtues*, Oxford, Clarendon Press, 1996, esp. pp. 6–7. For Railton's act-consequentialist view, see his 'Alienation, Consequentialism, and the Demands of Morality', in Samuel Scheffler (ed.), *Consequentialism and its Critics*, Oxford, Oxford University Press, 1988.

[22] See Richard B. Brandt, *Facts, Values, and Morality*, Cambridge, Cambridge University Press, 1996, e.g. pp. 145–55; and Brad Hooker, 'Rule-Consequentialism', *Mind* 99, 1990.

Our construal of a virtue ethics approach to professional roles should helpfully illuminate how virtue ethics can be applied to the ethics of professional roles in a way which is thoroughly within the spirit of its approach to ethics generally. A metatheoretical concern put to us by Michael Stocker queries how virtue ethicists who, having recognised that certain ordinary virtues seem unsuited to professional life, might then seek to overcome this problem by simply tacking on what seem to be appropriate guiding principles of certain professions to their conception of the virtuous agent. As Stocker puts it, virtue ethicists might be accused of preferring theft to honest toil in making such a move, much as many of us criticise consequentialists who seem to do so when they respond to certain apparent counterexamples by simply adding another intrinsic good to their list of values to maximise. Thus, those who seek to add apparently desirable role-generated features or character-traits to the picture of the virtuous agent at least owe us an account of how this might be done that is within the spirit of a virtue theory.[23] On our construal of virtue ethics' application to professional roles, however, it is not that one simply *adds* an account of professional roles to the general conception of the virtuous agent, but rather that this conception itself is both partly delivered by and constrains the virtues specific to a person's particular roles, relations, and activities. Thus, virtue ethics' account of the various characteristics of the virtuous agent is, in part, an account of what counts as excellence in certain roles characteristic of a flourishing human life, such as the role of a friend, and the application of virtue ethics to professional roles can be seen as an extension of this general approach. Indeed, by emphasising what counts as excellence within certain roles, virtue ethics sheds distinctive light on how a profession succeeds or fails to exhibit moral integrity by focusing on the ways in which it succeeds or fails to secure its guiding goals. Thus, it brings out how, for example, a lawyer's role-based violation of justice is a particularly acute kind of moral failing for a *lawyer*, and not just a violation of a value by which *any* good profession ought to be constrained.

One might accept that virtue ethics is particularly well suited to providing a plural, role-generated ethic of right conduct. But why think that it endorses broad-based moral guidance on the virtuous performance of certain roles, rather than guidance by values wholly within, and generated by, the excellent performance of those roles? In response, it is worth noting initially that nothing about recognising and accounting for the

---

[23] Stocker, 'Emotional Identification, Closeness, and Size'.

role-relativity of certain virtues entails that, as Shklar put it, 'we have no need for simple lists of vices and virtues' in evaluating the actions of individuals in their professional roles. In giving an account of the distinctive sensitivities and requirements of various professional roles, and of how those requirements may diverge from what broad-based morality would allow, one is in no way committed to the idea that those role requirements are absolute. While it is indeed 'naive' to use ordinary morality as the sole arbiter of people's behaviour in their professional roles, it is another thing to say that individuals can legitimately violate *the founding value of their profession*, in circumstances where their role seems to require such an action of them. One ought not to overvalue the good that might be claimed for excellent performance in certain professional roles. We accept, quite generally, that a person acting within a role may lose sight of how their acting within it promotes or in part constitutes their leading a good life, and that to the extent that they do so, the broad-based moral values making up the picture of a good life ought to correct this narrow vision. So, for instance, one may lose sight of how one's pursuit of friendship with another may be at the expense of leading a good life, and in this case the values that are violated ought to constrain one's pursuit of the friendship. Further, and specifically in relation to the value that might be attached to the role of the lawyer, in cases of conflicting and plural values, we may justifiably dirty our hands only where we act in pursuit of some good commensurate to that which we would violate by so acting. And certainly, it is hard to imagine how we could make this case for the lawyer's pursuit of their client's interest in, say, the rape cases we have sketched above. Now, any moral justification of allegedly valuable professional roles will appeal to some broad-based moral good or goal which ultimately makes the role a valuable one – such as the appeal to the promotion of human health, for the medical profession, or to justice, for the legal profession. And where this overarching good upon which the rightness of the role in part rests would, all things considered, be violated by practising certain characteristic features within the role, one's moral justification of the role – for virtue ethics, in terms of what a virtuous agent would do – will clearly recommend that the broad-based value have constraining force on the practice of the role.

Moreover, it should not be thought that such governing constraints on the practice of a particular role will negate the guiding normative force for the agent of relevant features of the role. Consider, for example, how, in the friendship case, the demands of an individual's overall well-being or flourishing might bear on the values or demands of friendship. People

can justifiably compromise their well-being or flourishing to some extent
on account of the demands of friendship; nevertheless, in cases where a
person's continuing with a friendship would seriously conflict with their
overall flourishing, we can plausibly think that they would be justified in
ending the friendship. However, that an individual's general flourishing
might trump the requirements of friendship in cases where continuing
the friendship would seriously conflict with their flourishing does not
entail that the requirements of friendship lack normative force in cases
where they do not seriously conflict with their flourishing. Thus, to use
a familiar example, if it was true that Gauguin's remaining with his wife
and children in Paris severely restricted the expression of his talents as
an artist, we might plausibly think it overall justified that he left them to
go and paint in Tahiti. But taking this as justified in no way entails that
Gauguin's role as husband and father lacked normative force where carrying out those roles did not so severely limit his work as an artist.[24]
Likewise, the fact that broad-based justice trumps the requirements of
the lawyer's role in cases where those role requirements would lead the
lawyer to carry out gross injustices does not entail that those role requirements lack normative force in cases where they would not lead the
lawyer to carry out gross injustices.

Some critics of virtue ethics have interpreted the view as defined
importantly by an approach to the determination of right action which
rejects appeals to principles and relies solely on modelling one's conduct
on some hypothetical exemplar, where a notion of character is thought
in some way to have primacy over rules or principles. However, those
who frame an ethics of character as necessarily opposed to an ethics of
principle have set up a false dichotomy.[25] For there is no reason why

---

[24] Aristotle brings out well how friendship carries its own distinctive demands, but in doing so he
also recognises that a friendship should be abandoned in some circumstances. (A similar claim
might be made about personal 'integrity', construed as wholeness.) See Aristotle's discussion of
'occasions for breaking off friendship', in *Nicomachean Ethics* IX. 3. For a related discussion of how
duty can govern friendship, without duty being part of the source of the goodness of friendship,
see Michael Stocker, 'Friendship and Duty: Some Difficult Relations', in Owen Flanagan and
Amélie O. Rorty (eds.), *Identity, Character, and Morality: Essays on Moral Psychology*, Cambridge, MA,
MIT Press, 1990, pp. 225–6. Indeed, those who (rightly) believe in dirty hands would hold that
those roles retain some normative force even when they are overridden by Gauguin's flourishing, and so can rationally ground moral emotions such as regret, etc. So too, (some) cases where
broad-based justice overrides what the lawyer's role requires them to do for their client may still
leave open the possibility of the lawyer's rationally regretting forgoing what zealous advocacy
would demand of them here.

[25] Note that some virtue ethicists themselves have invited this interpretation. See e.g. John
McDowell, 'Virtue and Reason', *The Monist* 62, no. 3, 1979; and (for a virtue ethics approach to
legal ethics) Thomas L. Shaffer, *Faith and the Professions*, Provo, Brigham Young University Press,
1987.

virtue ethics must hold that the character of the moral exemplar whose actions determine what it is right for us to do cannot have internalised and be guided by certain principles. In fact, this is precisely how one would expect certain excellences of character to be guided. So, for example, a good general practitioner will be guided in part by the principle of giving priority to their own patients over others. And a good friend will be guided in part by a distinctive and additional concern to promote the well-being of the friend.

Recent sophisticated versions of all broad-based moral theories – both Kantian and consequentialist – significantly emphasise the importance of having a certain character for right action. In particular, these accounts are concerned to show how the having of the kind of character required for various valuable activities, relations, and roles, such as friendship, or being a good lawyer or teacher, informs, is compatible with, and can be justified by the criterion of right action of these moral theories. So, for example, the good Kantian agent, in her role as a mother, would normally be guided by the concerns proper to and largely generated within the practice of motherhood, and not by her concern to do her duty. However, in the event that her particular, role-generated guiding concerns here would direct her to act against her overarching commitment to duty, the latter broad-based disposition would constrain her disposition specific to the domain of motherhood. On this model of the moral psyche, then, there is an interdependent connection between the criterion of rightness of the broad-based ethical theory and more particular role- and relation-sensitive dispositions. Thus, the connection between character and the criterion of right action of broad-based ethical theory posited here allows, at least *conceptually*, that role-generated values have significant scope in guiding an agent's moral deliberations, and so promises to remove the alleged dichotomy we mentioned at the outset between irreducible, particularistic, role-generated value and broad-based universal justification. And on this kind of plural-value model, virtue ethics construes the character of the virtuous agent as governed by a variety of principles, ranging from the general to the very specific, which are importantly informed, justified, and constrained by broad-based values and by particular role, relation, and practice-sensitive features. The alleged opposition, then, between an ethics of character and one of principle is rendered misguided and obsolete. And certainly, applied to virtue ethics, this model resists the characterisation of a virtue ethics approach as one which gives character primacy over principles.

This may help explain how virtue ethics may be properly understood as regarding the virtuous performance of certain professional roles to be constrained by broad-based moral concerns or virtues. One might well wonder, however, why this should be thought a distinctive feature of virtue ethics, or why virtue ethics should be thought distinctively well suited to this task. How, for example, would this virtue ethics approach differ from, and be preferable to, say, a rule-consequentialist approach to professional roles? For rule-consequentialism might also be thought to offer a plausible and consistent account both of the specific rules and requirements appropriate to particular professional roles and, as a teleo-logical theory, of how the good practice of a professional role would be importantly governed by the appropriate end of the profession. So, for example, a rule-consequentialist account of lawyers' roles might hold that a lawyer's action is right if and only if it is in accordance with a rule (or is done from a disposition) which, when followed by all lawyers in such circumstances, maximises the relevant good – such as justice. Thus, rule-consequentialists could hold that the rules and dispositions which consti-tute the lawyer's role are those which best serve the value of justice, and that the standard requirements of a lawyer's role are to be adjusted in circumstances in which the following of that role there by all lawyers would be likely to result in serious violations of justice. Indeed, the impor-tance of procedure in the law, and law's systemic nature as an institution, makes lawyers' roles a promising candidate for a rule-consequentialist approach, by comparison with, say, doctors' roles, where rules and pro-cedures are less central, and the framework under which doctors practise is perhaps less co-ordinated overall. And the urgency of one of the guiding ends of the law – viz., justice – might provide a further reason why teleological approaches such as rule-consequentialism (and virtue ethics) might offer particularly promising accounts of lawyers' roles, compared, say, to other professional roles, such as those of architects, where the ends of the profession are arguably less vital. Moreover, as we noted earlier, law's procedural and systemic nature also makes it a good candidate for testing the plausibility of the more agent-focused approach of virtue ethics, for it might be held that it is in the practice of law, above all, that considerations of individual virtuousness should take second place to the promotion of justice through one's role in the system. This, then, might provide some reason to prefer a rule-consequentialist focus on universal or general rules and behaviour to the more individualistic approach of the virtue ethics criterion of rightness.

We have not the space here adequately to argue the case for why our virtue ethics account of professional role morality should be preferred to a rule-consequentialist account. There are various unclear and complex issues here, deserving of detailed and lengthy discussion. For instance, it is not clear whether rule-consequentialism can properly be understood in such a way as to deliver the desired judgements in various specific cases. Take the rape cases discussed above, where defence lawyers may obtain the alleged victim's counselling records and present those records to the court. There is clearly much good to be gained by allowing defence lawyers in rape trials to have access to and use such records in defending their client. Indeed, there are good reasons for thinking that a rule which permits lawyers defending accused rapists to present such records would better promote justice overall, if followed by lawyers generally, than would a rule which declared such records off-limits to lawyers. For given that the facts (eg. about consent) surrounding an alleged rape may often be obscure and difficult to ascertain, and the grave injustice of incorrectly convicting someone of rape, the details contained in the alleged victim's counselling records are likely to be enlightening and crucial in such a substantial number of cases that justice may well be better served by a rule which, if generally followed, allows defence lawyers to present such records.

On the other hand, rule-consequentialists might claim that the rules governing defence lawyers' access to and use of alleged rape victims' counselling records can be more finely calibrated than this, so that these rules would not require (or perhaps even permit) defence lawyers to use those counselling records in certain cases. So, for example, rule-conse-quentialists might suggest that criminal lawyers' professional code of conduct could include the following rule:

If a lawyer acting for the accused in a rape case has good reason to believe that their client is guilty (although the client has not actu-ally confessed to the rape), the lawyer should not obtain and use as part of the defence records of any counselling which the alleged victim may have had, where the lawyer is using such records as a means to obscuring their client's apparent guilt.

It is not clear, however, that forbidding the use of counselling records in such circumstances would best serve justice overall, and so it is not clear that rule-consequentialism would advocate such a rule. One might hold, for instance, that given the grave injustice of an incorrect conviction of rape, and the oft-noted fallibility of defence lawyers' beliefs about the guilt or innocence of their clients, such a rule, as guide for general beha-viour, might well go against the maximisation of justice.

Further, there are detailed questions to consider concerning the appropriateness of a rule-consequentialist justification, in terms of universal or general rules or behaviour. In determining what the virtuous lawyer would do, virtue ethics focuses more on *this* individual lawyer, and the injustices *they* would be committing in this trial, by using counselling records inappropriately, or by using discovery provisions to delay proceedings advantageously. Rule-consequentialism would focus on the outcomes of *everyone's* following this rule. On virtue ethics' approach, then, the sorts of professional dispositions which a good lawyer would have (and the actions which those dispositions would prompt) might not be the sorts of dispositions which are likely to maximise justice (or just trial outcomes) when inculcated by lawyers generally. Whether or not justice would be maximised here remains an unclear empirical question. And whether or not the more individualistic justification given by virtue ethics is preferable to the more generalistic one of rule-consequentialism is a complex question which raises various issues concerning the nature of moral requirements, and how we should be understood to be guided by them. So, for example, many would think that whether or not rule-consequentialism would recommend a rule that, say, defence lawyers in the rape case are permitted or required to make use of counselling records where this might be advantageous to their clients' interests, the rule-consequentialist focus is irrelevant to the proper deliberations of the defence lawyer. That is, it would be irrelevant to their deliberations about the ethics of using counselling records to be told that, while the apparently genuine rape victim in this case is likely to suffer a serious injustice by your use of their counselling records, use of these records is nevertheless licensed or required by a rule which, if followed by lawyers generally, would maximise justice overall. Again, however, such issues deserve lengthy discussion, which we cannot pursue here.

In sum, then, in this chapter, we have argued first, that to do justice to the lawyer's role, this role should be understood as governed by broad-based moral values, most notably, by a broad-based conception of justice; and second, that virtue ethics' teleological approach offers a particularly promising way to deliver such an account, while retaining the determination of the guiding norms of professional exemplars by reference to the proper goals of the profession.

CHAPTER 6

Professional detachment in health care and legal practice[1]

People from a variety of professions commonly speak of how they distance themselves psychologically from various aspects of their professional roles. Indeed, such detachment is often seen as increasingly necessary by health-care and welfare professionals. However, the moral status of professional detachment itself is not very clear. Such detachment is sometimes regarded as a cornerstone of professionalism, where an ability to maintain an emotional distance from one's clients is thought by some to be a key part of what it means to have a professional attitude. For example, in an era of substantial cutbacks, state-employed social workers who deal with the impoverished and disadvantaged and often find themselves having to deliver bad news to their clients are urged to keep a significant degree of emotional separation between themselves and their clients, so that they are more able to carry out such requirements of their role. Similarly, doctors who regularly attend to the dying are taught how to remain somewhat emotionally removed from the plight of their patients, and relationship counsellors dealing with quarrelling couples are encouraged to provide constructive advice to both parties, without becoming 'judgemental' towards one party whose behaviour they might personally disapprove of. Lawyers, too, have often been told that they should not become personally concerned at the plight of their clients, but should instead, as Charles Curtis advised, strive to develop the sort of detachment displayed by the Stoics, regarding their clients' troubles 'vicariously', as if they were bystanders assisting in another's emergency. As Curtis puts it, 'if a lawyer is to be the best lawyer he is capable of being . . . the Stoic sage is his exemplar'.[2] Curtis exhorts lawyers to emulate the latter-day Stoic Montaigne, who cautioned that,

---

[1] Earlier versions of sections 1 and 2 of this chapter were presented at the Australasian Association for Professional and Applied Ethics Fifth National Conference, University of New South Wales, and at the Australian Institute for Health Law and Ethics Third Annual Conference, Melbourne. We are grateful to the audiences on those occasions for their helpful comments.

[2] Charles P. Curtis, 'The Ethics of Advocacy', *Stanford Law Review* 4, December 1951, p. 20.

137

in discharging the duties of public office, 'we carry ill what possesses and carries us'.[3] Indeed, Montaigne explicitly addressed his advice to lawyers, bankers, and priests, whom he urged to serve others 'only by way of loan . . . the mind holding itself ever in repose . . . not without action, but without vexation'.[4]

However, many writers have warned of the dangers of professional detachment, which they say can have extremely destructive effects on oneself and others with whom one deals. For example, some have argued that employing systematic detachment from one's clients or patients tends to have a broader desensitising effect on the person in carrying out their role, whereby they can become generally unresponsive or even oblivious to the nature and extent of their clients' or patients' troubles. It has also been argued that individuals who regularly adopt a detached stance towards their clients or patients risk becoming desensitised to the plight of others in a more generalised way, outside the context of their professional role. Other writers focus on the phenomenon of an individual becoming detached or perhaps alienated from the individual's role itself, a phenomenon sometimes thought more damaging than detachment from one's clients or patients. Detachment from one's role has been thought to sever one's capacity for moral judgement from the practice of one's role, and so make it more likely that one's role-based actions will seriously harm or wrong others, because one becomes incapable of distinguishing legitimate role-based actions from those which are illegitimate. In this chapter we show how our virtue ethics approach to professional roles offers a promising analysis of the morality of professional detachment.

I PROFESSIONAL DETACHMENT AND ARISTOTELIAN PSYCHIC HARMONY

Aristotle's virtue ethics is well known for its emphasis on the importance of psychic harmony and personal integrity in a good human life, and this might be suggested as a reason for thinking that virtue ethics could provide a promising general account of how to avoid the above-mentioned perils of detachment. For Aristotle shows how important it is that we care about what we do and what we value, and he argues that a

---

[3] Michel de Montaigne, 'Of Husbanding your Will', quoted ibid.
[4] 'Of Husbanding your Will', in *The Complete Essays of Montaigne*, trans. Donald Frame, London, Hamish Hamilton, 1958, p. 770. Montaigne continues, 'the body receives the loads that are placed on it exactly according as they are; the mind often extends them and makes them heavier to its cost, giving them the measurements it sees fit' (p. 770).

good person will not only act in accordance with what is right, but will do so in an appropriate spirit. As Aristotle puts it, when our beliefs, desires, and emotions are in harmony, they 'speak with the same voice' about what we value.[5] On the other hand, people who lack this psychic harmony, says Aristotle, are 'at variance with themselves . . . for their soul is rent by faction, and one element in it . . . grieves when it abstains from certain acts, while the other part is pleased, and one draws them this way and the other that, as if they were pulling them in pieces . . . to be thus is the height of wretchedness'.[6]

Now, Aristotle's emphasis on the importance of psychic harmony suggests that detachment from one's clients or patients, or from one's role altogether, would be categorically rejected by Aristotelian virtue ethics, as something which a good person should avoid or overcome, so as to integrate their professional life properly with their personal life. And indeed, many of those contemporary medical and nursing ethicists inspired by a virtues-based approach have emphasised the fundamental importance of doctors and nurses forming deep emotional connections and sometimes even friendship-like personal relations with their patients, and of health professionals identifying psychologically with the respective goals of their professions. For example, James Drane argues that 'the best medicine is personalized medicine . . . in which there is real affect in the relationship between doctor and patient', like the affects characteristic of friendship, which Drane believes the doctor–patient relationship is appropriately modelled upon.[7] Likewise, Edmund Pellegrino and David

---

[5] Aristotle, *Nicomachean Ethics*, trans. W. D. Ross, Oxford, Oxford University Press, 1980, 1102b28.

[6] *Nicomachean Ethics* 1166b8–27.

[7] James F. Drane, *Becoming a Good Doctor: The Place of Virtue and Character in Medical Ethics*, Kansas City, Sheed and Ward, 1988, p. 77. See also Charles Fried, *Medical Experimentation: Personal Integrity and Social Policy*, Amsterdam, North Holland Publishing Co., 1974, who, as we noted in chapter 4, argues that it is appropriate for a doctor to see themselves 'as a person who stands to his patients in a relation that is at least analogous to that of friend or lover' (p. 76). The idea that doctors should develop deep emotional connections with their patients, in ways at least analogous to personal relationships, is taken furthest in Michael Balint's highly influential psychodynamic model of doctor–patient relationships (see Michael Balint, *The Doctor, His Patient, and the Illness*, 2nd edn, London, Pitman Medical Books, 1964). Balint explicitly rejects professional detachment by doctors and believes that many doctors are unduly wary of becoming 'over-involved' with their patients. For Balint argues that (as one commentator puts it) 'it is impossible to avoid getting involved, particularly in the long-term relationships of general practice . . . [and there is] benefit from such involvement. No longer is the doctor the outside observer. She is part of the system, using her whole person in the therapy. This involves a higher degree of involvement from the doctor' (Peter D. Toon, *What is Good General Practice? A Philosophical Study of the Concept of High Quality Medical Care*, London, Royal College of General Practitioners, 1994, p. 29). Nevertheless, the Balint approach still draws a distinction between emotionally involved professional relationships and personal relationships. So, for example, 'unlike trainee analysts undergoing therapy, the doctor is discouraged from using the [psychotherapy training] group to deal with personal problems outside the consultation' (Toon, *What is Good General Practice?*, p. 29).

Thomasma argue that a virtuous doctor would have warm personal concern for each of their patients, would suffer with them to some extent, and must be 'a person of integrity' overall.[8] Similarly, Sally Gadow argues that a nurse ought to participate in caring for patients 'with her *entire* self, using every dimension of the person as a resource in the professional relation',[9] while Nel Noddings claims that caring relationships, such as those between teachers and students or nurses and patients, require that one become affectively 'engrossed' in the other.[10] In a comparable way, a virtues-based approach to legal ethics that emphasised Aristotelian psychic harmony would naturally appear to favour models of lawyer–client relationships and of the lawyer's role which recommend that lawyers develop deep emotional and perhaps even personal connections with their clients. So, for example, it might be suggested that a lawyer could achieve the kind of psychic harmony characterised by Aristotle if they modelled their relations with clients upon relationships of friendship, as Charles Fried recommends.[11]

However, it is misguided for health professionals or lawyers to think

---

[8] See Edmund Pellegrino and David Thomasma, *The Virtues in Medical Practice*, New York, Oxford University Press, 1993, pp. 80, 132. See also Gregory E. Pence, *Ethical Options in Medicine*, Oradell, NJ, Medical Economics Company, 1980, pp. 199, 208; and Priscilla Alderson, 'Abstract Bioethics Ignores Human Emotions', *Bulletin of Medical Ethics* 68, May 1991, esp. p. 20.

[9] Sally Gadow, 'Existential Advocacy: Philosophical Foundations of Nursing', in Stuart Spicker and Sally Gadow (eds.), *Nursing Images and Ideals*, New York, Springer, 1980, pp. 90–1.

[10] Nel Noddings, *Caring: A Feminine Approach to Ethics and Moral Education*, Berkeley, University of California Press, 1984, e.g. pp. 17, 30, 35–7, 73–4, 179–80; and Nel Noddings, 'In Defense of Caring', *Journal of Clinical Ethics* 3, no. 1, Spring 1992, pp. 15–18. Similar views are expressed by Jean Watson, who urges nurses 'to form a union with the other person on a level that transcends the physical . . . [where] there is a freeing of both persons from their separation and isolation', *Nursing: Human Science and Human Care*, Norwalk, Appleton-Century-Crofts, 1985, p. 66. See also Patricia Benner, *From Novice to Expert: Excellence and Power in Clinical Nursing Practice*, Menlo Park, CA, Addison-Wesley, 1984; Patricia Benner and Judith Wrubel, *The Primacy of Caring: Stress and Coping in Health and Illness*, Menlo Park, CA, Addison-Wesley, 1989; Sarah T. Fry, 'Response to "Virtue Ethics, Caring and Nursing"', *Scholarly Inquiry for Nursing Practice* 2, no. 2, 1988; and Per Nortvedt, 'Sensitive Judgement: An Inquiry into the Foundations of Nursing Ethics', *Nursing Ethics* 5, no. 5, 1998, e.g. p. 390.

[11] Charles Fried, 'The Lawyer as Friend: The Moral Foundations of the Lawyer–Client Relation', *Yale Law Journal* 85, no. 8, July 1976. In this article, Fried argues that a good lawyer, like a good doctor, should be the client's 'special-purpose' friend. Thus, according to Fried, in model lawyer–client relationships 'the intensity of [the lawyer's] identification with the client's interests is the same [as that which one has towards a friend]' (p. 1072). (Note that later in the article, Fried claims that lawyers should not feel that their job requires them to adopt an extreme partiality towards their clients, whereby a lawyer becomes an all-purpose instrument of a client, regardless of the morality of their client's demands or their moral character. Fried comments that this form of partisanship is experienced all too commonly by lawyers in the US legal system, many of whom Fried says feel as though they are 'totally bought' by their clients, whereas the British barrister/solicitor split, along with government hiring of barristers to pursue all manner of litigation in the UK, 'accomplish[es] the many-sidedness I call for here' (p. 1088 n. 40).)

that avoiding psychic disharmony requires that they strive to form deep emotional and personal attachments to their patients or clients. For, as we demonstrate below, health professionals and lawyers can integrate their personal and professional lives, and so achieve the psychic harmony Aristotle thought characteristic of a virtuous person, without always seeking to develop the sorts of intimate and personal relationships with their patients and clients suggested by the above accounts. The psychic harmony of a virtuous professional does not require them always to eschew an attitude of detachment from their clients or patients.

Let us examine professional detachment (and its various forms) in more detail. Consider the following four cases of professional detachment. Nurses who look after critically ill patients in intensive care often speak of the need to maintain a level of emotional detachment from their patients. As one intensive-care nurse said:

> I just could not take care of him. I just felt too bad for him. I just felt so overwhelmed by all these losses, and I felt so bad for his wife, I cried every time I saw her . . . When you can't step back far enough not to feel so devastated yourself . . . you're one step too close to the patient.[12]

Lawyers too, it is often claimed, must engage in certain sorts of professional detachment if they are to perform their role well. So, for example, where the evidence against one's client in a criminal defence case looks fairly convincing, many criminal lawyers talk about the importance of remaining somewhat aloof from the fact that here they are most probably helping, say, a murderer get off the hook. Such detachment is important, they say, since otherwise one might find it difficult to be an effective advocate for one's client, and so one might undermine the legal rights of one's clients to effective legal support and defence.[13]

In certain other circumstances however, some lawyers have found the

---

[12] From M. C. Ramos, 'The Nurse–Patient Relationship: Themes and Variations', *Journal of Advanced Nursing* 17, 1992, quoted in Louise de Raeve, 'Caring Intensively', in David Greaves and Hugh Upton (eds.), *Philosophical Problems in Health Care*, Aldershot, Avebury, 1996, p. 11. Of course, nurses also maintain this distance in order to provide more effective care for their patients. It can, for example, be difficult (e.g. embarrassing) to attend to the intimate bodily needs of someone whom one cares about fairly deeply – as with a partner (and so the motivation and justification for the detachment can be patient-centred as well as agent-centred).

[13] See, for example, New York lawyer Gerald Shargel's comments on defending Mafia members accused of murder: 'I have to be divorced from the underlying acts, because a man who's charged with not only killing someone but disembowelling the person or cutting the person up into little pieces – it's a horrendous, horrendous act. But if my mind is influenced by that act then I can't be a formidable advocate for that person' (Shargel, quoted in Fredric Dannen, 'Defending the Mafia', *The New Yorker*, 21 February 1994, p. 72).

detachment needed for effective legal advocacy intolerable. For example, one insurance company lawyer tells of how, once he began to appreciate the plight of the seemingly innocent car accident victims he had been defending his employer against, he decided to leave the profession altogether and drive taxis instead. Fortunately, this lawyer subsequently rejoined the profession and worked for Legal Aid in a slum area of Chicago. He explains how in doing so he no longer felt the sort of psychic disharmony he had to endure at the insurance company:

My work and my life, they've become one. No longer am I schizophrenic.[14]

Similarly, prostitutes have often referred to both the need for and psychological costs of certain sorts of detachment from their clients. As one prostitute puts it: 'The role one plays when one's hustling has nothing to do with who you are . . . The call-girl ethic is very strong. You were the lowest of the low if you allowed yourself to feel anything with a trick . . . the way you maintain your integrity is by acting all the way through.'[15] However, in cautioning against such psychic splits and disharmony, she also tells how after many years' work, 'I became cold, I became hard, I became turned off, I became numb. Even when I wasn't hustling, I was a hustler. I don't think it's terribly different from somebody who works on the assembly line forty hours a week and comes home cut off, numb, dehumanized. People aren't built to switch on and off like water faucets.'[16]

These four examples illustrate a variety of forms of detachment. In all four cases, the agent performing the role is somewhat detached from their client or patient, or from other individuals affected by their role-based behaviour (as in the insurance company lawyer's attitude towards the car accident victims). However, it is possible for someone not only to be psychologically detached from others affected by their role-based conduct, but also psychologically detached or at least somewhat alienated from their *role* itself, as seems to be evident in the case of the insurance lawyer. In discussions of the moral psychology of professional roles, these notions of role-detachment and role-alienation are not always distinguished from the notion of being detached from others affected by one's role-based conduct, but these forms of detachment are

---

[14] Philip da Vinci, quoted by Studs Terkel, in *Working*, New York, Avon Books, 1975, p. 697.
[15] Roberta Victor, quoted ibid., pp. 92, 94. It is interesting to compare this with George Orwell's description of the Paris waiters he worked with in *Down and Out in Paris and London* (Harmondsworth, Penguin, 1940), for, by contrast, it was their emotional *identification* with their wealthy customers that enabled the waiters to integrate their work with themselves, and to have a sense of dignity (and indeed, nobility) in carrying out their work.   [16] Ibid., p. 102.

importantly distinct. This can be appreciated when we consider that someone who, for example, finds detachment from clients and other parties to be a necessary part of fulfilling their role adequately need not also be psychologically detached or alienated from their role itself. For instance, the intensive-care nurse who finds it necessary to be somewhat detached from her patients need not also be psychologically detached or alienated from her role – indeed, she might closely identify with her role as an intensive-care nurse, and so might take considerable personal pride in, say, the efficiency with which she carries out the often urgent demands of her work. Similarly, the criminal defence lawyer who is detached from his clients may or may not also be psychologically detached or alienated from his role itself. We will return to the notion of role-detachment in section 3. In what immediately follows we concentrate on the notion of being psychologically detached from others with whom one deals in one's professional role – i.e. one's patients or clients, or other parties affected by one's role-based behaviour.

Now, to begin our analysis of the morality of professional detachment from others, it will be helpful to isolate some significant feature that is common to the nature of the various typical cases. One significant feature of the different cases of such detachment, which seems assumed by and common to all the agents in the above-mentioned four examples, is that the agent performing the role takes it to be a requirement of their proper performance of the role that they depart from an attitude towards those they deal with which otherwise (or at least, in other familiar sorts of relations) would be a morally appropriate attitude to take towards those people. Thus, the intensive care nurse thinks it a requirement of the proper performance of her role that in some significant sense, she departs from an attitude of empathetic concern for the dying man and his suffering wife. The criminal lawyer thinks that his role demands that he not take on a concern from justice about the likely guilt of his client. The insurance lawyer, if he is to advocate his employer's interests properly, must not concern himself with the apparent innocence of certain motor-accident victims. And the prostitute takes it to be a requirement of her role that she should not form certain emotional connections with clients. In all these cases, then, the attitudes from which the professional or role occupant is seemingly required to depart are attitudes which it would be morally, or at least psychologically, appropriate for a morally healthy person to take towards those concerned. Thus, in ordinary circumstances and relations between people, it would be appropriate for a morally healthy person to take an attitude of empathetic concern for the suffering of the dying man and his wife; to be disturbed by the injustice of the apparent guilt of the murderer not being punished; to be concerned for the claims of innocent motor-accident victims; and to form certain emotional connections with their sexual partners.

This feature of the professional detachment cases – namely, departing from what would, in other familiar and ordinary circumstances, be an appropriate attitude for a morally healthy person to take towards those whom they deal with – is significant in at least two related ways. First, it suggests that there is a justificatory burden to be met by the professional countenancing such detachment, to provide some compelling moral reason why such departures should be thought acceptable. If performing the professional role seems to require such departures from what would ordinarily be a morally appropriate attitude to take, the agent has prima facie reason to be concerned about the moral acceptability of such departures.[17] And second, the focus on a prima facie case for a compelling justification for such departures provides a promising ground for explaining the appropriateness or significance of the apparent psychic disharmony involved in various cases of detachment. For circumstances where one is being called to depart from an attitude which a morally healthy person would ordinarily have would seem to provide precisely the sorts of conditions in which we should expect problems of psychic disharmony to arise. Moreover, framing our understanding of the import of the experience of psychic disharmony for the morality of professional detachment in this way should be helpful, since, against various writers,[18] the experience of psychic disharmony itself need not show a moral failing in one's role. Rather, the latter will properly be shown by a failure to meet the above-mentioned justificatory burden. At best, the experience of psychic disharmony may (perhaps often) signal that such a failure exists in carrying out one's role. Let us now turn to providing an account that will address these two concerns over the justifiability of professional detachment and the significance of psychic disharmony in this context.

---

[17] Placing the justificatory burden squarely on those whose detachment would depart from what would ordinarily be thought an appropriate attitude to take toward those one deals with also seems a particularly appropriate way to frame a proper understanding of this issue, given our current times, where all sorts of workplace role-occupants – for example even real-estate agents and other salespeople – seem to be encouraged to think of themselves as 'professionals'.

[18] See, e.g., Andreas Eshete, 'Does a Lawyer's Character Matter?', in David Luban (ed.), *The Good Lawyer: Lawyers' Roles and Lawyers' Ethics*, Totowa, Rowman and Allanheld, 1984; and Gerald J. Postema, 'Moral Responsibility in Professional Ethics', *New York University Law Review* 55, no. 1, April 1980.

2 VIRTUE ETHICS AND PROFESSIONAL DETACHMENT

In our view, the moral status of a person's professional detachment from others in carrying out their role is importantly determined by whether their detachment serves the goal of their profession, and by the appropriateness of that professional goal itself. Our account of the justifiability of professional detachment can be stated as follows. Professional detachment from others can be justified, and so need not be morally defective, if and only if: (1) a particular professional role can be shown to serve the goals of that profession; (2) psychological detachment in carrying out that role helps one meet its requirements and so uphold those goals; and (3) these goals, all things considered, serve morally worthwhile ends. Thus, where the professional goals that one's detachment serves are themselves morally questionable or where the goals of one's profession *are* morally worthwhile but one's detachment does not help one meet those goals, such detachment should be regarded as morally defective.

In earlier chapters we argued that a virtue ethics approach to the evaluation of actions makes it a particularly appropriate ethical framework for capturing the distinctive nature and value of various professional roles. According to the Aristotelian virtue ethics we favour, acting well is determined by reference to what counts as excellence in performing various functions which are characteristic of a *humanly* flourishing life. And just as what counts as acting well in ordinary life can be judged by reference to characteristic human functions, so too what counts as acting well in the context of a professional role can be regarded as importantly determined by how well that role functions in serving the goals of the profession, and how those goals are connected with characteristic human activities. Thus, we have argued that a good profession, on this approach, would be one which involves a commitment to a key human good, and the justifiability of a particular role within that profession would be determined by how well it serves the key human goods which form the proper goals of that profession. We will now indicate how this sort of approach can also help bring out and explain why some forms of professional detachment in the service of one's role are morally defective, while other forms of professional detachment can be reconciled with the proper practice of one's role. In doing so, we hope to show how Aristotle's notion of psychic harmony can be plausibly applied to the problem of professional detachment, but only when supplemented by the functional account of particular virtuous dispositions given elsewhere in Aristotle's ethics.

First, the detachment that intensive-care nurses often report it necessary to maintain towards their patients. Such detachment might at first glance be thought somewhat disturbing, and some nurses working in this area seem indeed to have been troubled by it. However, many intensive-care nurses have been able to reconcile such detachment with the good practice of their role by seeing how nursing's proper goals of patient care, comfort, and welfare are well served by nurses remaining somewhat emotionally detached from their patients in this context.[19] Since many intensive-care patients are unlikely to survive, a nurse who maintains certain sorts of psychological detachment from critically ill patients, such as those referred to by the above-mentioned nurse, would generally be able to provide more effective care for such patients than would a nurse who allowed herself to become more emotionally involved with such patients and their plight.[20]

Similarly, some criminal defence lawyers who help, say, gangsters whom they have strong reason to believe guilty of murder to defeat a strong prosecution case may feel troubled by the psychological distance

---

[19] Of course (contrary to what Howard Curzer seems to suggest, in 'Is Care a Virtue for Health Care Professionals?', *Journal of Medicine and Philosophy* 18, no. 1, 1993), this sort of emotional detachment would not necessarily be appropriate for health professionals in other areas of their work, such as dealing with patients who have short-term acute illnesses. However, interestingly, where patients with intolerable conditions make a request for their life to be ended through an act of euthanasia, it seems of the utmost importance here that the doctor who is to perform such an act be emotionally *engaged* to a significant degree with their patient. As the authors of a recent Dutch study of the practice of euthanasia in the Netherlands report: 'Many respondents mentioned that an emotional bond is required for euthanasia, and this may be one reason why euthanasia was more common in general practice, where doctor and patient have often known each other for years and the doctor has shared part of the patient's suffering' (Paul van der Maas et al., 'Euthanasia and other Medical Decisions Concerning the End of Life', *The Lancet* 338, 14 September 1991, p. 673). Here the depth of the doctor's emotional engagement with the patient that is possible where euthanasia is carried out within an established doctor–patient relationship seems, at least for many patients, necessary for the patient to accept that the doctor has sufficient understanding of their plight to be trusted, both in their advice about what courses of action might be left and, where nothing else is to be done, to carry out the patient's request for euthanasia. (This also indicates that Roger Crisp's suggestion, that the conflict some see between euthanasia and the proper goals of the medical profession can be overcome by employing a specialist 'thanatologist' to carry out euthanasia, might be found unacceptable by significant numbers of patients, since such a person would not be acting within a long-established relationship with the patient. See Roger Crisp, 'A Good Death: Who Best to Bring it?', *Bioethics* 1, no. 1, 1987.)

[20] Note that intensive-care nurses should not be so detached from their patients that they are entirely uninvolved with them emotionally – as, for example, the investigators of clinical trials with intensive-care patients might be – since this would be likely to hinder their ability to respond adequately to their patients' needs. As de Raeve ('Caring Intensively', pp. 19–20) puts it: 'there can be, indeed often has to be, an oil and water mixture of the elements of attachment and detachment found in professional nursing care . . . It is entirely proper for nursing care to have as its purpose patient recovery from (or adjustment to) illness. To this end it is necessary for nurses to find a way of caring about their patients in order to care for them well but the extent of that caring about is properly limited.'

they need to maintain between themselves and the outcomes they secure for their clients. However, where it can be demonstrated that a lawyer who represents such clients and carries out their role with this detachment is better able to promote the proper goals of the criminal law, then the lawyer's professional detachment can be reconciled with the good performance of their role. So, for example, it is often argued that the goals of a just criminal legal system are well served by the presumption that a person is innocent of a crime until proven guilty beyond reasonable doubt, and that the zealous advocacy of their client which the criminal lawyer's detachment helps them to provide supports that presumption because it forces the prosecution to find and present compelling evidence of their client's guilt, thereby on the whole reducing the chances of convicting an innocent person. Thus, in seeing how the maintenance of professional detachment helps one carry out one's role, and how one's role thus performed is integral to serving the morally worthwhile goals of one's profession, one can properly become reconciled to a level of professional detachment in one's work, thereby dispel the apparent psychic disharmony initially presented by such a case, and render such detachment consistent with a level of professional integrity.[21]

However, for different reasons, this sort of reconciliation strategy cannot be so plausibly used to vindicate either the insurance company lawyer's psychological detachment from the plaintiffs whose claims he was employed to challenge or a claim that the prostitute performs a professional role requiring detachment of the above-mentioned sort. In the case of the insurance lawyer, while this lawyer's detachment from

---

[21] See David Luban, *Lawyers and Justice: An Ethical Study*, Princeton, Princeton University Press, 1988, p. 145. Tim Dare (in 'Virtue Ethics and Legal Ethics', *Victoria University of Wellington Law Review* 28, no. 1, March 1998, at pp. 154–5) also argues that if a lawyer can appreciate this derivative justification of their role, this can help prevent their sensitivity to the moral costs of their role and of their profession from becoming 'atrophied' (as Postema, 'Moral Responsibilities in Professional Ethics', p. 80, claims is likely), and so can preserve a sort of derivative moral integrity for the lawyer's role.

Note that notwithstanding this functional justification of professional detachment, one ought nevertheless to guard against such professional detachment becoming corrosive. Robert J. Lifton argues that a doctor's necessary distance from cutting up corpses may itself become corrupting (see Robert Jay Lifton, *The Nazi Doctors: Medical Killing and the Psychology of Genocide*, New York, Basic Books, 1986, p. 427). Robert Rader vividly describes the personal costs of the psychological detachment he developed in learning to become a criminal defence lawyer: '[I] learned more than I wanted to about having clients. Frankly, I didn't like it. Too much pressure. Maybe I just never wanted to "help" people, but I hated having other people's lives as part of my responsibility. Things I can't control . . . I've achieved detachment. But at what cost? Am I now a heartless, cynical lawyer? Yeah, but now I don't care . . . I don't have the time to care' (Robert Rader, 'Confessions of Guilt: A Clinic Student's Reflections on Representing Indigent Criminal Defendants', *Clinical Law Review* 1, Fall 1994, pp. 341–2). See also Barbara Babcock, 'Defending the Guilty', *Cleveland State Law Review* 32, 1983–4.

the plight of plaintiffs certainly helped him carry out his role, and so served this purpose, the particular nature of his role here as an insurance company lawyer cannot be shown to serve the morally worthwhile goals of the legal profession. For in requiring him to defend the company zealously against *all* claims, and so deprive innocent car-accident victims of their legitimate claims, the insurance company is assigning him role requirements that run contrary to the value of justice which constitutes a central goal of the legal profession. And, indeed, it was precisely because his detachment could not be construed as serving the proper goals of his profession that this lawyer found it and his role intolerable.[22] And, while one might make a plausible case for the role of the prostitute requiring emotional detachment from their clients, and indeed, also that such detachment does not violate the proper ends of their role, it is not so plausible, at least in normal circumstances, to claim that the prostitute's proper performance of their role serves morally worthwhile ends, or ends that are partly constitutive of a humanly flourishing life.[23]

It is also worth noting that while the lawyer overcame the detachment he suffered at the insurance company and was able to reconcile his professional role with his own values by working for Legal Aid, nevertheless, like the intensive-care nurses, he thought it important not to become *too* emotionally involved with the clients he then took on, lest he suffered from emotional 'burnout'.[24] Thus, both the Legal Aid lawyer and the intensive-care nurses were able to integrate their professional roles with their own values, whilst maintaining a degree of emotional detachment from their clients or patients. This is further confirmation of how psychic harmony or wholeness in professional life is more appropriately attained along the lines of the functional account we have sketched, rather than through aiming to forge deep personal relationships with clients or

---

[22] Indeed, he explains that it was through his perception of the injustices done to his new clients in his subsequent job at Legal Aid that he was able to overcome his disharmony and practise law wholeheartedly: 'Here you're aware of the suffering of your client. You know the type of landlord he has. You know what his apartment looks like. You know the pressure he's under. It makes you all the more committed' (da Vinci, quoted in Terkel, *Working*, p. 697).

[23] It is, in fact, often claimed that prostitution does provide worthwhile social service, or even has valuable therapeutic features. Of course, we would not deny that these ends might in certain circumstances attain some moral importance; however, in order to vindicate the detachment which prostitutes find necessary in carrying out their role, these ends would have to attain such significance as to outweigh the psychological costs involved. The case for prostitution gaining such significance might be stronger in certain extreme circumstances, for example wartime, in which prostitutes could be viewed as acting in the national interest. For a discussion of whether prostitution can sometimes be legitimate sexual therapy (and of the incursions into intimacy that prostitutes have to endure), see Debra Satz, 'Markets in Women's Sexual Labor', *Ethics* 106, no. 1, October 1995. [24] See da Vinci, in Terkel, *Working*, p. 698.

patients in every case (as some proponents of virtue- or care-based ethics, cited above, have urged lawyers and health professionals to do).

We have argued that psychological detachment in carrying out the requirements of a professional or occupational role is morally defensible only in cases where such detachment helps an individual uphold the overarching goals of their profession or occupation, and where those goals serve morally worthwhile ends. Thus, psychological detachment from clients and from other parties affected by one's role-based actions is not intrinsically valuable, and it is therefore a mistake to see such detachment as a cornerstone of professionalism.[25] Indeed, it is partly through retaining a capacity to empathise with the plight of clients and other parties that professionals can remain adequately sensitised to circumstances where their role-based actions might violate the proper goal of their profession. So, for example, it was the insurance lawyer's growing emotional appreciation of how his role-based behaviour affected innocent car accident victims that aroused his moral misgivings about the legitimacy of the role assigned to him. And where (as discussed in chapter 5) a defence lawyer in a rape trial knowingly misleads a jury by presenting the counselling records of a woman the lawyer believes is likely to be a genuine rape victim, the lawyer's confidence in the moral permissibility (indeed, on some views, obligatoriness) of their conduct here seems in many cases to be shielded from their critical scrutiny by their being psychologically detached from the woman they thereby impugn and humiliate.[26] Thus, accounts which confer value on professional detachment for its own sake risk depriving practitioners of a crucial means of determining *when* carrying out their role violates the proper overarching value or goal of their profession, and so oversteps the

[25] Also, as Arthur Applbaum argues (in *Ethics for Adversaries: The Morality of Roles in Public and Professional Life*, Princeton, Princeton University Press, 1999), using the figures of Charles-Henri Sanson – who served as the Executioner of Paris both before and after the fall of the monarchy in the French Revolution – and the character of Stevens the butler in Kazuo Ishiguro's *The Remains of the Day* (New York, Vintage, 1989), individuals who see their indifference to the moral status of the ends they serve as a mark of their 'professionalism' grotesquely misunderstand the way that morality bears upon their role.

[26] See Simon Bronitt and Bernadette McSherry, 'The Use and Abuse of Counseling Records in Sexual Assault Trials: Reconstructing the "Rape Shield"?' *Criminal Law Forum* 8, no. 2, 1997, esp. pp. 5–9. For discussions of other examples of a defence lawyer's emotional detachment from the plaintiffs they opposed seeming to prevent the lawyer from seeing that their role-based conduct violated their overall professional goal of justice, see the account by Justice Howard Nathan (at a panel on Legal Ethics, at the Australasian Association for Professional and Applied Ethics Fourth Annual Conference, Melbourne, 1997), where he seems to regret the manner in which he handled a defence brief in a rape trial involving a fourteen-year-old girl, summarised in Kerri Elgar, 'A Night at the Confessional', *Law Institute Journal* (Law Institute of Victoria) November 1997, p. 14; and Heidi Li Feldman, 'Codes and Virtues: Can Lawyers be Good Ethical Deliberators?', *Southern California Law Review* 69, March 1996, pp. 930–1.

boundaries of legitimate role-based behaviour and becomes, all things considered, unjustified. It is through regulating their detachment from others with a commitment to the proper goal of the profession, and thus retaining their capacity to empathise with those whom their role-based behaviour affects, that a practitioner is able to remain properly sensitised to the sorts of experiences by clients and others which can signal that the practitioner's behaviour may be violating the very goal of the profession which they represent.[27] An appropriately regulated detachment towards one's clients helps curb excesses carried out in the name of one's role.

At this point it might be suggested that enduring some level of detachment and perhaps psychic disharmony is simply the small price a professional must inevitably expect to pay given the nature and magnitude of the goods that they have embraced.[28] This might be put as a reason for thinking that Aristotle's ideal of psychic harmony and moral integration is both unrealistic and undesirable. On our account, however, an appropriate level of detachment from one's clients can be reconciled with psychic harmony, through an appreciation of how one's role serves the proper goals of one's profession. But whether or not such detachment is in this way integral to certain professional roles, it is sometimes argued that serving weighty social values requires individuals to allow their characters to become what we would ordinarily think of as morally *deformed*. For example, Montaigne argues that

[I]n every government there are necessary offices which are not only abject but also vicious. Vices find their place in it and are employed for sewing our society together, as are poisons for the preservation of our health. If they become excusable, inasmuch as we need them and the common necessity effaces their true quality, we still must let this part be played by the more vigorous and less fearful citizens, who sacrifice their honor and their conscience, as those ancients sacrificed their life, for the good of their country. We who are weaker, let us take roles that are both easier and less hazardous. The public welfare requires that a man betray and lie and massacre; let us resign this commission to more obedient and suppler people.[29]

---

[27] In 'The Conscience of Huckleberry Finn' (*Philosophy* 49, 1974), Jonathan Bennett illustrates powerfully how the maintenance of an active capacity for basic human sympathy and compassion helps serve as an important check on an overzealous commitment to principles, which otherwise might lead one to become inhumane.

[28] We thank Jennifer Radden for raising this point with us.

[29] Michel de Montaigne, 'Of the Useful and the Honorable', quoted in Applbaum, *Ethics for Adversaries*, p. 1. See also Aristotle: 'the more he [the brave man] is possessed of virtue in its entirety and the happier he is, the more he will be pained at the thought of death; for life is best worth living for such a man, and he is knowingly losing the greatest goods, and this is painful . . . But it is quite possible that the best soldiers may not be men of this sort but those who are less brave but have no other good; for these are ready to face danger, and they sell their life for trifling gains' (*Nicomachean Ethics* III.10.1117b10–17).

But although, as we discussed in chapter 5, the significance of matters of state and the exigencies of public life can undoubtedly sometimes necessitate that professionals develop certain character-traits that would be vices outside that context, it does not follow that the character-traits which a virtuous professional in such roles would have should be entirely determined by the goals of their profession. No matter how great the goals served, the character of a virtuous professional must also be governed to some extent by broad-based moral standards. So, for example, while the goal of health warrants doctors' developing a reliable disposition to save patients whose lives are endangered, doctors should not save patients' lives out of a medical beneficence which is unchecked by any dispositions to observe the side-constraints of respect for patient autonomy and justice in the allocation of health resources.

3 ROLE-DETACHMENT AND KANTIAN ACCOUNTS OF MORAL CHARACTER IN PROFESSIONAL LIFE

Let us now turn from the notion of being detached from one's clients and other parties to the idea of a professional being psychologically detached from their role itself. In the previous two chapters we critically discussed several utilitarian and Kantian arguments designed to show how certain conventional role demands of doctors and lawyers would turn out to be compatible with broad-based moral standards. We also outlined, in chapter 3, how virtue ethics can provide a plausible framework for justifying certain professional roles, and we have indicated in the current chapter how this framework can also be used to justify a professional's psychological detachment from patients and clients in certain contexts. In this final section we consider the nature of moral character in the context of professional roles, in the light of the various practical limitations of these strategies for moralising professional roles. We demonstrate how, in an environment of uncertainty over the ultimate moral justifiability of the demands of one's professional role, a Kantian account of moral character can encourage a pernicious and self-deceptive form of role-detachment that a virtue ethics approach is able to avoid.

Many philosophers have suggested that professionals should handle cases of prima facie conflict between the conventional demands of their role and broad-based moral standards by applying some form of 'reconciliation strategy', through which some conventional role demands might be shown to be compatible with, and indeed perhaps even expressions of, broad-based moral standards. In thus reconciling certain role

demands with broader moral standards, these strategies are also presented as ways of enabling an individual to integrate various prima facie
morally questionable demands of their role with their moral character,
and so as important ways in which a professional can come to regard the
institutional actions they bring about as their own. For example, as we
saw in chapter 5, Tim Dare puts forward the Kantian argument that
when a criminal defence lawyer succeeds in, say, gaining an acquittal for
a client who they have strong reason to believe is actually guilty, the
lawyer should see themselves as upholding the rule of public reason:

> Law is an essential part of the effort to secure stable and just political commu-
> nity between the advocates of diverse views of the good . . . [O]n the procedu-
> ral account the various law jobs are extraordinarily important in pluralist
> communities and hence are ones in which lawyers can and should take pride
> . . . [L]awyers . . . should be brought to appreciate the significance of the social
> roles they serve, and to understand and take pride in fulfilling the duties which
> flow from those roles.[30]

Similarly, Gerald Postema argues that a morally responsible lawyer will
regard the conventional demands of their role not as entirely predeter-
mined, but rather in terms of a 'recourse role', whereby they reflect on
the proper institutional objectives of the role, and fulfil only those conventional demands which are consistent with those objectives. In this
way, suggests Postema, 'a recourse role conception . . . integrat[es] to a
significant degree the moral personality of the individual with the performance of role responsibilities'.[31] These strategies are presented as
ways of recognising and acknowledging the moral validity of such role
demands, and are seen as giving the sort of bindingness which is usually
thought to be created by making an explicit contract or promise *de novo*.

Such strategies are undoubtedly useful, and serve as a timely reminder
not to prejudge the moral status of role demands and the actions of those
who fulfil them. Nevertheless, it is important to acknowledge that there
can be significant practical limitations on the application of such strategies to particular roles and to the individuals who occupy them.[32] It may

[30] Tim Dare, '"The Secret Courts of Men's Hearts": Legal Ethics and Harper Lee's *To Kill a Mockingbird*', in Kim Economides (ed.), *Ethical Challenges to Legal Education and Conduct*, Oxford, Hart Publishing, 1998, p. 57. (Dare cites John Rawls' 'Two Concepts of Rules', *Philosophical Review* 64, 1955 as providing a similar kind of strategy.) This sort of rationale for the lawyer's role is also given by Susan Wolf, 'Ethics, Legal Ethics, and the Ethics of Law', in David Luban (ed.), *The Good Lawyer: Lawyers' Roles and Lawyers' Ethics*, Totowa, Rowman and Allanheld, 1984.
[31] Postema, 'Moral Responsibility', p. 83. See also Michael Bayles, *Professional Ethics*, 2nd edn, Belmont, Wadsworth, 1989, p. 24; and Richard Wasserstrom, 'Roles and Morality', in Luban, *The Good Lawyer*, pp. 30–1.
[32] And our discussion in chapter 3 should not be taken as suggesting that determining the moral justifiability of one's role is a straightforward matter in any given case.

well, for instance, be very difficult for an individual to be in a position to be able to determine whether or not their carrying out the conventional demands of their professional role is, all things considered, morally justified.[33] Thus, consider again the role demands of the criminal defence lawyer. An individual carrying out such a role might find that while the demand, say, to advocate their client's case zealously is in general reconcilable with broader moral demands of justice, they might find it difficult to reconcile with justice what this demand is usually taken to require in certain particular cases – for example where, as we explained in chapter 5, criminal defence lawyers in rape trials commonly see it as incumbent on them to humiliate the complainant by presenting to the court the subpoenaed counselling records of the complainant, even where the lawyer has good reason to believe that she is innocent.[34] Or, while a criminal defence lawyer might perhaps accept that a reconciliation strategy of the kind suggested by Dare provides a sound justification of various conventional role demands *in theory*, they might (as we suggested in chapter 5) find such a strategy too idealised to justify their role demands in the actual legal system that they work in, where these role demands are so influenced by political expediency and other extrinsic factors that it is hardly plausible to claim that they express the 'rule of public reason'. Another problem is that the results of such reconciliation strategies can be indeterminate, not because the strategies are too general or unrealistic, but because they might provide equally reasonable arguments for diametrically opposed obligations in a particular role. For example, reasonable rights-based arguments exist both for and against the claim that doctors treating HIV-positive patients are morally obligated to breach confidentiality to protect third parties at risk of infection, in circumstances where those parties would not otherwise be aware of this risk.[35]

And, in the face of this uncertainty about the overall moral justifiability of fulfilling one's conventional role demands, there can be a strong

[33] So too, it can be difficult to see how 'systemic' justifications of *personal* roles bear on the justifiability of some particular relationship of *mine*. For example, I may well *know* that, generally speaking, the practice of friendship results in all sorts of good consequences – as Frank Jackson argues (in 'Decision-Theoretic Consequentialism and the Nearest and Dearest Objection', *Ethics* 101, no. 3, April 1991), friendship helps us to be better positioned to understand and help certain specified others, and facilitates social interaction; but such justifications do not speak to whether I ought, qua friendship, to maintain or terminate *this* relationship now. There is something of an action-guidingness problem here.

[34] To be bound here by the fact that the role demands are reconcilable *in general* with justice seems analogous to the well-known criticism of rule-worship which is commonly levelled at rule-utilitarianism.

[35] Thus, as Michael Hardimon acknowledges, 'different individuals occupying the same contractual role may reasonably disagree about the contents of their roles': 'Role Obligations', *Journal of Philosophy* 91, no. 7, July 1994, p. 355.

temptation to withdraw one's conscience (or even one's sense of self) from the institutional role-based actions one carries out, and to come to regard one's moral character as constituted by what one does *outside* one's professional role (in, for example, the ways one conducts one's personal and family relations), where the moral status of what one does may well seem more transparent and within one's control. In this environment of moral uncertainty about the overall defensibility of one's professional doings, a Kantian account of moral character, we suggest, has the potential to encourage an alarming level of self-deception about the nature of one's involvement in such actions. A virtue ethics approach to moral character can better handle this moral uncertainty in professional life, for while it may be unclear in some cases whether one's conventional role demands are, all things considered, morally justified, virtue ethics can nevertheless recognise that having internalised those demands and carrying them out are things that individuals can reasonably be held morally accountable for.

The self-deception that Kantian accounts of moral character can be seen to foster is not only due to the perceived *moral uncertainty* of professional roles, but also facilitated by a tendency amongst some professionals to deflect evaluations of the outcomes they bring about through their roles to *the institution* within which they act, whether they regard the outcome for a client as morally uncertain or as clearly morally wrong. Montaigne's endorsement of this attitude captures it well:

I have been able to concern myself with public affairs without moving the length of my nail from myself, and give myself to others without taking anything from myself . . . The mayor and Montaigne have always been two people, clearly separated. There's no reason why a lawyer or a banker should not recognize the knavery that is part of his vocation. An honest man is not responsible for the vices or the stupidity of his calling, and need not refuse to practise them. They are customs in his country and there is profit in them. A man must live in the world and avail himself of what he finds there.[36]

Few these days would seriously defend the suggestion that a professional is shielded by their role from *moral responsibility* for carrying out role demands which they acknowledge are irreconcilably vicious. Nonetheless, we find it difficult to give up the idea that the sorts of evaluations properly made of individuals for discharging the conventional demands of a professional role may be importantly different from the sorts of evaluations appropriately made of individuals for actions they

---

[36] Michel de Montaigne, 'Of Husbanding your Will', quoted in Curtis, 'The Ethics of Advocacy', p. 20.

perform outside the context of such a role. A typical context where this arises is in legal practice, particularly with lawyers working within adversarial legal systems. For example, criminal defence lawyers commonly talk of their misgivings about what 'the adversarial system' requires them to do. Thus, a retired judge recently spoke of how the adversarial system enabled him, as a young barrister defending a man accused of raping a fourteen-year-old girl, to secure an acquittal for his client, even though this barrister at some point seemed to realize that she was telling the truth:

> In front of a jury . . . I say . . . 'She didn't complain. Did you think she wasn't provocative . . . ? She was flaunting herself at the baths!' This was standard defence at the time . . . That system, with my skills, allowed the most appalling injustice, as far as that girl was concerned, to go unrequited. What sort of system is this? [37]

Examples of this kind abound.[38] Implicit in this sort of talk is the suggestion that when someone is wronged as a result of a lawyer's fulfilling the conventional demands of their role, it is not *the lawyer* themselves who wrongs that individual but rather *the institution* within which the lawyer's particular role demands are located – here, the adversarial system of litigation. Some may even go so far as to claim that the lawyer cannot in any way be held *morally responsible* for whatever they do in such circumstances. Commonly, however, the suggestion is not this[39] – the lawyer's zealous actions in defending their client are, after all, voluntary and intentional, and so they are not claiming to be acting as an automaton. Rather, the suggestion being made here is that whatever wrongs occur through the lawyer discharging their conventionally defined role are to be laid at the door not of the lawyer but of the institution itself. Thus, in dealing with circumstances where a lawyer's conduct during a trial knowingly causes harm to specific persons, Charles Fried distinguishes between wrongs *personally* committed by the lawyer in the course of their

---

[37] Justice Howard Nathan, quoted in Elgar, 'A Night at the Confessional', p. 14.

[38] See, for example, New York criminal defence lawyer Gerald Shargel's account of his attitude if his advocacy enables a guilty person to go free (as reported in Fredric Dannen, 'Defending the Mafia', *The New Yorker*, 21 February 1994, esp. p. 72). See also the examples discussed by David Luban, 'The Adversary System Excuse', in Luban, *The Good Lawyer*. For examples from other professions, see Michael Quinlan, 'Ethics in the Public Service', *Governance* 6, 1993, and Applbaum's critique in *Ethics for Adversaries* of Quinlan's endorsement of the 'person-neutrality' of roles in the British civil service.

[39] This is a corrective to Postema's characterisation (p. 80) of this kind of view, where he says that advocates of this kind of view of the lawyer's role are, in effect, advocating that a lawyer should regard their role in a manner akin to a spectator at an unfortunate traffic accident (i.e. regret as a bystander). Such a characterisation (involving 'bad faith') goes too far towards passivity really to capture the lawyers' attitude that we are focusing on here.

professional activities and *institutional* wrongs brought about by the rules of the legal system.[40]

Many professionals find Montaigne's role-detachment strategy very attractive, and the sort of stance implicit in the ex-barrister's account of his actions in the rape trial is commonly taken by criminal defence lawyers seeking to achieve the separation of moral character from various role-based actions as recommended by Montaigne.[41] Indeed, in his speech to graduating students at Harvard Law School (referred to at the beginning of this chapter), Charles Curtis explicitly invokes Montaigne in advising lawyers to recognise the 'knavery' inherent in their calling and to treat litigation like a game, from which the moral self is detached: 'Never blame a lawyer for treating litigation as a game.'[42] Other writers have brought out vividly how the cultivation of such detachment from one's role can be extremely damaging, both to oneself and to others.[43] And Gerald Postema has shown well how the use of

[40] See Fried, 'The Lawyer as Friend', pp. 1084–6. There are certain obvious limits to any such suggestion of a transfer of reprehensibility from the individual to the institution. Nobody would regard an individual as exempt from moral assessment for implementing clearly racist role demands (as in South Africa under apartheid), or, particularly, for carrying out the dictates of an institution whose very *goal* was an evil one (as with the 'racial hygiene' eugenics in Nazi medicine). Nevertheless, doubts often persist about the moral assessability of individuals who carry out less grievously wrong (by ordinary standards) role demands within an institution that aims to serve some great *good*, as the legal system does with justice.

[41] See, for example, the criminal defence lawyers described by Charles Ogletree, 'Beyond Justifications: Seeking Motivations to Sustain Public Defenders', *Harvard Law Review* 106, 1993. See also Lisa J. McIntyre, *The Public Defender: The Practice of Law in the Shadows of Repute*, Chicago, University of Chicago Press, 1987; and Seymour Wishman, *Confessions of a Criminal Lawyer*, New York, Times Books, 1981, pp. 238–9. An illuminating first-hand discussion can be found in Rader, 'Confessions of Guilt'. We see later, however, that barrister Nathan, 'after years of contemplation and education', and defence lawyer Wishman, eventually came to reject any such Montaignean stance.   [42] Curtis, 'The Ethics of Advocacy', p. 21.

[43] Andreas Eshete discusses how lawyers working within adversarial legal systems might deal with their development of various 'unsavory' professional traits such as deceitfulness, unfairness, callousness, and ill-will towards others, which he suggests those systems tend to breed in lawyers. Eshete suggests that lawyers commonly find it necessary to make attempts to shield their character from such traits and the actions they motivate, by creating a separate 'legal self' to distance themselves from their role as a lawyer and from the causes of the clients whom they represent; but he argues that the attempt to insulate one's character from those negative traits enables those traits to become entrenched and to persist without adequate scrutiny from one's moral character (see Eshete, 'Does a Lawyer's Character Matter?', esp. pp. 274–6, 279–80). Gerald Postema also draws attention to the detrimental effects of lawyers' distancing themselves from their professional roles. Postema argues forcefully that lawyers who pursue the detachment strategies advocated by Curtis and Montaigne are likely to become desensitised to circumstances in which role-based actions that might appear justified by reference to their role alone are in fact all things considered immoral, for a lawyer who managed to attain this level of detachment would effectively sever their capacity for ordinary moral judgement from their professional actions as a lawyer, leaving themselves with a distorted grasp of broader moral questions raised by their work – or perhaps even a 'deep moral skepticism' about such broader issues (see Postema, 'Moral

psychological detachment from one's role as a means of evading moral responsibility involves a form of Sartrean 'bad faith'.[44] Our focus here, however, is on how the attractiveness of such detachment strategies makes certain accounts of moral character more problematic. The enduring appeal of Montaigne's role-detachment strategy for sidestepping moral condemnation for what one does to others in the name of one's role creates a hazard in the path of attempts to develop and apply a compelling account of the nature of moral character in the context of professional roles. But these detachment strategies find an ally in Kantian accounts of moral character and their constructivist view of the self.

Kant praises the self-sufficiency he says we can achieve only by rising above or repudiating heteronomous influences, such as our natural temperament and our inclinations emanating from the phenomenal world:

Responsibility in Professional Ethics', esp. pp. 73–81; and Gerald Postema, 'Self-Image, Integrity, and Professional Responsibility', in Luban, *The Good Lawyer*, pp. 301–2, 309–10). A more extreme example of the destructive effects of role-detachment is provided in Robert Jay Lifton's well-known account of the Nazi doctors. Lifton demonstrates in chilling detail how the Nazi doctors' psychological detachment from the plight of the concentration-camp prisoners enabled these doctors ruthlessly to select which of the many arriving prisoners would be sent to the gas chambers, and to perform hideous experiments on some of the remaining prisoners without their consent. Lifton describes how the Nazi doctors in Auschwitz distanced themselves from their murderous actions by developing a separate 'Auschwitz-self', which they saw themselves as acting through when they carried out their killings and their experiments. Lifton calls such detachment 'doubling', and says that 'the ideal doctor remains warm and humane by keeping [any such] "doubling" to a minimum' (Lifton, p. 427). Note that, as Lifton explains, 'doubling' is less extreme than 'dissociation' or 'splitting', where (unlike the Auschwitz-self which the Nazi doctors developed) the 'split-off' element 'ceases to respond to the environment or else is in some way at odds with the remainder of the self'(p. 419), as with a segmented-off automatism.

[44] See Postema, 'Moral Responsibility in Professional Ethics', pp. 74–9; and Postema, 'Self-Image, Integrity, and Professional Responsibility', pp. 289, 299–306. Eshete also argues that a lawyer who makes a claim to role-detachment in an attempt to screen their character from the unsavoury legal traits bred in them by the adversarial system is being disingenuous or even engaging in outright self-deception: 'the lawyer's claim to be merely acting rings hollow: there is no way in which the official words and deeds can be fastened to the role [such that the lawyer's own character escapes unscathed]' ('Does a Lawyer's Character Matter?', p. 276).

Another strategy sometimes employed by professionals to evade moral responsibility for their role-based behaviour is simply to redescribe their action in terms that seem morally unobjectionable, where the latter act-description is intended to squeeze out the former. A famous example of such a ploy is found in the case of *Annesley* v. *Anglesea* (1743). When the murder prosecution of James Annesley for shooting another man begins to falter – as the shooting appears to be accidental – the Earl of Anglesea instructs his lawyer James Giffard, who is prosecuting Annesley, to make an offer of £10,000 to have Annesley hanged (as Annesley is the Earl's rival for the Anglesea estate, and its rightful heir). When this offer is later discovered and Giffard himself is put on the stand for making it, he is asked: 'Did you not apprehend it to be a bad purpose to lay out money to compass the death of another man?' Giffard responds 'I make a distinction between carrying on a prosecution and compassing the death of a man.' The fallaciousness of this sort of strategy is well exposed by Applbaum *Ethics for Adversaries*, chapter 5.

[Character is a matter not] of what nature makes of man, but of what man makes of himself . . . What nature makes of him belongs to the temperament (where the subject is for the most part passive); only by what man makes of himself can we recognize that he has character . . . Temperament has a fancy price; one can have a good time with such a man, he is a pleasant companion. But character has an intrinsic worth and is exalted beyond any price.[45]

In *The Doctrine of Virtue*, Kant makes clear how he thinks that one can wilfully build a character of one's own choosing:

In so far as virtue is based on inner freedom it thus contains a positive command for man, over and above the prohibition against letting himself be ruled by his feelings and inclinations: the command, namely, to bring all his powers and inclinations under his (that is, reason's) control – hence the command of self-mastery . . . The principle . . . of positive duties to oneself [lies] in the saying: *make yourself more perfect* than mere nature made you.[46]

In the context of professional roles, one implication of this Kantian emphasis on *agency* in constituting moral character seems to be that unless an individual has been able successfully to carry out a 'reconciliation strategy' regarding the conventional demands of their professional role, then any role demands that they might have internalised are not, properly speaking, part of their moral character. For Kantians are inclined to regard being subject to the unreconciled conventional demands of an institutional role as failing to be the author of one's own actions. And clearly, when someone believes that they are not in a position adequately to evaluate or change their conventional but morally irreconcilable role demands, Kantianism offers them a way in which they can seemingly relinquish authorship of those role-based actions,

[45] *Anthropology from a Pragmatic Point of View*, trans M. J. Gregor, The Hague, Nijhoff, 1974, Ak. p. 292. See also Ak. p. 293: 'The imitator (as far as morals are concerned) is without character, because character has its being in the originality of the mode of thinking' (trans. V. L. Dowdell).
[46] *The Metaphysics of Morals – Part II: The Doctrine of Virtue*, trans. M. J. Gregor, Cambridge, Cambridge University Press, 1991, Ak. pp. 407, 419. See also the following passages: 'Reason must regard itself as the author of its principles, independently of foreign influences' (*Foundations of the Metaphysics of Morals*, trans. L. W. Beck, Indianapolis, Bobbs-Merrill, 1959, Ak. p. 448); 'Any transgression of the law can and must be explained only as arising from a maxim of the criminal . . . for if we were to derive it from a sensible impulse, he would not be committing it as a *free* being and it could not be imputed to him' (*The Metaphysics of Morals – Part I: The Doctrine of Right*, trans. M. J. Gregor, Cambridge, Cambridge University Press, 1991, Ak. p. 320n; and 'The vices contrary to this duty are lying, avarice, and false humility (servility). Since these vices are directly contrary to man's character as a moral being (according to its very form) – that is, contrary to inner freedom, the inherent dignity of man – to take them as one's principles amounts to making it one's principle to have no principle and so no character' (*The Metaphysics of Morals – Part II: The Doctrine of Virtue*, trans. Gregor, Ak. p. 420). Note that, as here, Kant and Kantians often conflate 'character' and 'moral character' (as though a through-and-through immoral person really has *no* character).

while reaffirming authorship of their actions outside those conventional confines of their role – that is, by changing *themselves*, so that they regard what they do in their role as superfluous to a true estimation of themselves, of who they *really* are. Thus, when a client is wronged by my carrying out the conventional but morally unreconciled demands of my role, I can regard that as a problem with the system, from which my real self is detached, just as Kant says I should Stoically regard human tragedies that I can do nothing about – I should turn away, and say 'it is no concern of mine', that it is a 'misfortune' that I can do nothing about.[47] Indeed, in 'What is Enlightenment?' Kant looks scornfully upon those who would rely in their actions on the dictates of mere conventions: 'rules and formulas, those mechanical instruments of a rational use, or misuse, of our natural gifts are the shackles of unending immaturity'.[48]

This reliance on agency in the constitution of the self is also a feature of contemporary Kantian constructivist approaches to the self. For example, on Christine Korsgaard's development of this approach,

> There is some principle or way of choosing that you regard as expressive of *yourself*. . . To identify with such a principle or way of choosing is . . . to be unified as such. This . . . is a practical necessity imposed upon you by the nature of the deliberative standpoint . . . It is practical reason that requires me to construct an identity for myself.[49]

Korsgaard draws an analogy with how the practical necessity involved in needing to execute an act *at a time* requires one to deliberate about the various conflicting forces within one at that time (desires to y, beliefs about x, the varying intensities of different desires for x, y, z), and decide which is going to move oneself. Then, in emphasising how achieving many of the things that matter morally requires agency over time, Korsgaard argues that

---

[47] See Kant, *Lectures on Ethics*, trans. L. Infield, New York, Harper & Row, 1963, p. 200.
[48] 'What is Enlightenment?', in *Foundations of the Metaphysics of Morals and 'What is Enlightenment?'*, trans. Beck, p. 86. This is not, of course, to deny that Kant can find a way for his ethics to accommodate an obligation to obey the law. In *The Metaphysics of Morals – Part I: The Doctrine of Right*, Kant argues that we have an obligation to be law-abiding – at least in an ideally just state – since he holds that it is possible for anyone to come to see how the laws in such a state arise from or conform with universalisable rules, and in doing so we can regard those laws as expressions of our own rational will (see Ak. pp. 255ff). See also Ak. p. 315: '[W]hatever sort of positive laws the citizens might vote for, these laws must still not be contrary to the natural laws of freedom and of the equality of everyone in the people corresponding to this freedom, namely that anyone can work his way up from this passive condition to an active one'.
[49] Christine M. Korsgaard, 'Personal Identity and the Unity of Agency: A Kantian Response to Parfit', *Philosophy and Public Affairs* 18, no. 2, Spring 1989, pp. 111–12.

Pragmatic necessity can be overwhelming. When a group of human beings occupy the same territory, for instance, they have an imperative need to form a unified state. And when a group of psychological functions occupy the same human body, they have an even more imperative need to become a unified person.[50]

But as is well known, this very overwhelmingness of practical necessity which can stimulate moves to integrate and unify disparate forces in the self can also have the opposite effect of self-fragmentation. Thus, for instance, individuals who have been subjected to gross violations as children sometimes deal with the need to make and carry out plans of action by partitioning off the *self-as-subject-of-abuse*.[51] However, where the disparate forces involved are one's personal moral values and the conventional demands of one's professional role, a less extreme response to the pragmatic necessity described by Korsgaard is to continue to discharge those conventional role demands, but with a level of psychological detachment designed to insulate one's 'real' self from what one does in carrying out the conventional demands of one's role. Thus, the insurance lawyer described earlier in this chapter initially reacted to what his role demanded of him – namely, to deprive people who (in many cases) were innocent car-accident victims of their legitimate claims – by bracketing off what he did in that role from his self-conception, although he subsequently found it impossible to maintain this psychological separation and so he left the profession.

Korsgaard herself need not, of course, endorse Montaigne's Stoic view of professional roles, nor need she approve of the specific advice Charles Curtis gave to lawyers. Nevertheless, the ideas expressed by Korsgaard are not simply a feature of how she happens to put the constructivist view – rather, they are an intrinsic part of Kantianism and Kantian ethics. This becomes more apparent when one acknowledges the deep and pervasive influence of Stoic ideas on Kant's ethics.[52] Kant emphasises acquiring something as a feature of oneself through gaining control over it, but when he finds some aspect of our psyche that seems

---

[50] Ibid., p. 115.

[51] For further discussion of this phenomenon, see Jennifer Radden, *Divided Minds and Successive Selves: Ethical Issues in Disorders of Identity and Personality*, Cambridge, MA, MIT Press, 1996; and Steve Matthews, 'Personal Identity, Multiple Personality Disorder, and Moral Personhood', *Philosophical Psychology* 11, no. 1, 1998.

[52] For discussions of the extent to which Kant's ethics is influenced by Stoic ideas, see Nancy Sherman, *Making a Necessity of Virtue: Aristotle and Kant on Virtue*, Cambridge, Cambridge University Press, 1997, esp. chapters 3 and 4; and Marcia Baron, *Kantian Ethics Almost Without Apology*, Ithaca, NY, Cornell University Press, 1995, pp. 137ff.

to him beyond our control, such as recalcitrant inclinations, he resorts to Stoicism, and says that these are not, properly speaking, features of me, are not *really* relevant to the moral status of my character. The connection between Montaigne and Kantian constructivism is thus by no means merely incidental – both are founded on the Stoic attempt to liberate oneself from heteronomous influences through psychological distancing.[53]

At this point, however, Kantians might protest that they *can* consistently hold individuals morally accountable for acting to fulfil conventional role demands which they try to 'disown'. After all, such actions involve voluntary and intentional movements of our bodies, and Kant might be thought able to concede that such actions can be imputed to our characters, just as he regards lacking sufficient control over one's emotions as an 'indulgence' that can be ascribed to one's will:

[Man] does not even hold himself responsible for these inclinations and impulses or attribute them to his proper self, i.e. his will, *though he does ascribe to his will the indulgence which he may grant to them when he permits them an influence on his maxims to the detriment of the rational laws of his will.*[54]

By analogy, then, Kant might be thought able consistently to condemn an individual for unthinkingly allowing their professional conduct to be determined by the conventional demands of their role. This suggestion is further supported by Kant's occasional comments indicating that he thinks it proper for individuals critically to evaluate the conventional demands of their roles. For example, in his discussion of how priests might permissibly deal with role demands they find contentious, Kant acknowledges the importance of making room for dissent from those demands in such circumstances – though he maintains that such dissent is morally acceptable only *outside* the context of the role:

---

[53] Interestingly, in one of his few references to Montaigne, Kant writes approvingly in his *Vorlesungen über Anthropologie* (*(Lectures on Anthropology)*, ed. Reinhard Brandt and Werner Stark, in *Gesammelte Schriften*, vol. xxv, Berlin, Walter de Gruyter, 1997, at Ak. pp. 472, 735) of Montaigne's dispassionate approach to self-contemplation. As Allen Wood explains, Kant cautions against becoming too involved in self-examination, which he thinks is likely to be self-indulgent and is in any case ultimately futile (since Kant thinks that we can never have adequate empirical knowledge of the self). See Allen Wood, *Kant's Ethical Thought*, Cambridge, Cambridge University Press, 1999, p. 201.

[54] *Foundations of the Metaphysics of Morals*, trans. Beck, Ak. pp. 457–8 (our italics). See also Kant, *The Metaphysics of Morals*, p. 226: 'although experience shows that man as a *sensible being* has the capacity to choose *in opposition to* as well as *in conformity with* the law, his freedom as an *intelligible being* cannot be *defined* by this . . . Freedom can never be located in a rational subject's being able to make a choice in opposition to his (lawgiving) reason, even though experience proves often enough that this happens (though we still cannot conceive how this is possible).' See also the *Critique of Practical Reason*, trans. L. W. Beck, Indianapolis, Bobbs-Merrill, 1956, Ak. p. 30.

[A clergyman who, outside the church] communicate[s] . . . all his carefully tested and well-meaning thoughts on that which is erroneous in the symbol [of the church] and . . . make[s] suggestions for the better organization of the religious body and church . . . [but who] make[s] his sermon to his pupils in catechism and his congregation conform to the symbol of the church . . . [does] nothing that could be laid as a burden on his conscience. For what he teaches as a consequence of his office as a representative of the church, this he considers something about which he has no freedom to teach according to his own lights.[55]

Such examples do suggest that Kant saw it as important not to discourage individuals from reflecting critically on what their roles are commonly thought to demand of them. However, to allow criticism of individuals for failing to publicise – in a non-professional context – their misgivings about the contentious aspects of their role is not yet to allow that individuals are properly condemned for continuing to fulfil those contentious role demands themselves, which, in the case of the priest, is condemnation Kant is clearly not prepared to make. Also, we might well question the plausibility of the suggestion that a professional who continues to adhere to morally contentious role demands is beyond reproach, or 'does nothing that could be laid as a burden on his conscience', simply because he is, outside his role, protesting against those demands.

[55] 'What is Enlightenment?', p. 88. One argument Kant offers in defence of this sort of obedience by role-occupants appeals to the importance of the ends thereby served: 'Many affairs which are conducted in the interest of the community require a certain mechanism through which some members of the community must passively conduct themselves with an artificial unanimity, so that the government may direct them to public ends, or at least prevent them from destroying those ends. Here argument is certainly not allowed – one must obey' ('What is Enlightenment?', p. 87).

Thus, where the institutional ends served by their role are of sufficient importance, a good Kantian professional should stifle the expression in a professional context of any moral misgivings they might have about their role (though they may make attempts outside their role to gather support for reforming the received demands of their role). Kant's stance here is analogous to his vehement condemnation of any kind of civil disobedience or conscientious objection, in his discussion of his Ideal State: 'the presently existing legislative authority ought to be obeyed, whatever its origin . . . a people cannot offer any resistance to the legislative head of state that would be consistent with right, since a rightful condition is possible only by submission to its general legislative will . . . The reason a people has a duty to put up with even what is held to be an unbearable abuse of supreme authority is that its resistance to the highest legislation can never be regarded as other than contrary to law, and indeed as abolishing the entire legal constitution', (*The Metaphysics of Morals – Part I: The Doctrine of Right*, Ak. pp. 319–20).

This Kantian argument is too general, and enables (e.g.) lawyers too easily to shift accountability for their fulfilling morally questionable role demands to the institution itself and the importance of the ends it serves, rather than encouraging (e.g.) lawyers to realise that meeting such role demands not only serves as an occasion for attempting to rally others to support institutional reforms, but can be a stain on one's character as well.

To his credit, Kant does seem to suggest that if after proper reflection one found a particular conventional demand of one's role morally or personally *unsupportable*, then one ought to abandon one's post.[56] So, perhaps Kant could claim that an individual would be morally account- able if they continued to carry out role demands that they sincerely believed to be morally indefensible.[57] But while this would be a welcome acknowledgement, limiting moral accountability for role-based actions to such extreme cases fails to do justice to what, arguably, are the more common cases, where individuals fulfil conventional role demands that they might suspect are morally dubious, without being convinced that those demands are out-and-out morally indefensible. For there are many factors which can strongly motivate individuals to avoid deeply scrutin- ising, and to continue to act on, the conventional demands of their pro- fessional roles. Some individuals seem unwilling to make a genuine attempt to think through one of the strategies mentioned at the begin- ning of this section, to see whether certain demands of their role really are reconcilable with broad-based moral standards, because, as Richard Wasserstrom points out, the degree of moral simplification offered by thinking only in terms of one's role demands can be very appealing, and indeed, at times, seductive.[58] And in any case, the level of personal investment many professionals have made in their careers is likely to act as a strong disincentive to their engaging in rigorous evaluation of their role demands which they suspect are morally questionable (and an even stronger disincentive to their being prepared to resign from their role, should its conventional demands turn out to be irreconcilable with

---

[56] Kant says that while a priest would not tarnish his conscience by enunciating to his congrega- tion statutes about which he lacks full conviction, nevertheless 'he could not conscientiously dis- charge the duties of his office' if he continued to enunciate statutes in which he had found something that was 'contradictory to inner religion' ('What is Enlightenment?', p. 88).

[57] See Kant's example of the soldier who spots corruption in the military but does not expose it, in the soldier's capacity as a member of the community at large ('What is Enlightenment?', p. 87). In this respect Kant differs from Montaigne – who would simply toss his hands in the air and say 'what business of mine is this entrenched knavery?' – and Kant is to be commended for this. Thus, Kant is not, of course, against reconciliation strategies per se; it is simply that his Stoic urgings to self-sufficiency by rising above the trappings of the phenomenal world (and to create the self via one's rational/moral interactions with clients through one's role) make it tempting for a professional who is uncertain about where morality leaves the conventional demands of their role to take refuge in some allegedly 'real' noumenal self.

[58] Wasserstrom, 'Roles and Morality', p. 29. Indeed, barrister Nathan's account of his behaviour during the rape trial suggests that such a factor might have been operative in this case. Another factor here is that some professionals complacently accept a role 'reconciliation' which is, in fact, false. See Wasserstrom's discussion (p. 36) of how utilitarian justifications have continued to be offered for certain particular demands of lawyers' roles, even though the demands of those roles have been reversed.

morality).[59] For such individuals, the strategy of role-detachment recommended by Montaigne – and facilitated by Kant's narrow conception of moral character – is likely to appear an attractive refuge.

At most, then, when we have emotions which are beyond our immediate control, or we unreflectively follow the conventional dictates of our professional role, Kant would seem to hold us morally accountable for being indulgent, morally weak, or unthinking, but he would not, it seems, regard us as morally reprehensible for what we thereby actually *feel* or *do*. Having, for example, uncontrolled excessive anger would on this view not itself be a feature of my character, nor would having undue fear that is beyond my immediate control, and I could not be thought poorly of on account of what it is I am angry or fearful about here. Similarly, Kant could condemn individuals who passively acquiesce in the conventional demands of their role as unthinking and indolent, but not as themselves *wronging* other people by their institutional actions. Thus, when a lawyer's unthinking adherence to what is 'the standard defence at the time' helps to bring about a seemingly unjust outcome for a litigant, the Kantian approach seems to tell us that we can regard the lawyer as personally accountable for being insufficiently reflective here, but not as in any way accountable for the injustice to the litigant – that, properly speaking, is an injustice of the system itself. The fourteen-year-old rape victim in our earlier example is wronged by the adversarial system, not by barrister Nathan himself. And indeed, as we saw earlier, this is exactly how Kantians like Charles Fried talk.[60]

But while many criminal defence lawyers may see their part in the injustice done to a crime victim in this way during court proceedings, they sometimes come to regard their actions in such cases quite differently. It is quite common for defence lawyers, looking back over their careers, to talk of feeling strong regret and sometimes shame at their involvement in certain trial outcomes.[61] And the shame expressed in such accounts is not shame simply at having aped convention, or about having been insufficiently reflective. Rather, these lawyers feel shame over *what they did* through unthinkingly following convention – that is, they are ashamed of how their manner of conducting a particular case treated the crime victim: that they were able, for example, to secure an acquittal for a client by, say, humiliating a complainant whom they knew

---

[59] For a summary of the extensive empirical research indicating how individual career choices tend to be self-reinforcing, see Irving L. Janis and Leon Mann, *Decision Making: A Psychological Analysis of Conflict, Choice, and Commitment*, New York, The Free Press, 1977.

[60] See Fried, 'The Lawyer as Friend', pp. 1084–6.

[61] For good examples of such accounts, see Wishman, *Confessions of a Criminal Lawyer*, esp. pp. 16–18, 69, 151–2, 222–3, 240, and Jennifer Hall [pseud.], quoted in R. Jack and D. C. Jack, *Moral Visions*

was telling the truth. And the shame expressed in such accounts shows that these lawyers take themselves to be *morally* reprehensible for the way they conducted a particular case, and not merely, as Kant might have it, an unhappy influence on others.[62] Whatever the reason a professional's conventional role demands remain unreconciled, where he has internalised those demands in such a way that he can be relied upon to act upon them, we should be clear that his having and acting upon those unreconciled role demands do reflect on him, and indeed are still part of the moral fabric of his character.

Our claim is that the sorts of traits which are involved in fulfilling the demands – even the conventional demands – of professional roles are such that those traits must, conceptually, form part of one's character. This claim is distinct from the empirical claim, sometimes made, that, as a matter of psychological fact, individuals will be unlikely to be able to prevent their professional traits from 'spilling over' and *influencing* (for example, corrupting) them outside their professional role.[63] Regarding

and *Professional Decisions: The Changing Values of Women and Men Lawyers*, Cambridge, Cambridge University Press, 1989, p. 114. Also, Howard Nathan's comments about the way he defended the man accused of raping a fourteen-year-old girl suggest that he feels (at least) regret at the way he conducted his client's defence, and at the outcome that this helped bring about.

[62] Suppose that we were sitting in the public gallery at a rape trial like this, watching the barrister use his advocacy skills to persuade the jury that the young girl had 'asked for it', while we knew (say, from having overheard a conversation the barrister had had with one of his colleagues outside the court) that he strongly believed his client was guilty. It seems rather far-fetched to suppose that we would regard the moral outrage we would probably feel towards the barrister for what he brought about as no longer *moral* outrage, if we learnt that the barrister was just unthinkingly following what he took to be 'the standard defence at the time', rather than embracing role demands that he had reflectively accepted (or that our moral outrage was simply at his 'thoughtlessness', but not directed at him for what his thoughtlessness helped to bring about).

[63] Andreas Eshete argues ('Does a Lawyer's Character Matter', pp. 274–9) that a lawyer's attempts to contain their entrenched negative legal traits within a legal self are in the end likely to fail, and that those traits will therefore eventually most probably 'leave their trace' upon their character generally and so come to be expressed outside the context of their legal practice, in ways which are clearly wrong. Eshete sees this non-containment claim about lawyers as an instance of 'a simple and plausible hypothesis in moral psychology', which he cites Rawls formulating as follows: 'When an individual decides what to be, what occupation or profession to enter, say, he adopts a particular plan of life. In time his choice will lead him to acquire a definite pattern of wants and aspirations (or the lack thereof), some aspects of which are peculiar to him while others are typical of his occupation or way of life' (John Rawls, *A Theory of Justice*, Oxford, Oxford University Press, 1972, pp. 415–16). (Eshete also refers to the use which Marx and Mill make of this sort of claim.)

Gerald Postema ('Moral Responsibility in Professional Ethics') agrees with Eshete's 'plausible hypothesis in moral psychology'. That is, Postema holds that 'Acting and deliberating within the special moral universe of any role that involves a large investment of one's moral faculties will tend to shape one's moral personality' (p. 75), and he argues that it is therefore difficult for lawyers to keep their characters entirely immune from the corrupting influences of any negative professional traits they may have developed – any such traits a lawyer has will tend to find their way into their character outside their professional role. However, Postema is less sceptical than Eshete about the ability of lawyers to contain those negative traits solely within the legal sphere

this empirical claim, we remain agnostic (although it does seem to us quite possible that, for example, the psychological detachment from patients that surgeons commonly say is necessary for operating success-fully need not in any way carry over into, say, their relationships with their family or friends). Carrying out the demands of professional roles, even when one has not scrutinised their reconcilability with broad-based moral standards, necessitates the development of standing dispositions and a level of deliberation, practical judgement, and decision-making that makes it implausible for an individual to claim that their character is not thereby involved. After all, it is because a criminal defence lawyer takes his character to have this level of involvement in (say) humiliating a crime victim that, even though he may have presented what was 'the standard defence at the time', he may nevertheless subsequently regard his behaviour here as proper grounds for shame.[64] As Anthony Kronman has acknowledged:

To be a lawyer is to be a person of a particular sort, a person with a distinctive set of character traits as well as an expertise. I believe that something like this is true, in a general way, of other professions as well and that the very notion of a profession – as distinguished from a mere technique – implies the possession of certain character-defining traits or qualities . . . A lawyer's profession is part of his identity and can't be put on or off like a suit of clothes.[65]

Footnote 63 (*cont.*)

(although Postema is not primarily interested in determining the truth about that issue). Nevertheless, Postema argues that when such quarantining can be accomplished, it comes at great cost (see our n. 43 above).

While we find much of what Eshete and Postema say here plausible, it is important to bear in mind here that, as the extensive research reported by Ross and Nisbett shows, situational factors – including features of the *role* a person occupies – are often a far better predictor of people's behaviour in different circumstances than is commonly assumed (and often enable far better pre-dictions to be made of individual behaviour in different situations than predictions based on the assumptions made about underlying dispositions or character-traits of particular individuals). See Lee Ross and Richard Nisbett, *The Person and the Situation: Perspectives of Social Psychology*, New York, McGraw-Hill, 1991, esp. chapters 4 and 5.

[64] Of course, being ashamed of something one did when one reviews one's career does not itself establish that one's conduct was in that instance morally wrong. Sometimes one's shame at what one did in carrying out one's role may be misplaced – one may simply have failed to see how what one did there was, in fact, all things considered morally justified. (The same sort of point can also be made about *pride* in one's professional doings.) We are not, however, arguing that shame at some past role-based action shows our behaviour there to be wrong; rather, our argu-ment is that being ashamed at having met certain conventional demands of our role provides strong evidence that our *character* was involved in our actions here, and that we are indeed there-fore properly morally assessable – as, e.g., morally reprehensible – on account of those actions.

[65] Anthony Kronman, 'Living in the Law', *University of Chicago Law Review* 54, 1987, pp. 841, 845. See also Anthony Kronman, *The Lost Lawyer: Failing Ideals of the Legal Profession*, Cambridge, MA, Harvard University Press, 1993, e.g. pp. 14–17. Indeed, Kronman seems to regard this as a con-ceptual truth – a person who tries to hold their character apart from carrying out their profes-sional role is being, in some sense, unprofessional; is, in an important sense, not acting as a professional.

So, even if we accepted that an individual's professional wrongs were in some sense not due to the individual's *will*, they are still *their* doings, and they still reflect on them morally.

Another argument which undermines suggestions that an individual's character can coherently be held apart from what they do in their professional role would point to how the demands of such roles can often test and challenge the individuals within them. Consider first how, outside the context of professional roles, an individual's standing dispositions can often be relatively inconspicuous and, in interpreting people's character-traits, we are inclined to place considerable weight upon how people are disposed to act under conditions of significant adversity, or when competing values are particularly weighty. That is, we often take what people do and are prepared to do in such circumstances as revealing something of their standing dispositions and what their fundamental priorities are. For example, when 'the chips are down' and we turn to those we think of as friends for help, we tend to cast doubt on our earlier impression that someone had the dispositions of friendship towards us when they fail to provide any support in our hour of need. We are inclined to take their failure to help, when the relationship becomes more challenging, as telling us something important about their character, at least insofar as it relates to us. (As we sometimes say, their 'true colours' come out.) Now, one feature widely thought distinctive of *professional* roles is that they are (in some way) directed towards serving significant human goods, and this gives us reason to think that the stakes involved in the decision-making within such roles can be expected to be, at times, fairly high and therefore quite challenging to the individuals within them. People may well be suffering great personal hardship when they turn to lawyers and doctors, and important values such as fairness and welfare may need to be weighed against each other. As professionals often note, meeting the dictates of one's role in such difficult circumstances tends to demand reaching into the depths of one's character, and this can indeed reveal standing dispositions that one did not realise one had – and, of course, it can also reveal that one *lacks* certain dispositions (such as courageousness) which one liked to think of oneself as having. Either way, though, these considerations make it plausible to think that involvement of an individual's character in various role-based actions is a pervasive feature of professional life.

An important merit of a virtue ethics approach is that it can recognise how role demands that one has internalised are part of one's character, and that one remains morally accountable for them, whether or not one has employed any strategy to reconcile those demands with broad-based morality. Of course, a virtue ethics approach does not deny the importance of agency in constituting moral character in, say, professional life. Indeed, we suggested in chapter 3 one way in which various professional roles may be reconciled with or grounded in broad-based human goods and virtues, and Aristotle himself spends much time in his ethics discussing how we can take steps to acquire virtues through habituation. But virtue ethics has no commitment to the notion that people cannot reasonably be held morally accountable for features they have acquired more passively – whether they have uncontrolled emotions, or have unthinkingly adopted 'the standard demands of the time'. For as Aristotle puts it, 'moral virtue . . . is concerned with passions and actions';[66] 'the actions which proceed from anger or appetite are the man's actions', and 'the irrational passions are thought not less human than reason is'.[67] Kantianism emphasises self-creation, whereas an Aristotelian approach to ethics emphasises self-improvement, whereby unchosen features may still reflect on us morally.[68] As Aristotle argues, there are, for example, things at which one ought to be angry, such as great injustices, and if one fails to be angered by great injustices, even where this is not for want of trying, one's unirascibility is nevertheless a fault, and a moral fault, in one's character.[69] Similarly, some people find it harder to grieve than others, though they may not have tried to become like this. Nevertheless, we naturally take the manner of someone's grieving as indicating something about their character.

Aspects of the self sometimes pre-date any active attempts that we might make to create them. As the experiences of adoptees searching for their biological parents can attest, it is sometimes by our *discovering* some feature that was, in a sense, already there that we encounter the self, rather than by *making* that feature part of us with our wills.[70] And these aspects of the self can reflect on us morally. For example, as Tom Nagel

---

[66] *Nicomachean Ethics* II.6.1106b15.   [67] *Nicomachean Ethics* III.1.1111b1–2.
[68] For further defence of this moral relevance of our unchosen features, see Justin Oakley, *Morality and the Emotions*, London, Routledge, 1992, chapter 5.
[69] See *Nicomachean Ethics* IV.5.1125b30–5.
[70] Thus, when asked why they are going to such trouble to find out who their biological parents are, adopted children often respond by saying 'I want to find out who I am.' Another example in support of the role of passivity in constituting the self can be found in the non-contractual (prima facie) role obligations adult children are thought to have, to help provide some kind of (e.g. emotional) support for their elderly parents. For if an adult child decided, say on frivolous grounds, to *reject* all such role obligations towards their elderly parents, we would commonly think that the child is, in some sense, thereby denying a part of *themselves*. Some significant features of our selves seem to be (almost) inalienable.

says of himself, being an American citizen during the Vietnam War reflects poorly on one, and is properly grounds for shame, even if one found the conventional role demands of being an American citizen at that time reflectively *unacceptable*, and so tried (as he did) to distance oneself from the US intervention in Vietnam.[71] As Michael Hardimon says about our roles as family members and citizens, 'the depth of these bonds is in part a reflection of the fact that they are not chosen'.[72] And Robert Adams makes a similar point about the authenticity of unchosen psychological features: 'in many cases . . . direct voluntary control over our desires and emotions . . . would undermine the sincerity or genuineness of the desire or emotion produced'.[73]

It is an indictment of Kantian accounts of moral character that they encourage professionals to regard the habituated conventional demands of their roles that they cannot rationally share as heteronomous influences that are irrelevant to a true moral estimation of their character. For one cannot plausibly (or even coherently) evade moral accountability for one's role-based actions, simply by erecting some psychological barrier between that role and one's putative 'real' self. Indeed, it is telling that such wilful psychological barriers are wont eventually to collapse, as many real and fictional examples attest. For instance, the perplexed Reverend Dimmesdale in *The Scarlet Letter* finds that despite his best efforts to shun it, his capacity for sin, expressed in his adulterous encounter with Mrs Hester Prynne, is an irrepressible part of who he is. As Hawthorne memorably puts it late in the novel, when Dimmesdale finds himself uncustomarily moved to utter obscenities and blasphemies at innocent members of his congregation as he returns from the forest: 'No man, for any considerable period, can wear one face to himself, and another to the multitude, without finally getting bewildered as to which may be the true'.[74]

---

[71] Thomas Nagel, 'Moral Luck', in Thomas Nagel, *Mortal Questions*, Cambridge, Cambridge University Press, 1979, p. 34 n. 10.   [72] Hardimon, 'Moral Obligations', p. 353.

[73] Robert M. Adams, 'Involuntary Sins', *Philosophical Review* 94, no. 1, January 1985, p. 10.

[74] Nathaniel Hawthorne, *The Scarlet Letter*, New York, Signet Books, 1970, p. 203. As Edward Davidson puts it, '[the Calvinist theologian] Jonathan Edwards' inquiries into the process of salvation, or damnation, would have found no more fitting memorial than Hawthorne's obsessed man [Rev. Dimmesdale] . . . man is saved or damned, not by the dislodgement of one portion of his life from another, but by his knowing in all humility that what he is in his fleshly being he reflects in his soul, and the state of his spirit is manifest every instant in the outward demeanour of his daily experience. This thought tortures Dimmesdale beyond endurance' (Edward H. Davidson, 'Dimmesdale's Fall', *New England Quarterly* 36, September 1963, p. 360; reprinted in John C. Gerber (ed.), *Twentieth-Century Interpretations of The Scarlet Letter*, Englewood Cliffs, Prentice-Hall, 1968, p. 84). Davidson (in Gerber) describes Dimmesdale's 'fall' thus: 'It begins for Dimmesdale during the forest interview when he pledges with Hester that the two would

Kant has a vested interest in regarding dispositions to carry out morally unreconciled conventional role demands as superfluous to who we really are, and to what we are properly morally answerable for. It is a defect of Kantian constructivism – and Kant's Stoic attitude towards those aspects of 'us' which we lack control over – that through facilitating a kind of selective self-presentation, it serves as a useful device for deflecting a degree of moral disapproval and shame for submitting to immoral conventional role demands which one is unprepared to relinquish.[75] In their haste to reject the passivity approach to personal identity and character commonly given by empiricist philosophers and utilitarian ethicists, Kantian constructivists like Korsgaard go too far the other way to activism, and neglect how the passive may reflect on us. Hume was well aware of the significance of passivity here: 'many of those qualities, which all moralists, especially the ancients, comprehend under the title of moral virtues, are equally involuntary and necessary, with the qualities of the judgement and imagination. Of this nature are constancy, fortitude, magnanimity; and, in short, all the qualities which form the *great* man.'[76]

Footnote 74 (*cont.*)

    leave Boston and thereby live for "self". Then Dimmesdale walks to the village and undergoes a sudden transformation which would delight the gloating eyes of Satan or Chillingworth. In yielding himself "with deliberate choice" to do that which "he knew was deadly sin", Dimmesdale finally acknowledged the long-hidden secrets of his bestial, fleshy nature. He never had effected a separation of flesh from spirit; the wickedness of one was the evil of the other; "the infectious poison of that sin", Hawthorne says, "[was] rapidly diffused throughout his moral system"' (p. 90).

[75] Note that we are not claiming that Kantians' emphasis on agency in constituting moral character entails that they are committed to viewing a given set of conventional role demands as morally binding on a person only if they have explicitly contracted into or 'signed on' for them. We recognise that a Kantian agent needn't regard non-contractual conventional role demands – such as a requirement to assist with their elderly parents – as non-binding, simply because they have not *contracted into* these. For Kantians can consider whether these and other non-contractual role requirements are, as Hardimon puts it, 'reflectively acceptable'. And indeed, that is the sort of thing a Kantian would be doing with institutional roles when the Kantian makes use of the sort of 'reconciliation strategy' suggested by, e.g., Dare earlier. Rather, we are claiming that the Kantian view of the centrality of agency in constituting moral character makes the moral evaluation of individuals for their role-based behaviour too dependent on their having voluntarily accepted or successfully carried out 'reflective acceptance' of their role. And, for professionals who have not engaged in or completed such a process, the Kantian account makes it too easy for them to take their role as set, and as not reflecting on who they really are. This point applies to any conventional role demands, whether contractual or non-contractual – it is just that it is more likely to arise regarding the non-contractual role demands, since we are less likely to have subjected these sorts of demands on us to explicit scrutiny. Our point about how Kantianism can lead us to make misguided judgements about moral character could equally be made using non-contractual conventional role demands outside an instutional or professional context (as we have above).

[76] Hume, *A Treatise of Human Nature*, Book III, chapter ii, section 4. Hume's account of personal identity brings out well how and why non-voluntary features of our psyche can be integral to some notion of the self (built up through, e.g., the emotion of pride).

Unlike Kant, Aristotelian virtue ethics does not have a vested interest in denying the relevance of our unchosen features to our moral character, and to what we are morally accountable for. Lacking any need to transcend the empirical aspects of our nature, and recognising that internalised habits of deliberation and acting become part of us, no matter how much we attempt to insulate some 'real self' from them, Aristotelian virtue ethics would regard Montaigne's detachment strategy simply as self-deception on a grand scale. A virtue ethics approach to professional roles shows how a person who has developed habits of acting on professional dispositions which cannot be reconciled with broad-based virtues, or serve key human goods, has changed their moral character, no matter how detached from those dispositions they may regard themselves as being. Contrary to Montaigne, *unless* one refuses to practise them, the vices of one's calling become the vices of oneself.

Bibliography

Ackrill, J. L., 'Aristotle on *Eudaimonia*', in Amélie O. Rorty (ed.), *Essays on Aristotle's Ethics*, Berkeley, University of California Press, 1980.

Adams, Robert M., 'Motive Utilitarianism', *Journal of Philosophy* 73, 1976.

'Involuntary Sins', *Philophical Review* 94, no. 1, January 1985.

Alderson, Priscilla, 'Abstract Bioethics Ignores Human Emotions', *Bulletin of Medical Ethics* 68, May 1991.

Anechiarico, Frank, and Jacobs, James B., *The Pursuit of Absolute Integrity: How Corruption Control Makes Government Ineffective*, Chicago, University of Chicago Press, 1996.

Anscombe, G. E. M., 'Modern Moral Philosophy', *Philosophy* 33, 1958.

Applbaum, Arthur, *Ethics for Adversaries: The Morality of Roles in Public and Professional Life*, Princeton, Princeton University Press, 1999.

Aristotle, *The Politics*, trans. T. A. Sinclair, Harmondsworth, Penguin, 1962.

The Nicomachean Ethics, trans. W. D. Ross, Oxford, Oxford University Press, 1980.

Australian Law Reform Commission, *Review of the Adversarial System of Litigation: Rethinking Legal Education and Training*, ALRC Issues Paper no. 21, August 1997.

Babcock, Barbara, 'Defending the Guilty', *Cleveland State Law Review* 32, 1983–4.

Badhwar, Neera Kapur, 'Introduction' to Neera Kapur Badhwar (ed.), *Friendship: A Philosophical Reader*, Ithaca, NY, Cornell University Press, 1993.

Baier, Kurt, 'Radical Virtue Ethics', in Peter A. French, Theodore E. Uehling, and Howard K. Wettstein (eds.), *Midwest Studies in Philosophy, Volume 13: Ethical Theory: Character and Virtue*, Notre Dame, Notre Dame University Press, 1988.

Balint, Michael, *The Doctor, His Patient, and the Illness*, 2nd edn, London, Pitman Medical Books, 1964.

Baron, Marcia, 'The Alleged Moral Repugnance of Acting from Duty', *Journal of Philosophy* 81, 1984.

'Kantian Ethics and Supererogation', *Journal of Philosophy* 84, 1987.

Kantian Ethics Almost Without Apology, Ithaca, NY, Cornell University Press, 1995.

Baron, Marcia W., Pettit, Philip, and Slote, Michael, *Three Methods of Ethics: A Debate*, Oxford, Blackwell, 1997.

Bayles, Michael, *Professional Ethics*, 2nd edn, Belmont, Wadsworth, 1989.

Beauchamp, Tom L., and Childress, James F., *Principles of Biomedical Ethics*, 4th edn, New York, Oxford University Press, 1994.

Becker, Lawrence, *Reciprocity*, London, Routledge & Kegan Paul, 1986.

Benner, Patricia, *From Novice to Expert: Excellence and Power in Clinical Nursing Practice*, Menlo Park, CA, Addison-Wesley, 1984.

Benner, Patricia, and Wrubel, Judith, *The Primacy of Caring: Stress and Coping in Health and Illness*, Menlo Park, CA, Addison-Wesley, 1989.

Bennett, Jonathan, 'The Conscience of Huckleberry Finn', *Philosophy* 49, 1974.

Benson, Paul, 'Moral Worth', *Philosophical Studies* 51, 1987.

Bickenbach, Jerome E., 'Law and Morality', *Law and Philosophy* 8, no. 3, December 1989.

'The Redemption of the Moral Mandate of the Profession of Law', *Canadian Journal of Law and Jurisprudence* 9, 1996.

Blum, Lawrence, *Friendship, Altruism and Morality*, London, Routledge & Kegan Paul, 1980.

'Vocation, Friendship, and Community: Limitations of the Personal–Impersonal Framework', in Owen Flanagan and Amélie O. Rorty (eds.), *Identity, Character, and Morality: Essays in Moral Psychology*, Cambridge, MA, MIT Press, 1990.

Blustein, Jeffrey, 'Doing what the Patient Orders: Maintaining Integrity in the Doctor–Patient Relationship', *Bioethics* 7, no. 4, 1993.

Boorse, Christopher, 'On the Distinction Between Disease and Illness', *Philosophy and Public Affairs* 5, Fall 1975.

'What a Theory of Mental Health should be', *Journal for the Theory of Social Behaviour* 6, no. 1, 1976.

'Health as a Theoretical Concept', *Philosophy of Science* 44, 1977.

Brandt, Richard, 'Morality and its Critics', *American Philosophical Quarterly* 26, 1989.

Facts, Values, and Morality, Cambridge, Cambridge University Press, 1996.

Brink, David O., 'Utilitarian Morality and the Personal Point of View', *Journal of Philosophy* 83, 1986.

Bronitt, Simon, and McSherry, Bernadette, 'The Use and Abuse of Counseling Records in Sexual Assault Trials: Reconstructing the "Rape Shield"?', *Criminal Law Forum* 8, no. 2, 1997.

Broome, John, *Weighing Goods*, Oxford, Blackwell, 1991.

Camenisch, Paul R., 'On Being a Professional, Morally Speaking', in Bernard Baumrin and Benjamin Freedman (eds.), *Moral Responsibility and the Professions*, New York, Haven Publications, 1983.

Campbell, John, 'Can Philosophical Accounts of Altruism Accommodate Experimental Data on Helping Behaviour?', *Australasian Journal of Philosophy* 77, no. 1, March 1999.

Care, Norman, 'Career Choice', *Ethics* 94, no. 2, January 1984.

Christie, Ronald J., and Hoffmaster, C. Barry, *Ethical Issues in Family Medicine*, New York, Oxford University Press, 1986.

Churchill, Larry R. 'Reviving a Distinctive Medical Ethic', *Hastings Center Report* 19, no. 3, May/June 1989.

Cocking, Dean, and Kennett, Jeanette, 'Friendship and the Self', *Ethics* 108, no. 3, April 1998.

'Friendship and Moral Danger', *Journal of Philosophy* 97, no. 5, May 2000.

Cocking, Dean, and Oakley, Justin, 'Indirect Consequentialism, Friendship, and the Problem of Alienation', *Ethics* 106, no. 1, October 1995.

'The Ethics of Professional Detachment', *Journal of Law and Medicine* 7, no. 2, November 1999.

Cohen, Joshua, 'Deliberation and Democratic Legitimacy', in Alan Hamlin and Philip Pettit (eds.), *The Good Polity*, Oxford, Blackwell, 1989.

Cooper, John, 'Aristotle on Friendship', in Amélie O. Rorty (ed.), *Essays on Aristotle's Ethics*, Berkeley, University of California Press, 1980.

Reason and Human Good in Aristotle, Indianapolis, Hackett, 1986.

Cottingham, John, 'Medicine, Virtues and Consequences', in David S. Oderberg and Jacqueline A. Laing (eds.), *Human Lives: Critical Essays on Consequentialist Bioethics*, Basingstoke, Macmillan, 1997.

Crisp, Roger, 'A Good Death: Who Best to Bring it?', *Bioethics* 1, no. 1, 1987.

'Utilitarianism and the Life of Virtue', *Philosophical Quarterly* 42, 1992.

'Modern Moral Philosophy and the Virtues', in Roger Crisp (ed.), *How Should One Live? Essays on the Virtues*, Oxford, Clarendon Press, 1996.

Crisp, Roger, and Slote, Michael (eds.), *Virtue Ethics*, Oxford, Oxford University Press, 1997.

Curtis, Charles P., 'The Ethics of Advocacy', *Stanford Law Review* 4, December 1951.

Curzer, Howard, 'Is Care a Virtue for Health Care Professionals?', *Journal of Medicine and Philosophy* 18, no. 1, 1993.

Dancy, Jonathan, 'The Role of Imaginary Cases in Ethics', *Pacific Philosophical Quarterly* 66, 1985.

Daniels, Norman, *Just Health Care*, Cambridge, Cambridge University Press, 1985.

Dannen, Fredric, 'Defending the Mafia', *The New Yorker*, 21 February 1994.

Dare, Tim, '"The Secret Courts of Men's Hearts": Legal Ethics and Harper Lee's *To Kill a Mockingbird*', in Kim Economides (ed.), *Ethical Challenges to Legal Education and Conduct*, Oxford, Hart Publishing, 1998.

'Virtue Ethics and Legal Ethics', *Victoria University of Wellington Law Review* 28, no. 1, March 1998.

Davidson, Edward H., 'Dimmesdale's Fall', *New England Quarterly* 36, September 1963; reprinted in John C. Gerber (ed.), *Twentieth-Century Interpretations of The Scarlet Letter*, Englewood Cliffs, Prentice-Hall, 1968.

Dent, N. J. H., *The Moral Psychology of the Virtues*, Cambridge, Cambridge University Press, 1984.

de Raeve, Louise, 'Caring Intensively', in David Greaves and Hugh Upton (eds.), *Philosophical Problems in Health Care*, Aldershot, Avebury, 1996.

Doris, John M., 'Persons, Situations, and Virtue Ethics', *Nous* 32, no. 4, 1998.
Lack of Character: Personality and Moral Behaviour, New York, Cambridge University Press, 2001.
Drane, James F., *Becoming a Good Doctor: The Place of Virtue and Character in Medical Ethics*, Kansas City, Sheed and Ward, 1988.
Dreier, James, 'Structures of Normative Theories', *The Monist* 76, 1993.
Driver, Julia, 'Monkeying with Motives: Agent-Basing Virtue Ethics', *Utilitas* 7, 1995.
Dworkin, Ronald, *Life's Dominion: An Argument about Abortion, Euthanasia and Individual Freedom*, New York, Knopf, 1993.
Elgar, Kerri, 'A Night at the Confessional', *Law Institute Journal* (Law Institute of Victoria), November 1997.
Emanuel, Ezekiel J., and Emanuel, Linda L., 'Four Models of the Physician–Patient Relationship', *Journal of the American Medical Association* 267, no. 16, 22–9 April 1992.
Emmet, Dorothy, *Function, Purpose and Powers*, 2nd edn, Philadelphia, Temple University Press, 1972.
Eshete, Andreas, 'Does a Lawyer's Character Matter?', in David Luban (ed.), *The Good Lawyer: Lawyers' Roles and Lawyers' Ethics*, Totowa, Rowman and Allanheld, 1984.
Ewing, A. C., *Ethics*, London, English Universities Press, 1953.
Feldman, Heidi Li, 'Codes and Virtues: Can Lawyers be Good Ethical Deliberators?', *Southern California Law Review* 69, March 1996.
Firth, Roderick, 'Ethical Absolutism and the Ideal Observer', *Philosophy and Phenomenological Research* 12, 1952.
Fiske, Pat, and Johnson, Michael, *Memories of Fred*, Sydney, ABC Books, 1995.
Flanagan, Owen, *Varieties of Moral Personality*, Cambridge, MA, Harvard University Press, 1991.
Foot, Philippa, 'A Reply to Professor Frankena', in Philippa Foot, *Virtues and Vices*, Berkeley, University of California Press, 1978.
'Euthanasia', in Philippa Foot, *Virtues and Vices*, Berkeley, University of California Press, 1978.
'Goodness and Choice', in Philippa Foot, *Virtues and Vices*, Berkeley, University of California Press, 1978.
'Moral Beliefs', in Philippa Foot, *Virtues and Vices*, Berkeley, University of California Press, 1978.
'Morality as a System of Hypothetical Imperatives', in Philippa Foot, *Virtues and Vices*, Berkeley, University of California Press, 1978.
'Virtues and Vices', in Philippa Foot, *Virtues and Vices*, Berkeley, University of California Press, 1978.
Virtues and Vices, Berkeley, University of California Press, 1978.
'Utilitarianism and the Virtues', in Samuel Scheffler (ed.), *Consequentialism and its Critics*, Oxford, Oxford University Press, 1988.
Frankena, William, *Ethics*, 2nd edn, Englewood Cliffs, Prentice-Hall, 1973.

Freedman, Monroe H., 'Professional Responsibility of the Criminal Defense Lawyer: The Three Hardest Questions', *Michigan Law Review* 64, 1969.

Lawyers' Ethics in an Adversary System, Indianapolis, Bobbs-Merrill, 1975.

French, Peter A., Uehling, Theodore E., and Wettstein, Howard K. (eds.), *Midwest Studies in Philosophy, Volume 13: Ethical Theory: Character and Virtue*, Notre Dame, Notre Dame University Press, 1988.

Fried, Charles, *Medical Experimentation: Personal Integrity and Social Policy*, Amsterdam, North Holland Publishing Co., 1974.

'The Lawyer as Friend: The Moral Foundations of the Lawyer–Client Relation', *Yale Law Journal* 85, no. 8, July 1976.

Fry, Sarah T., 'Response to "Virtue Ethics, Caring and Nursing"', *Scholarly Inquiry for Nursing Practice* 2, no. 2, 1988.

Furman, Wyndol, Brown, B. Bradford, and Feiring, Candice (eds.), *The Development of Romantic Relationships in Adolescence*, Cambridge, Cambridge University Press, 1999.

Gadow, Sally, 'Existential Advocacy: Philosophical Foundations of Nursing', in Stuart Spicker and Sally Gadow (eds.), *Nursing Images and Ideals*, New York, Springer, 1980.

Griffin, James, *Well-Being: Its Meaning, Measurement, and Moral Importance*, Oxford, Clarendon Press, 1986.

Hardie, W. F. R., 'The Final Good in Aristotle's Ethics', *Philosophy* 40, 1965.

Hardimon, Michael, 'Role Obligations', *Journal of Philosophy* 91, no. 7, July 1994.

Hare, R. M., *Moral Thinking*, Oxford, Oxford University Press, 1981.

'Comments', in D. Seanor and N. Fotion (eds.), *Hare and Critics*, Oxford, Clarendon Press, 1988.

'Health', in R. M. Hare, *Essays on Bioethics*, Oxford, Clarendon Press, 1993.

'Moral Problems about the Control of Behaviour', in R. M. Hare, *Essays on Bioethics*, Oxford, Clarendon Press, 1993.

'The Philosophical Basis of Psychiatric Ethics', in R. M. Hare, *Essays on Bioethics*, Oxford, Clarendon Press, 1993.

'Methods of Bioethics: Some Defective Proposals', in L. W. Sumner and Joseph Boyle (eds.), *Philosophical Perspectives on Bioethics*, Toronto, University of Toronto Press, 1996.

Harman, Gilbert, 'Moral Philosophy Meets Social Psychology: Virtue Ethics and the Fundamental Attribution Error', *Proceedings of the Aristotelian Society* 99, 1998–1999.

Hart, H. L. A., *The Concept of Law*, Oxford, Oxford University Press, 1961.

Hawthorne, Nathaniel, *The Scarlet Letter*, New York, Signet Books, 1970.

Herman, Barbara, 'On the Value of Acting from the Motive of Duty', *Philosophical Review* 90, no. 3, 1981.

'Integrity and Impartiality', *The Monist* 66, 1983.

'Rules, Motives, and Helping Actions', *Philosophical Studies* 45, 1984.

'Agency, Attachment, and Difference', *Ethics* 101, 1991 (reprinted in Barbara Herman, *The Practice of Moral Judgment*, Cambridge, MA, Harvard University Press, 1993).

'Leaving Deontology Behind', in Barbara Herman, *The Practice of Moral Judgment*, Cambridge, MA, Harvard University Press, 1993.

'The Practice of Moral Judgment', *Journal of Philosophy* 82, 1985 (reprinted in Barbara Herman, *The Practice of Moral Judgment*, Cambridge, MA, Harvard University Press, 1993).

The Practice of Moral Judgment, Cambridge, MA, Harvard University Press, 1993.

Hollows, Fred, *An Autobiography* (with Peter Corris), Melbourne, John Kerr, 1991.

Hooker, Brad, 'Rule-Consequentialism', *Mind* 99, 1990.

Hume, David, *A Treatise of Human Nature*, ed. L. A. Selby-Bigge, Oxford, Oxford University Press, 1978.

Hurka, Thomas, 'Consequentialism and Content', *American Philosophical Quarterly* 29, 1992.

'Virtue as Loving the Good', in Ellen F. Paul, Fred D. Miller and Jeffrey Paul (eds.), *The Good Life and the Human Good*, Cambridge, Cambridge University Press, 1992.

Perfectionism, New York, Oxford University Press, 1993.

Hursthouse, Rosalind, 'Virtue Theory and Abortion', *Philosophy and Public Affairs* 20, 1991.

'Normative Virtue Ethics', in Roger Crisp (ed.), *How Should One Live? Essays on the Virtues*, Oxford, Clarendon Press, 1996.

Illingworth, Patricia M. L., 'The Friendship Model of Physician/Patient Relationship and Patient Autonomy', *Bioethics* 2, no. 1, January 1988.

Inness, Julie, *Privacy, Intimacy, and Isolation*, New York, Oxford University Press, 1992.

Ipp, David, 'Reforms to the Adversarial Process in Civil Litigation – Part I', *Australian Law Journal* 69, 1995.

Irwin, T. H., 'Reason and Responsibility in Aristotle', in Amélie O. Rorty (ed.), *Essays on Aristotle's Ethics*, Berkeley, University of California Press, 1980.

Ishiguro, Kazuo, *The Remains of the Day*, New York, Vintage, 1989.

Jack, R., and Jack, D. C., *Moral Visions and Professional Decisions: The Changing Values of Women and Men Lawyers*, Cambridge, Cambridge University Press, 1989.

Jackson, Frank, 'Decision-Theoretic Consequentialism and the Nearest and Dearest Objection', *Ethics* 101, no. 3, April 1991.

Janis, Irving L., and Mann, Leon, *Decision Making: A Psychological Analysis of Conflict, Choice, and Commitment*, New York, The Free Press, 1977.

Kagan, Shelly, 'The Additive Fallacy', *Ethics* 99, October 1988.

The Limits of Morality, Oxford, Clarendon Press, 1989.

Kant, Immanuel, *Critique of Practical Reason*, trans. L. W. Beck, Indianapolis, Bobbs-Merrill, 1956.

Foundations of the Metaphysics of Morals, trans. L. W. Beck, Indianapolis, Bobbs-Merrill, 1959.

'What is Enlightenment?', trans. L. W. Beck, in *Foundations of the Metaphysics of Morals and 'What is Enlightenment?'*, Indianapolis, Bobbs-Merrill, 1959.

Lectures on Ethics, trans. L. Infield, New York, Harper & Row, 1963.

Anthropology from a Pragmatic Point of View, trans. M. J. Gregor, The Hague, Nijhoff, 1974.

The Metaphysics of Morals, trans. M. J. Gregor, Cambridge, Cambridge University Press, 1991.

Vorlesungen über Anthropologie (*Lectures on Anthropology*), ed. Reinhard Brandt and Werner Stark, in *Gesammelte Schriften*, vol. xxv, Berlin, Walter de Gruyter, 1997.

Kapur, Neera Badhwar, 'Why it is Wrong to be Always Guided by the Best: Consequentialism and Friendship', *Ethics* 101, 1991.

Kass, Leon, 'Neither for Love nor Money: Why Doctors must not Kill', *The Public Interest* 94, Winter 1989.

Kirby, Michael, 'Billable Hours in a Noble Calling?', *Alternative Law Journal* 21, no. 6, December 1996.

Korsgaard, Christine, 'Two Distinctions in Goodness', *Philosophical Review* 92, 1983.

'Aristotle on Function and Virtue', *History of Philosophy Quarterly* 3, no. 3, 1986.

'Personal Identity and the Unity of Agency: A Kantian Response to Parfit', *Philosophy and Public Affairs* 18, no. 2, Spring 1989.

Kristjansson, Kristjan, 'Virtue Ethics and Emotional Conflict', *American Philosophical Quarterly* 37, no. 3, July 2000.

Kronman, Anthony, 'Living in the Law', *University of Chicago Law Review* 54, 1987.

The Lost Lawyer: Failing Ideals of the Legal Profession, Cambridge, MA, Harvard University Press, 1993.

Kruschwitz, Robert B., and Roberts, Robert C., *The Virtues: Contemporary Essays on Moral Character*, Belmont, Wadsworth, 1987.

Kymlicka, Will, *Contemporary Political Philosophy*, Oxford, Clarendon Press, 1990.

Lifton, Robert Jay, *The Nazi Doctors: Medical Killing and the Psychology of Genocide*, New York, Basic Books, 1986.

Louden, Robert B., 'On Some Vices of Virtue Ethics', *American Philosophical Quarterly* 21, 1984.

'Kant's Virtue Ethics', *Philosophy* 61, 1986.

'Can we be too Moral?', *Ethics* 98, 1988.

Luban, David, 'The Adversary System Excuse', in David Luban (ed.), *The Good Lawyer: Lawyers' Roles and Lawyers' Ethics*, Totowa, Rowman and Allanheld, 1984.

Lawyers and Justice: An Ethical Study, Princeton, Princeton University Press, 1988.

Maas, Paul van der, et al., 'Euthanasia and other Medical Decisions Concerning the End of Life', *The Lancet* 338, 14 September 1991.

McCloskey, H. J., 'A Note on Utilitarian Punishment', *Mind* 72, 1963.

McDowell, John, 'Virtue and Reason', *The Monist* 62, no. 3, 1979.

'The Role of *Eudaimonia* in Aristotle's Ethics', in Amélie O. Rorty (ed.), *Essays on Aristotle's Ethics*, Berkeley, University of California Press, 1980.

Machiavelli, Niccolò, *The Prince*, trans. George Bull, Harmondsworth, Penguin, 1975.

Macintosh, David, 'Trust and Betrayal in the Physician–Patient Relationship', Ph.D. thesis, Centre for Human Bioethics, Monash University, 2000.

MacIntyre, Alasdair, *After Virtue*, 2nd edn, Notre Dame, University of Notre Dame Press, 1984.

McIntyre, Lisa J., *The Public Defender: The Practice of Law in the Shadows of Repute*, Chicago, University of Chicago Press, 1987.

McNaughton, David, and Rawling, Piers, 'Agent-relativity and the Doing–Happening Distinction', *Philosophical Studies* 63, 1991.

McWhinney, I. R., 'General Practice as an Academic Discipline', *The Lancet* 1, 1966.

Matthews, Steve, 'Personal Identity, Multiple Personality Disorder, and Moral Personhood', *Philosophical Psychology* 11, no. 1, 1998.

May, William, 'The Beleaguered Rulers: The Public Obligation of the Professional', *Kennedy Institute of Ethics Journal* 2, no. 1, 1992.

Miller, Franklin G., and Brody, Howard, 'Professional Integrity and Physician-Assisted Death', *Hastings Center Report* 25, no. 3, May–June 1995.

Momeyer, Richard, 'Does Physician-Assisted Suicide Violate the Integrity of Medicine?', *Journal of Medicine and Philosophy* 20, 1995.

Montaigne, Michel de, 'Of Husbanding your Will', in *The Complete Essays of Montaigne*, trans. Donald Frame, London, Hamish Hamilton, 1958.

'Of the Useful and the Honorable', in *The Complete Essays of Montaigne*, trans. Donald Frame, London, Hamish Hamilton, 1958.

Moore, G. E., *Principia Ethica*, Cambridge, Cambridge University Press, 1903.

Ethics, London, Oxford University Press, 1978.

Moore, Mark H., and Sparrow, Malcolm K., *Ethics in Government: The Moral Challenge of Public Leadership*, Englewood Cliffs, Prentice-Hall, 1990.

Nagel, Thomas, 'Moral Luck', in Thomas Nagel, *Mortal Questions*, Cambridge, Cambridge University Press, 1979.

'Ruthlessness in Public Life', in Joan C. Callahan (ed.), *Ethical Issues in Professional Life*, New York, Oxford University Press, 1988.

Nightingale, J. (ed.), *The Trial of Queen Caroline*, vol. II, London, J. Robins & Co., Albion Press, 1821.

Nisselle, Paul, 'Difficult Patients – The Games they Play', *Australian Doctor Weekly*, 7 July 1989.

Noddings, Nel, *Caring: A Feminine Approach to Ethics and Moral Education*, Berkeley, University of California Press, 1984.

'In Defense of Caring', *Journal of Clinical Ethics* 3, no. 1, Spring 1992.

Nortvedt, Per, 'Sensitive Judgement: An Inquiry into the Foundations of Nursing Ethics', *Nursing Ethics* 5, no. 5, 1998.

Nussbaum, Martha, *The Fragility of Goodness*, Cambridge, Cambridge University Press, 1986.

'The Discernment of Perception: An Aristotelian Conception of Private and

Public Rationality', in Martha Nussbaum, *Love's Knowledge*, New York, Oxford University Press, 1990.

Nussbaum, Martha, and Sen, Amartya (eds.), *The Quality of Life*, Oxford, Clarendon Press, 1993.

Oakley, Justin, *Morality and the Emotions*, London, Routledge, 1992.

'Varieties of Virtue Ethics', *Ratio* 9, no. 2, September 1996.

'A Virtue Ethics Approach', in Helga Kuhse and Peter Singer (eds.), *A Companion to Bioethics*, Oxford, Blackwell, 1998.

Oddie, Graham, and Menzies, Peter, 'An Objectivist's Guide to Subjectivist Value', *Ethics* 102, no. 3, April 1992.

Ogletree, Charles, 'Beyond Justifications: Seeking Motivations to Sustain Public Defenders', *Harvard Law Review* 106, 1993.

O'Neill, Onora, 'Consistency in Action', in N. Potter and M. Timmons (eds.), *Morality and Universality*, Dordrecht, Reidel, 1985.

Orwell, George, *Down and out in Paris and London*, Harmondsworth, Penguin, 1940.

Parfit, Derek, *Reasons and Persons*, Oxford, Clarendon Press, 1984.

Paton, H. J., 'Kant on Friendship', *Proceedings of the British Academy* 42, 1956.

Pellegrino, Edmund, and Thomasma, David, *A Philosophical Basis of Medical Practice*, New York, Oxford University Press, 1981.

The Virtues in Medical Practice, New York, Oxford University Press, 1993.

Pence, Gregory E., *Ethical Options in Medicine*, Oradell, NJ, Medical Economics Company, 1980.

'Recent Work on the Virtues', *American Philosophical Quarterly* 21, 1984.

'Virtue Theory', in Peter Singer (ed.), *A Companion to Ethics*, Oxford, Blackwell, 1991.

Pettit, Philip, 'Satisficing Consequentialism', Part II, *Proceedings of the Aristotelian Society*, Supplementary Volume 58, 1984.

Piper, Adrian M. S., 'Moral Theory and Moral Alienation', *Journal of Philosophy* 84, 1987.

Postema, Gerald J., 'Moral Responsibility in Professional Ethics', *New York University Law Review* 55, no. 1, April 1980.

'Self-Image, Integrity, and Professional Responsibility', in David Luban (ed.), *The Good Lawyer: Lawyers' Roles and Lawyers' Ethics*, Totowa, Rowman and Allanheld, 1984.

Quinlan, Michael, 'Ethics in the Public Service', *Governance* 6, 1993.

Rachels, James, *The Elements of Moral Philosophy*, 2nd edn, Englewood Cliffs, Prentice-Hall, 1993.

Radden, Jennifer, *Divided Minds and Successive Selves: Ethical Issues in Disorders of Identity and Personality*, Cambridge, MA, MIT Press, 1996.

Rader, Robert, 'Confessions of Guilt: A Clinic Student's Reflections on Representing Indigent Criminal Defendants', *Clinical Law Review* 1, Fall 1994.

Railton, Peter, 'Alienation, Consequentialism, and the Demands of Morality', in Samuel Scheffler (ed.), *Consequentialism and its Critics*, Oxford, Oxford University Press, 1988.

Ramos, M. C., 'The Nurse–Patient Relationship: Themes and Variations', *Journal of Advanced Nursing* 17, 1992.

Ramsey, Paul, *The Patient as Person*, New Haven, Yale University Press, 1970.

Rashdall, Hastings, *The Theory of Good and Evil*, vol. i, Oxford, Oxford University Press, 1907.

The Theory of Good and Evil, vol. ii, 2nd edn, London, Oxford University Press, 1924.

Rawls, John, 'Two Concepts of Rules', *Philosophical Review* 64, 1955.

A Theory of Justice, Oxford, Oxford University Press, 1972.

Political Liberalism, New York, Columbia University Press, 1993.

Ross, Lee, and Nisbett, Richard, *The Person and the Situation: Perspectives of Social Psychology*, New York, McGraw-Hill, 1991.

Ross, W. D., *The Right and the Good*, Oxford, Clarendon Press, 1930.

Satz, Debra, 'Markets in Women's Sexual Labor', *Ethics* 106, no. 1, October 1995.

Scanlon, T. M., 'Rights, Goals and Fairness', in Samuel Scheffler (ed.), *Consequentialism and its Critics*, Oxford, Oxford University Press, 1988.

Schaller, W. E., 'Kant on Virtue and Moral Worth', *Southern Journal of Philosophy* 25, 1987.

Scheffler, Samuel, *The Rejection of Consequentialism*, Oxford, Oxford University Press, 1982.

'Introduction' to Samuel Scheffler (ed.), *Consequentialism and its Critics*, Oxford, Oxford University Press, 1988.

Human Morality, New York, Oxford University Press, 1992.

Schweitzer, Albert, *My Life and Thought: An Autobiography*, trans. C. T. Campion, London, Allen & Unwin, 1933.

On the Edge of the Primeval Forest, trans. C. T. Campion, London, A. & C. Black, 1949.

Shaffer, Thomas L., *Faith and the Professions*, Provo, Brigham Young University Press, 1987.

Sherman, Nancy, *The Fabric of Character*, Oxford, Clarendon Press, 1989.

'The Place of Emotions in Kantian Morality', in Owen Flanagan and Amélie O. Rorty (eds.), *Identity, Character, and Morality: Essays in Moral Psychology*, Cambridge, MA, MIT Press, 1990.

'Aristotle and the Shared Life', in Neera K. Badhwar (ed.), *Friendship: A Philosophical Reader*, Ithaca, Cornell University Press, 1993.

Making a Necessity of Virtue: Aristotle and Kant on Virtue, Cambridge, Cambridge University Press, 1997.

Shklar, Judith N., 'Bad Characters for Good Liberals', in Judith N. Shklar, *Ordinary Vices*, Cambridge, MA, Harvard University Press, 1984.

Sidgwick, Henry, *The Methods of Ethics*, 7th edn, Indianapolis, Hackett, 1981.

Simon, William H., 'The Ideology of Advocacy: Procedural Justice and Professional Ethics', *Wisconsin Law Review* 29, 1978.

Slote, Michael, *Goods and Virtues*, Oxford, Clarendon Press, 1983.

'Satisficing Consequentialism', Part I, *Proceedings of the Aristotelian Society*, Supplementary Volume 58, 1984.

Beyond Optimizing: A Study of Rational Choice, Cambridge, MA, Harvard University Press, 1989.
From Morality to Virtue, New York, Oxford University Press, 1992.
'Agent-Basing Virtue Ethics', in Peter A. French, Theodore E. Uehling, and Howard K. Wettstein (eds.), *Midwest Studies in Philosophy, Volume 20: Moral Concepts*, Notre Dame, University of Notre Dame Press, 1995.
'Law in Virtue Ethics', *Law and Philosophy* 14, no. 1, February 1995.
Sorabji, Richard, 'Aristotle on the Role of Intellect in Virtue', in Amélie O. Rorty (ed.), *Essays on Aristotle's Ethics*, Berkeley, University of California Press, 1980.
Sosa, David, 'Consequences of Consequentialism', *Mind* 102, 1993.
Statman, Daniel, *Virtue Ethics: A Critical Reader*, Edinburgh, Edinburgh University Press, 1997.
Stocker, Michael, 'The Schizophrenia of Modern Ethical Theories', *Journal of Philosophy* 73, 1976.
'Values and Purposes: The Limits of Teleology and the Ends of Friendship', *Journal of Philosophy* 78, 1981.
'Some Problems with Counter-Examples in Ethics', *Synthese* 72, 1987.
'Friendship and Duty: Some Difficult Relations', in Owen Flanagan and Amélie O. Rorty (eds.), *Identity, Character, and Morality: Essays in Moral Psychology*, Cambridge, MA, MIT Press, 1990.
Plural and Conflicting Values, Oxford, Clarendon Press, 1990.
'Emotional Identification, Closeness, and Size: Some Contributions to Virtue Ethics', in Daniel Statman (ed.), *Virtue Ethics*, Edinburgh, Edinburgh University Press, 1997.
Stocker, Michael, with Hegeman, Elizabeth, *Valuing Emotions*, Cambridge, Cambridge University Press, 1996.
Sumner, L. W., 'Two Theories of the Good', in Ellen F. Paul, Fred D. Miller, and Jeffrey Paul (eds.), *The Good Life and the Human Good*, Cambridge, Cambridge University Press, 1992.
Terkel, Studs, *Working*, New York, Avon Books, 1975.
Thomas, Laurence, *Living Morally: A Psychology of Moral Character*, Philadelphia, Temple University Press, 1989.
Toon, Peter D., *What is Good General Practice? A Philosophical Study of the Concept of High Quality Medical Care*, London, Royal College of General Practitioners, 1994.
Trianosky, Gregory, 'Rightly Ordered Appetites: How to Live Morally and Live Well', *American Philosophical Quarterly* 25, 1988.
'What is Virtue Ethics all About?', *American Philosophical Quarterly* 27, 1990.
Trioli, Virginia, 'Assault Victims not Protected, say Counsellors', *The Sunday Age*, Melbourne, 19 April 1998.
Veatch, Robert M., *A Theory of Medical Ethics*, New York, Basic Books, 1981.
'The Physician as Stranger: The Ethics of the Anonymous Patient-Physician Relationship', in Earl Shelp (ed.), *The Clinical Encounter*, Dordrecht, Reidel, 1985.

'The Danger of Virtue', *Journal of Medicine and Philosophy* 13, 1988.

Wallace, James D., *Virtues and Vices*, Ithaca, Cornell University Press, 1978.

Wasserstrom, Richard, 'Roles and Morality', in David Luban (ed.), *The Good Lawyer: Lawyers' Roles and Lawyers' Ethics*, Totowa, Rowman and Allanheld, 1984.

Watson, Gary, 'On the Primacy of Character', in Owen Flanagan and Amélie O. Rorty (eds.), *Identity, Character, and Morality: Essays in Moral Psychology*, Cambridge, MA, MIT Press, 1990.

Watson, Jean, *Nursing: Human Science and Human Care*, Norwalk, Appleton-Century-Crofts, 1985.

Wiggins, David, 'Deliberation and Practical Reason', in Amélie O. Rorty (ed.), *Essays on Aristotle's Ethics*, Berkeley, University of California Press, 1980.

Williams, Bernard, 'A Critique of Utilitarianism', in J. J. C. Smart and Bernard Williams, *Utilitarianism: For and Against*, Cambridge, Cambridge University Press, 1973.

'Moral Luck', in Bernard Williams, *Moral Luck*, Cambridge, Cambridge University Press, 1981.

'Persons, Character, and Morality', in Bernard Williams, *Moral Luck*, Cambridge, Cambridge University Press, 1981.

'Politics and Moral Character', in Joan C. Callahan (ed.), *Ethical Issues in Professional Life*, New York, Oxford University Press, 1988.

Wishman, Seymour, *Confessions of a Criminal Lawyer*, New York, Times Books, 1981.

Wolf, Susan, 'Ethics, Legal Ethics, and the Ethics of Law', in David Luban (ed.), *The Good Lawyer: Lawyers' Roles and Lawyers' Ethics*, Totowa, Rowman and Allanheld, 1984.

Wood, Allen, *Kant's Ethical Thought*, Cambridge, Cambridge University Press, 1999.

Wulff, H. R., Pedersen, S. A., and Rosenberg, R., *Philosophy of Medicine: An Introduction*, Oxford, Blackwell Scientific Publications, 1990.

Index

Index

Printed in the United Kingdom
by Lightning Source UK Ltd.
124390UK00002B/89/A

9 780521 027298